"We carry the genes and the culture of our ancestors, and what we think about them shapes the way we think about ourselves."

HILARY MANTEL, REITH LECTURE, 2017

THE NORTHERN LINE

The History of a Provincial Jewish Family

To Deborah
with love from
Judy

JUDY SIMONS

Matador
9 Priory Business Park,
Wistow Road, Kibworth Beauchamp,
Leicestershire. LE8 0RX
Tel: 0116 279 2299
Email: books@troubador.co.uk
Web: www.troubador.co.uk/matador
Twitter: @matadorbooks

ISBN 978 1800460 928

British Library Cataloguing in Publication Data.
A catalogue record for this book is available from the British Library.

Printed and bound in the UK by TJ Books Limited, Padstow, Cornwall
Typeset in 12pt Minion Pro by Troubador Publishing Ltd, Leicester, UK

Matador is an imprint of Troubador Publishing Ltd

For my grandchildren

Contents

Family Trees

Brown Family Tree

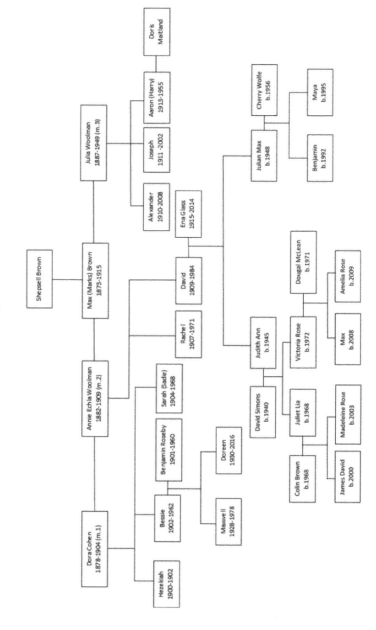

Glass Family Tree

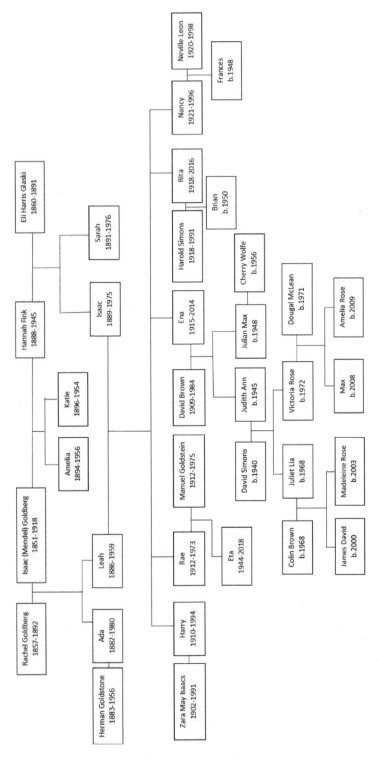

Sophia Woolman Family Tree

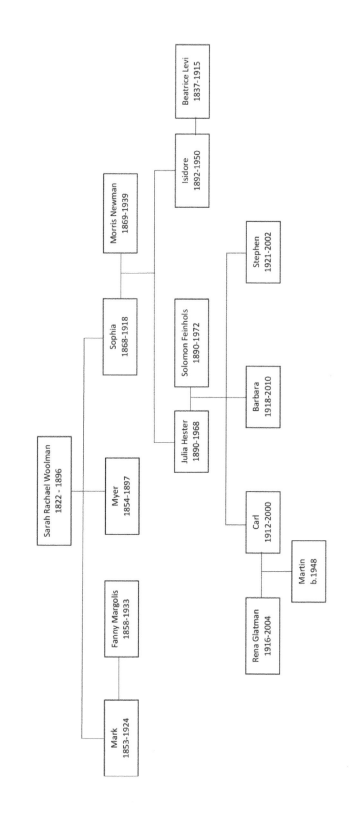

Woolman Family Tree

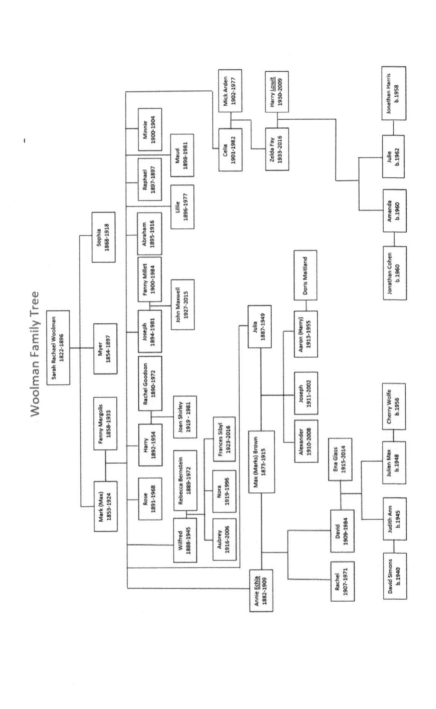

Prologue

Sheffield 1947

"I have done nothing about finding my past. It isn't 'my past', is it? I have written over it. I have recorded on top of it. I have repainted it. Life is layers, fluid, unfixed, fragments."

JEANETTE WINTERSON, *WHY BE HAPPY WHEN YOU COULD BE NORMAL?*

Even though it was the middle of the day, the dining room was dark. My mother lifted me up onto the windowsill in the big bay window so that I could see the snow. It had piled halfway up the glass to block out the light. It was the winter of 1947 and when I went outside the snow was higher than I was. I wore a red siren suit with a hood to keep warm. My woolly gloves were on a string that went around my neck and through the armholes of my coat. I held my mother's hand when we walked up the hill, across the cinder track and crunched through the loose chippings in the old stone quarry to meet my father coming home from work. I was two and a half.

When my mother disappeared, my father took me to stay at Grandma's house. Jack Frost made white patterns on the inside of the bedroom windows. We dressed quietly because Grandma and Grandad were still asleep. In the kitchen Daddy made porridge on the black cast-iron range. He told me stories as we walked to my Montessori nursery school. That afternoon, we walked to a big house, and there was my mother, not disappeared at all but in bed. She showed me a cradle. Inside was a baby. Apparently, this was my brother, Julian. He didn't do much. I was more interested in the enormous basket of fruit on the tall table. It was covered with cellophane paper that rustled when you touched it, and someone had undone the glossy red ribbon that hung round it. The fruit nestled in a little mountain of straw and blue tissue paper; there were apples and oranges and huge purple grapes and a fruit I had never see before, which was called a peach. Mummy gave me one to take home. It was white with pink patches and a furry skin but back at Grandma's house when Daddy cut into it, it was bad.

Although I was born on May 6th, 1945, one of the very last days of the Second World War, I don't have any clear memories before that winter of 1947, the coldest and longest in living memory. And the arrival of my little brother in February 1948 marked the start of the family in which I grew up. My childhood was spent with my parents and my brother in a three-bedroomed, semi-detached house on a steep hill in a Sheffield suburb. Most houses in Sheffield were on hills. Ours, 123 Dobcroft Road, was the same as its neighbour except the other way round. "How can you tell which one is yours?" asked my friend, Dianne, one day when her father gave me a lift home. "Don't you ever go into the wrong house by mistake?" How could she think such a thing? My house had a brown door and a yellow laburnum tree at the gate. It easily stood out from the crowd.

What I loved most about the house though was at the back. At the very end of the long, thin garden, a path opened straight into the woods beyond. If you went past the metal swing, walked round the roses, and carried on past the humped, moss-covered air raid shelter, you came to strawberry beds, raspberry canes and brambles. This was where it stopped being a garden and became an adventure. The gap between the dark holly bushes and the knobbled tree trunks was my gateway to freedom, the equivalent of the space at the back of the wardrobe without any danger of meeting either a lion or a witch. From the age of five I went into the forest to explore. No grown-ups ever thought it necessary to hold my hand or caution me not to talk to strange men or warn me not to get lost.

In fact, no one bothered me at all. I was free to go by myself, which was best, or with other children from our street, whose parents, like mine, didn't seem to care where they were from morning till night. The woods were never threatening in spite of the twisted roots waiting to trip you up and the swathes of boggy ground which regularly swallowed up at least one of my wellies, while I scrambled frantically to safety in my sodden socks. I wore shorts or skirts, which made my knees chapped. Jeans didn't make their appearance in children's wear departments until the 1960s, and little girls only wore trousers if they went horse riding, like the ones in Thelwell cartoons. I stayed out for hours, climbing trees, paddling in the streams that criss-crossed the paths and making secret houses in the dim, leafy hollows of bushes, where I would take cover, safe and enclosed, watching out for passers-by, and knowing for absolute certain that no one could see me. It was a perfect breeding ground for a budding spy.

The house where my family lived on the other hand had rules and rooms and toys that had to be shared. Private places were few and far between, although I could disappear behind the long curtains at the French windows, where, like Jane Eyre, I could read in secret or listen to adult conversations, polishing my spy technique. Although I never noticed the cold when I was racing around in the open air, inside the house life was a struggle to keep warm. The fireplace was the focus for each downstairs room, though the grate in the dining room was hardly ever lit, usually only when we had guests or at Christmas. The open fire in the tiny kitchen was supposed to heat a bread oven built into the wall next to it, not that my mother ever baked a single loaf. She used the white-mottled gas cooker for everything, except when we toasted pikelets by stretching out a long-handled toasting fork to the flames for a tea-time treat. I later used this fork in my spartan hall of residence at university to make toast in front of a pathetic gas fire, which gave off smelly fumes – when I could afford the shilling for the meter – in an attempt to bring some comfort to my cheerless surroundings. The Dobcroft Road kitchen was dismantled in 1956 to make way for a smart blue and white Hygena galley with worktops that joined on to one another to make a single surface, the ultimate in chic.

Before then, on winter evenings my father would carry a shovel full of glowing coals from the kitchen into the living room to light the fire. My brother and I stood with our backs pressed against the wall in case one of the embers spat at us. The coal arrived in a cart, which lurched unevenly up the road, spraying dust as it went. The coalman's face was black, as if he had just emerged from down the pit, which was only a few miles away, at Handsworth, a less salubrious Sheffield suburb than ours. He lugged the sacks on his back and emptied them into the coal hole near the back door on the outside of the house wall from where we heard the lumps rattle down the chute into the cellar beneath. Once a year, my mother covered all the furniture with dust sheets to prepare for the chimney sweep, who came with his mop-headed spiky brush, which he pushed through the flue so we could watch it reappear like Struwwelpeter on the roof at the other end. My abiding dread was that, as happened once, he would dislodge a dead bird or nest with chicks still inside, charred and trapped in the angles of the chimney until they fell, showering soot and blackened feathers into the hearth.

I ran between rooms in search of warmth. The hallway was an ice kingdom. I was Gerda in Hans Andersen's *The Snow Queen* as she shivered on her quest to find her little brother. I longed for her furs. Prime position in any room was the hearth, with two chairs positioned on either side to capture the waves of heat that flared up when my father stretched a sheet of newspaper across the opening. Permanent chilblains tickled my toes because I put them too near the fire to defrost when I got home from school. Before venturing outside, we held the lining of our coats and gloves up to the blaze to thaw. At night my frozen feet rested on a rubber hot water bottle, which my father filled from the boiling kettle. I arranged my clothes on the end of the bed so that I could stretch out my hand to reach them when I woke next morning, and I got dressed under the covers without ever having to touch down on the chilly linoleum that covered the floor.

Everything was rationed in post-war England, and everything ran to its own routine. I glugged National Health orange juice, dark and viscous, from small medicine-like bottles, and tried bravely to swallow the bright-yellow powdered egg that scrambled into a lurid, desiccated mess, even when my mother followed the instructions on the tin to mix well with water. I was nourished on cod liver oil to make me strong (it didn't work) and slurped liquid paraffin from a tablespoon to make me 'go' when I was constipated (which did). When I was ill, the doctor came to our house to examine me. Even after the NHS was introduced in 1948, he liked to keep to his habit of home visits, especially when he could rely on tea and biscuits and a chat with the young patient's mother. He was bluff and breezy with little or no bedside manner and even less tact. When I contracted whooping cough at the age of five months, he briskly reassured my mother that there was no cause for concern as whooping cough was only fatal in cases of babies less than six months old. This did little to allay her fears.

The whole of Dobcroft Road belonged to the Wentworth estate, and our landlord was Earl Fitzwilliam. He lived at Wentworth Woodhouse, a property near Rotherham that has the longest frontage of any country house in England. Manny Shinwell, who was the government minister in charge of power, had sunk pits in the grounds so that coal mines reached almost to its front door. I knew that Sir Thomas Wentworth had his head chopped off by Oliver Cromwell because he had supported King Charles in the English Civil War. We were on Wentworth's side because he had disapproved of the king's extravagance, and extravagance was wrong. It was wanting new shoes when the old ones still fitted. Even so, I was less certain why my parents had to hand over £4 every year to the man whom Earl

Fitzwilliam sent round to collect the ground rent. I was always being told that we couldn't afford things. Manny Shinwell on the other hand was Jewish, like us, so when he came to address a meeting in Sheffield, my father went to hear him. I was already quite used to the aristocracy and their splendid homes, as Chatsworth, the family seat of the Duke of Devonshire, was only a bus ride away from where we lived. It had been taken over by a girls' school, Penrhos College from Wales, during the war, and on my first visit there, when I was about seven, evidence of their occupation was still visible. I particularly remember a large stone bath standing in the main hallway, and to this day am still slightly uncertain if this was an antique treasure on display for admiring visitors, or a remnant from the school that had been left behind by careless removals men. I did think it was a bit odd that dukes, who were supposed to be rich, had to take a bath in the hall.

My brother and I had our weekly bath on Friday evenings. The bathroom, like every other room in our house, was freezing, but my father, who was no handyman, had rigged up an ingenious heating system of a two-bar electric fire, which was attached precariously to the wall opposite the bath, its wires dangling down to the plug that was on the landing outside the door. It never occurred to anyone that this might be just a bit dangerous. Hot water was strictly limited because it was expensive to heat the boiler, and only a few inches were allowed in the tub to make sure there was enough to go around the family. As children, we shared the bath, seated one at either end, fighting not to sit on the plug. On alternate Fridays this ritual was combined with a hair wash, as my mother rubbed soap – I never saw a bottle of shampoo until I started going to the hairdresser in the 1960s – into our scalps and then poured water from a beaker over our heads whilst we sat with eyes screwed tight so that suds didn't seep into our eyes. Soap in your eyes could send you blind for at least a minute, a lifetime of agony. With damp hair and wrapped in dressing gowns, cords tied around our waists, we sat with our parents in front of the fire and listened to the wireless or played Snap and Happy Families. We were the picture on the front of the Janet and John reading scheme or Enid

Blyton's bright-eyed, docile siblings, the incarnation of untroubled post-war Englishness.

Yet this serene family image screened a history of disruption and fear of which my brother and I were innocent. It had taken over half a century to assemble and would be another half century before I would feel able to deconstruct it to find out the truth behind the enigmatic allusions that were code for "not in front of the children" whenever my parents talked amongst themselves. *Pas devant les domestiques*", my mother would say, meaning us – she had studied French at university. Perhaps all family histories are made up of secrets and lies. Why should mine be any different?

Dobcroft Road was over a mile long, and the top part of it remained unmade until 1955. This meant that the surface was just stones and rubble and very bumpy for cars to manoeuvre. Whenever my friends' fathers drove me home, they grumbled that "this road is ruining my tyres". I knew from their tone that this was my fault and remained uncertain what I could do about it. But in the spring of 1955, when I was ten and Julian was seven, tractors arrived and began to crush and flatten the stones. Then came the massive steamrollers, which trundled noisily up and down the hill, leaving the sweet acrid smell of hot pitch in our nostrils. Once the lumbering machinery had disappeared, the tarmac solidified into a black, shiny and perfectly matt surface, which we were all expressly forbidden to walk on, although Miles Linley, the wild boy of the street, carved his initials in the still warm tar in an act of spectacular bravado. Overnight Dobcroft Road was transformed into a perfect roller-skating rink with a surface as smooth as glass. We spent summer evenings racing one another and sliding down the slope on clunky pieces of metal attached to our feet by wide leather straps. We never worried about speeding cars or having to dodge vehicles that assumed they took priority over zooming children. "You are a very lucky girl," my father never tired of reminding me. I knew I was lucky to have roller skates. Did he mean something else?

Now the road is a main bus route. In 1970, a primary school was built on the playing fields and over the abandoned stone quarry, and today traffic wardens police the crossing while yummy mummies collect their offspring in four-by-fours. The uneven rubble and the sharp-edged stone chippings that made drivers curse, now form the substratum for pavements shaded by flowering cherry trees, which in May drip pale pink blossom over the grey asphalt. The jagged shards that could pierce rubber have been buried for over sixty years, and you would never know what lay underneath the smooth surface unless you dug down to the crude materials at the base. As children, we skated blithely over the top without a thought of the debris below our feet. Out of sight, out of mind is a child's natural solipsistic habitat.

Nowadays, when writing memoirs has become a national pastime, Dobcroft Road, with its submerged mass of unexcavated materials, mirrors my own uneven processes of recollection. Autobiographers construct narratives along chronological timelines. We create connections between the isolated flashbacks and remembered anecdotes, and fuse together the loose splinters of memory. Yet the orderliness is a fiction. We search for form to lend meaning to our stories and those of our ancestors, smoothing out the awkward angles so that we can glide over the fissures from a recent, well-documented perspective where Wikipedia can supply all the answers at the click of a mouse. Except of course it can't. How lucky was I? It's only in retrospect I can see clearly.

My father went to work early every morning except at weekends and every evening he came home at six o'clock on the dot. At precisely ten minutes to six my brother and I had to tidy away our toys before sitting down at the kitchen table for supper. My father had a pathological abhorrence of mess, and everything had to be in its proper place, including us, when he walked through the door. I knew he worked in a factory that made knives and forks but it took me a long time before I found out what he actually did there. Sometimes on Saturday mornings, he would take me and Julian to "the works", where he had a big desk at one end of a large open plan office, separated by a frosted glass partition from the desks of everyone else who worked there, mostly young women with typewriters. If we were truly in luck, we were allowed out of the office area, which was pretty dull, with not much to look at except more desks, and through the double soundproofed doors into the part of the factory where the knives and forks were made. As the doors creaked open, we could hear the din of machinery so loud that we had to shout if we wanted to speak – even then no one could really make out what we were saying. Once inside, the noise was deafening. We would climb onto the knees of the buffer girls (the women who polished the items of cutlery to make them shiny), who sat in a long row in front of clattering machines, and we watched the shapes rattle their way towards us along a rolling trolley. The women wore brown paper aprons over their overalls, which crackled as we wriggled, and scarves swathed round their heads like turbans to protect them from the dust. No masks or eyeshades though. A health and safety inspector today would have a fit. The buffer girls were warm and friendly. They tucked us in close to their cushiony bosoms and shouted to us and across the benches to one another, and they gave us Fox's Glacier Mints from the pockets in their overalls. If you wanted to go upstairs, you stepped into a cavernous lift with two sets of folding concertina metal doors that creaked. Everything in the factory had its own special noise. A grown-up had to pull the handles to make the doors open and close because they were much too heavy and awkward for children to use.

Sunday mornings though were for me and my father alone. We would get up early, leave my mother tucked up in bed with Julian, and walk to the open-air lido in Millhouses Park for my swimming lesson. We would arrive as the gates opened, when the only other person there was Sam, the pool attendant. My father's method of tuition was simple. He would stand on the side of the pool, throw an inflated rubber ring into the water, and then throw me in after it, while he stood and chatted to Sam, sporadically applauding my exertions as I splashed about at the deep end. I thought this was terrific fun, even though the water was unheated, and in the spring months, and indeed for much of the Sheffield summer, its temperature was glacial. My mother, who was quite content to send me off at seven o'clock on a nippy April morning at the age of three with my swimming costume rolled in a towel, claimed not to have known about the throwing-in until I described it to her many years later as an approach not necessarily recommended for young children. But then my ancestors had been forced to sink or swim in much choppier waters.

My mother didn't go out to work. Despite her university education, her job was to stay at home and look after us. She cleaned the house and did the washing and cooked our dinner. The nearest shops were about a mile and a half away. On Tuesdays and Fridays, Mr Squires, the greengrocer, parked his lorry on our road, and we could climb up the little wooden slope into the back, and choose vegetables and fruit for my mother to buy. In winter there were tangerines, laid out in a wooden box that smelled of sawdust, each one wrapped in its own personal tissue-paper parcel. Supermarkets were at least ten years in the future and Ocado too remote to be even a sci-fi fantasy. There was no electric mixer or microwave and no vacuum cleaner or washing machine in our house. Yet food was, as we expected it to be, on the table at mealtimes, home-made spice biscuits lived in a tin, and freshly laundered clothes hung on the drying rack attached by a pulley to the kitchen ceiling, ready for ironing before they made their way to the airing cupboard, the one guaranteed warm place in the whole house.

In the evenings my mother sat in her upright chair with its wooden arms, and knitted from balls of coloured wool, clicking long plastic needles, and peering at bits of paper with hieroglyphic instructions written on them and pictures of women with waved hair and complicated cardigans. My home-made jumpers, scarves and gloves all gave off a special wet dog smell when they were washed or were accidentally dropped in puddles, in my case a frequent occurrence. One winter she knitted my vests, which was a total disaster, as not only were they horribly scratchy on my skin but when I got changed for PE, the sight of them, baggy with irregular holes, made all the other girls at school laugh. In contrast, they wore liberty bodices, wonderful fleecy cotton undergarments, which had little rubber buttons that fastened the vest to their knickers in a single harmonious outfit. I yearned for one but was never allowed. My mother thought they were common and an unnecessary expense. As well as knitting, cooking, washing and ironing, she also spent hours in the garden, where she sprinkled seeds from twists of brown paper into the freshly raked soil from which, months later, flowers grew, although it took me some time to connect these two events. She planted bulbs with a trowel and took cuttings – whatever they might be. She was responsible for the strawberries and raspberries, which I picked in the summer, as well as the lettuces for tea and the string beans which had scarlet flowers and grew up high on long poles. Often when I opened the back door of the house as I got home from school – the front door was reserved for visitors – I would be greeted by the sound of a Chopin sonata as my mother played the upright piano during her one free hour in the afternoon.

It was only much later that I understood that this calm and seemingly uncomplicated English middle-class upbringing was a privilege in those post-war years, and for Jews like us even a miracle. For my family's history was anything but uncomplicated. Both my mother and father were the children of European immigrants, who came to England to seek a better life, and on both sides these displaced families could tell stories that today would have the neighbours calling out the social services. Put them together and they resemble the plot of a sensational nineteenth-century novel with banished orphans, clandestine marriages, premature and violent deaths, and abandoned women incarcerated in lunatic asylums. So, what you are about to read is not for the fainthearted. Rather it is a story of poverty, injustice, loneliness, adultery, madness and suicide, and it has its share of remarkable heroes and heroines, who triumph over grim circumstance. It is also a story with gaps and patches of darkness, where very little is known, and where occasional speculation has to substitute for fact. Although we are now fascinated by the tales of the past, those who actually lived it mostly tried to forget the harsh backgrounds they came from. Certainly they did not dwell on it or tell their secrets to their children. We have to read meaning into the empty spaces as best we can and try to piece together the fragments of the family scrapbook if we are to understand how, with luck on our side, we came to be here at all.

One

A Vanished World: The Pale of Settlement 1899

"He sat at his desk and attempted a Memoir but found it impossible. Opinions, Judgements had made him famous, but how to write without opinion or judgement? Statement of facts – easy. But how to decide which were the facts?"

JANE GARDAM, OLD FILTH

I am trying to assemble a jigsaw from old boxes of memories and half-remembered tales my mother told me, from torn letters with indistinct signatures and from yellowing photographs of people in old-fashioned clothes, whose names are sometimes but not always written on the back in faded pencil. I am trying to recall scraps of conversations I overheard as a child and pull them together so that they will form a coherent narrative. It's not easy to complete the picture when half the pieces are missing or hidden in the unrecovered minds of the dead. There's no perfect image on the front of the jigsaw box to guide me as to the correct sequence or signpost what I should be looking for. I can't find the four corners of the puzzle that will hold the rest in place and I'm struggling to locate the straight-edged pieces that would help to construct a stable frame. So instead I'm starting with the solitary image that doesn't seem to have any natural matches, and I'm working backwards by examining the colours, the background and the shapes protruding from it that might just lock into another section where the correspondence is clearer. I'm receiving conflicting accounts from various sources, especially when my cousins offer me what they think is helpful advice. I'm making mistakes and my meticulous research still manages to put people in the wrong timeframe or even in the wrong family. Despite these setbacks, I hope that when I've deviated up and down the avenues that take me continually in different directions, a picture will emerge not just of a single family but of a generation of survivors, immigrants from a vanished world who have bequeathed to my own grandchildren their patchwork identity. But where to start?

A portrait in a heavy wooden frame hung for years in my mother's hallway. It is of a girl with long auburn hair tied in a ribbon, a thick plait tumbling down over her left shoulder. She is shown head and shoulders only. Her expression is solemn and her olive dress is thrown into relief by a wide creamy collar and neckerchief tied in a bow that frames her throat. Around her neck is a black silk or velvet ribbon, from which hangs an oval locket with a circlet of tiny turquoise stones. Unmistakeably she has the full face, slightly protruding lower lip and large, grave eyes that have been inherited by some of her descendants, though not by me. The picture is a hand-coloured version of a photograph taken towards the end of the nineteenth century, and then probably tinted in the early 1900s, a period when over-painting in oils was popular and before the commercial invention of colour photography itself.

This young woman is Rachel, my great-grandmother, who lived and died in Jagielnica, a village in Eastern Galicia. It was here that my mother's mother, Lea Goldberg, was born on 28 November 1886, the younger of two sisters. Or at least I think so. Birth, marriage, census and death records all provide different accounts of her timeline. As an adult, Lea never openly disclosed her real birthdate and always claimed to be younger than she actually was. She lived in an era when it was unbecoming for women to admit to their real age, and she certainly didn't want anyone to know that she was older than her husband. So, in the absence of cosmetic fillers and a decent hair dye, she resorted to other forms of subterfuge. My grandmother persisted in this fiction right up to her dying day, and on her death certificate in July 1959 her age is inscribed fraudulently as seventy years, putting her a good two years younger than I believe she actually was. Lies and secrets. Secrets and lies. Each family has its share. Whatever the truth of the matter, she always seemed old to me.

Eastern Galicia, in the Ukraine, was an area that had been ruled by Austria for over 200 years as part of the vast Austro-Hungarian Empire. About 3,000 people lived in Jagielnica, and between 1880 and 1890, Jews formed more than half of these. On my Google map, the village lies on the borders of Russia, Lithuania and Poland in the vast expanse that was known as the Pale of Settlement, an area as large as France and the UK combined, and with a population of about forty-two million. According to my Aunt Rita, who died recently at the age of ninety-eight but whose long-term memory remained supremely intact, its name kept being altered throughout the nineteenth century, an event which must have been deeply puzzling for its inhabitants. Despite all this chopping and changing, I am pretty certain I have the facts more or less right. I inherited a faded nineteenth-century document, which my grandmother carried with her when she left Europe in 1899, and which gives her birthplace unequivocally as Jagielnica. She continued to describe herself as Austrian, although the Viennese Jews were apt to sneer at this designation. To make matters worse, different official records give Lea's nationality as variously Austrian, Russian or Polish, even occasionally English, depending on who happened to be completing the form at the time. Lea herself never learned to write.

This sort of misconstruction is typical of my family history, where names of both places and individuals keep mutating, and where marriages take place within the same family so that brothers, sisters, cousins and aunts are often closer than anyone might comfortably expect. It is a history characterised by instability from which has evolved a remarkably steady set of high achievers, twenty-first century professionals – lawyers, doctors, teachers, pharmacists and engineers. "What's the difference between a tailor and a lawyer?" goes the Jewish joke. Answer: "A generation." The contours of my jigsaw resemble those of many of today's British Jews who share a heritage of dislocation. But within that outline, rickety at best once I try to reassemble it, are the personal dramas that breathe life into ancestry. My jigsaw is populated by ghosts who glide alongside me and whisper their secrets in my ear as I search for pieces that will fit together to reanimate their youth. They are skulking in the belongings they left behind them, in my grandmother's black sable muff, which resonates with icy winters but also with her love of fashion, and in the delicate hand-painted tea cups in my kitchen cupboard, too precious for everyday use. How can I read their story?

From the late eighteenth century onwards, Jews had been banished from the major cities in Imperial Russia and forced to live in the Pale, where they were subject to widespread discrimination. Not only were there restrictions on their movement from place to place, but they were also forbidden from entering certain professions or trades and were denied a proper education. After 1882, the number of Jewish students allowed to enter secondary schools for instance was limited to ten per cent of the national population. As a result, the Goldbergs were like many other Jewish families at that time, both uneducated and denied any prospect of advancement. My great-grandfather, Mendel Goldberg, made his living selling fish in the local market, but trade became harder when his Ukrainian fellow citizens pooled their resources and worked together as a collective from which Jews were excluded. So when Lea was a child, her father decided to follow in the footsteps of friends and neighbours, and go to England. He took with him his elder daughter, Ada, who aged eleven was less of a burden, whilst Lea and her mother were left behind to be sent for once he was settled.

This decision was not at all unusual in an age when families were regularly being broken up and dispersed across continents, when passports were expensive and difficult to come by and when many people could barely afford steamship tickets for themselves, let alone their loved ones. It finds its present-day parallel in the hardworking and enterprising Eastern European migrants, the reliable Polish builders and charming Romanian baristas, who flock to the major UK cities, leaving their homelands for the attractions of the Western economy. As I write, refugees wait, caged in camps for the approach of winter. They fight for fresh water, bread and clean clothes, and stream in their thousands across borders as European leaders argue over their fate. Their presence is a visible reminder of the less public but equally momentous obstacles my predecessors had to contend with as they stepped falteringly into a dimly realised future.

It is estimated that in the years 1880 to 1910, over two million Jews emigrated from Russia and its territories, which included parts of Austro-Hungary. In Jagielnica living conditions were gradually becoming intolerable for Jews as indeed they were throughout the Pale. Violence against Jewish homes and businesses was widespread, and the authorities did not merely turn a blind eye to the atrocities being committed but actively encouraged them. It was around 1892 when Mendel and Ada set sail for their new country. They took with them the picture that later hung in my mother's house of the young wife and mother they had left behind.

After her husband had packed and gone, my great-grandmother carried on with the business of selling fish, eking out a hand-to-mouth existence, haggling with local suppliers and waiting for customers in the market square with its few miserable stalls, seated day after day on a stool, with her basket of pike and carp, the fish most readily obtainable from the local ponds. I have a postcard of this square dated 1900, with the rabbi's house clearly marked, and showing the market, with its open sides and the roofed area, which gave some respite from the harsh weather. Great-grandma's hands would have been chapped and red, covered most likely with stinging cuts from the knife she used to gut the merchandise. The village was exposed to the biting winds driven in from the Russian Steppes, and just a few months after her husband's departure, Rachel Goldberg succumbed to the unforgiving conditions, and died. There are no eyewitness accounts and no medical certificate that might confirm the cause of her untimely death. What age would she have been? Twenty-eight or nine? Thirty-two at most? No doubt she was weakened by poverty and by sitting out in the open, wrapped in nothing more substantial than a shawl to protect her from the fierce chill and temperatures that could fall as low as minus 20°C. Lea was taken in by her mother's sister, while they waited for her father to send word from his new country.

It did not take long for Mendel Goldberg to find his feet. He made his way to Manchester, where there was a flourishing Jewish community of about 30,000, approximately the same number as today. He changed his name to Isaac Golding – both Mendel and Goldberg smacked too much of the *shtetl* – and around 1893 re-married Hannah (Annie) Glaskie or Glaski, nee Fink, a widow who had two children of her own, Isaac and Sarah. Their father had been Eli Harris Glaski, a mackintosh maker, who fortuitously passed away around the time his daughter was born, creating room for my great-grandfather to step promptly into his place. Annie and Isaac Golding, together with their new names, set up home in Cheetham, a district conveniently close to the Manchester wholesale fish market. When Lea was twelve, the age at which she was thought sufficiently responsible to travel unaccompanied and, more importantly, could be guaranteed to pay for her keep, her father sent her a one-way ticket to England. In the autumn of 1899 just before the dawn of the new century, she started out alone on her daunting journey from Eastern Europe into the unknown.

She was lucky to get out when she did. On the last day of the Jewish Passover in 1903, which coincided that year with Easter, just over three years after her departure, a particularly savage pogrom took place in the region. Easter was always a particularly nerve-wracking period for Jews in the Pale. They had to contend annually with the belief that Jews were Christ killers, an excuse for increased hostility and attacks on Jewish property. There was also the persistent blood libel, dating from medieval times, that Jews used the blood of a murdered Christian child as a ritual element in their Passover feast. This fiction was so deeply rooted that it endured well into the 1970s, when a young Polish girl from a simple Catholic and deeply superstitious family, told me gravely that her mother knew personally a family whose child had been killed for just such a purpose. It is well known that the pogrom, a Russian word, literally meaning "destruction", was essentially a legalised riot, giving licence for mobs to attack Jewish neighbourhoods, murdering householders, raping women and butchering children. Houses were looted and set on fire, and property, including livestock, stolen or killed. As peasants from neighbouring villages rampaged through the streets of Jagielnica, brandishing knives and flaming torches, terrified mothers hid their babies in cupboards or under beds or in farmyards under bales of hay in fear of their lives. After two days of incessant violence, a deathly quiet fell over the village. Shaken survivors emerged from their hiding places to view their ruined homes. The place looked as if it had been hit by a snowstorm, the ground white with the feathers drifting from mattresses that had been ripped open, spilling their contents across the narrow roads. The scale of the destruction was immortalised in a Yiddish song.

A house three-storeys high
Was destroyed to the ground.
Bedding was torn apart;
The feathers blew in the wind.
In the feathers they walked
As in winter in snow.
Women were beaten;
Men torn in two.
Sweet God in heaven
Look already down to the earth.
Have the Jews so sinned
That they are of no worth?

Lea left behind her a way of life that has since been obliterated. A generation later, on June 7 1941, the Germans entered Jagielnica as part of their inexorable progress across occupied Europe, systematically destroying the rich Jewish culture that had accumulated over centuries. For the next six months Jews were compelled to work in designated labour camps or on farms, where they harvested a rubber substitute. By early 1942, when the supply of forced labour had been exhausted, any remaining Jews were either shot summarily during two focused *Aktions* as the German forces methodically evacuated the last of the inhabited Jewish homes, driving their occupants out onto the streets, or they were rounded up and sent to the camp that had been built at Belzec, now in Poland.

Belzec was the first of the Nazi extermination camps, a pioneer in the horrific implementation of Hitler's Final Solution. It was in operation for a mere nine months, from March to December 1942. In that brief period, it is estimated that between 430,000 and 500,000 Jews were murdered there, including the entire community from Jagielnica, the remnants of my family, the aunt who had given my grandmother shelter, her uncles and all her cousins. Although the name became infamous in the vicinity and despite its gruesome record of brutal efficiency, Belzec is virtually unheard of today in comparison with the adjacent death camps of Auschwitz-Birkenau and Treblinka, which, with their harrowing tales of mass slaughter, have become bywords for evil. The Nazi machine had done its work too well, ensuring that there were virtually no witnesses after the war who might give evidence about the atrocities committed there. Out of the almost half a million Jews who passed through its gates, a total of precisely seven survived Belzec, only two of whom were capable of coming forward to testify at the Nuremberg trials. The bodies of victims, which initially had been flung into crudely dug pits for mass graves, fresh corpses casually heaped on top of their barely decomposing friends and neighbours, were exhumed in 1943 and burned, reducing the human remains to ash, and effectively covering the traces of the executioners. This is where my past is buried. Today, the only evidence that there has ever been a Jewish community at Jagielnica rests in the old cemetery with its desolate tombstones and their mostly indecipherable inscriptions, inviting visitors to remember the dead who lie beneath them with their unspoken histories intact.

I try to imagine what it must have been like to leave the only place you had ever known and to travel across the sea to a foreign country where you didn't speak a word of the language. Lea, not much more than a child, had to trek 1,500 kilometres to Hamburg, the German port, where ships were harboured, waiting to convey thousands of hopeful emigrants to England. Hamburg was enjoying an economic boom, created by the invasion of these transient and mostly unworldly Jews, many of whom were ripe for exploitation. Whilst arrangements for authorising exit papers and issuing travel documents were all formally in place, the city was nonetheless full of potential hazards. Corrupt officials were everywhere, targeting the gullible and disoriented new arrivals. "When you get to Hamburg," wrote one recent New Yorker in 1891 to the wife who was preparing to join him, "a policeman will show you the way to the office. Everything is pre-paid... Do not pay any more. And should you have to pay anyway, then ask for a receipt because in Hamburg they are all robbers and thieves."

The streets near the docks were swarming with ticket touts, cheats and sham officials trying to swindle frightened and credulous Jews out of their paltry savings by selling them fake papers. Cautions are repeated again and again in letters to prospective travellers from their more seasoned relatives. "When you arrive in Hamburg agents will want a great deal of money from you," warned a mother to her daughter who was travelling alone that same year. "Even if you have it do not hand it over, just say that your tickets are already pre-paid, 'my mother paid'. If they will absolutely not yield, then pay at the most 2 marks. As to the rest do not let on what you have to anyone."

Clinging on to her few possessions, and successfully negotiating the pitfalls of crooks, foreign currency and Hamburg's unfamiliar thoroughfares, my not quite teenage grandmother showed the authorities her papers, taken from the official Jagielnica birth register, written in German and Polish, and prepared for her by the Jewish Council. This yellowing document, dated 8 October 1899, folded and unfolded many times, and now sellotaped together to stop it falling apart, was her exit visa. Petrified that if they knew she was only twelve, she might be refused permission to travel, she added three years on to her natural age, a ruse which appears to have worked. She had to undergo a health check at a control station and have her clothes disinfected in a fumigation centre. Many migrants were turned back at the point of embarkation if they were deemed to be too weak to survive the voyage, if they were lice-ridden or were suffering from any of the common illnesses from diphtheria to dysentery. Once she was pronounced well enough to sail, she waited along with the hordes of other hopefuls to secure her passage on the boat. Hamburg lodging houses, which had mushroomed to meet demand, offered a bed for the night at exorbitant prices, usually to be shared with other travel-worn strangers. A river town, Hamburg was too far upstream to be navigable by ocean-going vessels, so Lea also had to endure a cramped, overcrowded ferry journey before arriving at the port itself.

In common with many of my contemporaries, who are second-generation immigrants, I knew that my grandmother had made this journey but it had never occurred to me to ask what it would have involved. It was a time of mass migration across Europe and the weekly crossings of emigrant ships from Hamburg to England, which could accommodate 450 passengers at a time, dramatically changed the face of its human landscape. After London, the Humber ports of Hull and Grimsby, where Lea was headed, were the most popular destinations. In 1899, she was one of more than 65,000 who landed there that year, even if many of the passengers were merely using the UK as a transit point on their more ambitious journeys to America, Canada or South Africa. The steamship journey from the Continent normally took about two days by sea, although in poor weather it could be much longer, and conditions on the ships, which were often converted or even unconverted cattle ships, were primitive, with poor Jewish migrants crowded into steerage between and below decks, accessed by ladders. They slept on boards placed around the sides of the ship. Many of the ships were also transporting freight, usually horses or cattle, in which case the animals, much more valuable than the human cargo, were given first-class treatment, while the Jews had to fend for themselves in filthy and poisonous conditions.

"There is no separation of the sexes, the whole of the immigrants occupying the one space by day, and at night sleeping on a common bench or shelf," the Royal Commission on Alien Immigration heard in 1902, while "the foulness arising from the condition of the people and their surroundings was made worse by the drainage of urine etc from the horses, which occupied adjoining parts of the hold." It was not unusual for passengers to die on the short voyage – babies and young children were the most vulnerable – especially during the winter months when temperatures dropped below freezing and rough weather caused extreme sea-sickness, leaving the floor of the hold awash with human waste. Even without the extreme weather, the travel conditions were appalling. A reporter from *The Evening News and Post* braved the journey "in the interests of his readers" and found himself on board a floating hovel packed with men and women "so enfeebled that one might have fixed their age at nearer seventy than thirty."

Third-class passengers on these crossings had to take their own food, mostly salt herrings, sausage and black bread. My grandmother guarded her few possessions in a makeshift bundle that she kept constantly by her side in case of thieves. Poles had a particularly bad reputation for pilfering, and she was careful to keep her distance. When her ship eventually arrived at Grimsby's Royal Dock – her name is there in the passenger list for 1899 – she stood patiently in line for the Customs Officers with her papers as proof of her identity, date of birth and place of origin. Jewish immigration officials, who could translate from Yiddish, also met the boat, ascertained where passengers were going on the next stage of their journey and helped direct them to the best route and the correct trains. In Lea's case, this interrogation turned out to be a godsend.

Despite the medical checks in Hamburg, the reports of the English Port Medical Officers of Health show that many immigrants arrived in a shocking state, suffering from cholera, typhus or smallpox. Those who arrived at Hull were sent to the floating isolation hospital, which was moored in the River Humber. This was an old whaling ship, the *Earl of Mar and Kellie*, which had been converted in August 1893 when eight cases of the most virulent kind of cholera were discovered on craft arriving from Hamburg in that year. It had a ward with berths for twenty patients plus facilities for disinfecting their clothing and luggage. In Grimsby, any suspicious cases were transferred immediately to the local fever hospital on the mainland. The port authorities were still raw from the memory of epidemics that had hit the region a few years before, and fear of disease was rife. When Lea's boat docked, she was only permitted to climb up from her quarters once all the first-class passengers had disembarked. Only when she had been declared fit and healthy was my grandmother finally allowed to set foot in the country she had dreamed of, and which was to offer her permanent refuge, a home and a reinvented family life.

Lea could heave a sigh of relief that she had finally made it this far. Relatively small in comparison to London, both Hull and Grimsby had been put under huge pressures to cope with the unprecedented numbers of Jews and other hopefuls who spilled off the boats and into the Victorian provincial consciousness. They would have presented an extraordinary sight to English eyes, these orthodox Jews, some of them wearing outlandish clothing in styles dating back to the eighteenth century, men sporting long earlocks dangling below the brims of their fur hats. Women of all ages, their heads adorned with horsehair wigs, mingled with young girls like Lea, wrapped in shawls and clutching bundles, all the while babbling in Yiddish. In neighbouring Hull, the authorities were so desperate to move travellers on as quickly as possible, fearing that they might contaminate respectable citizens, that they provided no lodgings or solid shelter for these weary souls. In contrast, Grimsby had established an immigrants' hostel at the dockside, the first welcoming port of call for the refugees, many of whom were destitute and dropping from fatigue. It was here, in the waiting room at Grimsby Town station, that Lea was able to wash away the grime. Clutching the piece of paper with her father's new address, she knew she had to make her way by train to an unknown city, hoping that the man who now called himself Isaac Golding would be expecting her. She had last seen him half her lifetime ago. She was worn out and fearful as she clung to her possessions, ready to board the Manchester, Sheffield and Lincolnshire Railway across the Pennines. At the same time, if her behaviour during the rest of her life is anything to go by, she was buoyed up, excited and ready for anything. With the characteristic cheerfulness that was to serve her well in the days ahead, she looked to the future not the past, and there was only one more stage of her journey to go.

Two

A New World: Manchester 1899

"There is something fascinating about investigating your ancestry if nothing is known about them other than what can be gleaned from certificates of birth, marriage and death, because all you end up with is a list of names, dates and occupations. You know nothing about them as people, their lives, what they were like as human beings, and you have no way of finding out."

BRIAN MAGEE, CLOUDS OF GLORY

If people are the figures in bold in the foreground of my family jigsaw, then its background is strewn with objects. A silver sovereign case, school prizes with gilt insignia, and tattered recipe books provide the clues that help me reconstruct the world which past generations inhabited. They give substance not just to the individual life but to the community and culture in which they lived. On my bookshelf at home, for instance, slotted in between the copy of Josephus' *History of the Jews* and the leather-bound volumes used for synagogue services, which were a present from my grandparents on my twelfth birthday, is a miniature prayer book with an exquisite inlaid ivory cover. Its pages are wafer-thin, fragile and covered with tiny black Hebrew characters. There is no English translation or guide as to their meaning. This would have been considered redundant at a time when every Jewish boy was expected to have absorbed the ancient language along with his first mouthful of chopped herring.

The little book was given to my mother's father, Isaac Glass, in 1902 on the occasion of his bar mitzvah, along with a prayer shawl, two watches and three silk handkerchiefs. People in the *shtetl* communities of the Pale continued to respect the tradition of learning, at least for boys, who were expected to play their full part in religious services once they had reached the age of thirteen, and this tradition was perpetuated in the English diaspora. Yet that book was probably one of the very few in my grandfather's childhood home, where only he and his stepfather were able to read. It connects me with a past I never knew, with dark streets and homes without soap or electric light, where books were a male privilege, blessings were recited by boys over every morsel of food, and children were raised in awe of autocratic fathers, whose every word was law.

The history of Jewish immigration into Manchester during this period is well documented, and I am not going to rehearse it here except where it touches on those closest to me. Their fortunes echo the movement of migrant peoples across the continent, as they sought permanence and a sense of belonging, and sowed the seeds for future dynasties, generating a revitalised culture from the blend of inherited European traditions with a fresh, contemporary milieu. In 1893 my mother's grandparents, Isaac Golding, the widower, and Annie Glaski, the widow, had married and put down roots. Cheetham Hill had been a magnet for poor immigrants since the 1850s, and Jewish businesses were growing at a rate of knots in a new, turn-of-the-century industrial revolution. All around them Russian, Austrian, Hungarian, Ukrainian and Lithuanian refugees were pouring into the North of England, transforming the face of the city and swelling its total population to nearly 800,000.

Census records of the period, together with the City Directories, paint an eloquent picture of the tenements around Strangeways and

Cheetham Hill Road, crammed to overflowing with generations of relatives plus incidental lodgers, often young men like my great-grandfather, who had come on ahead of their wives or children to find work and make something of themselves. The expanse of North Manchester they colonised became a ghetto in all but name. Although signs of Christian life remained in the area, with a sprinkling of churches and gentile-owned shops, these gradually gave way to the all-consuming influx of the thousands of Jews who populated the narrow enclaves off York Street, Bury Old Road and Bury New Road. By the 1890s there were already five major synagogues in Cheetham Hill alone. There were Jewish schools, kosher butchers selling salt beef and sticks of *wurst*, bakeries specialising in rye bread garnished with poppy seeds, and grocers with their trays of pickled cucumbers, matzo meal and sides of smoked salmon. The doctors, dentists, lawyers and accountants came later.

The address that Lea had kept safe during her long and hazardous voyage across Europe, 126 Moreton Street, was right in the midst of this teeming, multi-ethnic hive of activity. The building was one in a line of terraced dwellings, and in 1899 it housed my great-grandfather and his daughter, Ada, his wife and her children, Isaac and Sarah, and two more daughters, Millie and Katy, aged five and three, from the second marriage. The street itself was packed with Jews. On one side of them was the Brunswitch family with their lodgers, Joseph Flasch and Bertha Goldstein. On the other side lived the Padirewskis, and next door to them the Hobsbaums. All were of Russian origin and all were working in the garment trade as tailors' pressers or cap-makers. It was an enclave in which Lea was immediately at home.

The morning of Friday the thirteenth of October, the date her boat docked in Grimsby, was cool, and as the travellers emerged from below deck, the gusts of a gale were blowing on the northern coast. Once Lea had got through the seemingly endless complications of the immigration processes, it was getting late, and even later by the time she climbed into the wooden railway carriage at Grimsby Station, and heard the doors slide and bolt behind her. Locking migrants into their coaches for the duration of the journey was regular practice, both a safety precaution for them and a form of insurance for the railway company, who did not want to be responsible for fatalities if panicky aliens decided to jump the train or attempted to get from one coach to another. Corridors connecting adjoining carriages were not introduced until the 1920s. At the end of the nineteenth century it was not unusual for a hundred people a year to die on the railways, and rail company barons were defensive about their safety record. Seats, which in third class consisted of wooden benches in closed compartments, were at a premium, and often it was standing room only with passengers holding on to a handrail for the length of the journey. Carriages were heated using steam from the engine, and were lit by gas, a hazardous facility in a wooden coach. In comparison with the earlier stages of Grandma's journey, however, the English railway trip was pure luxury.

It is at this point that Lea's story becomes the stuff of family legend. Her train had been due to arrive in Manchester around midday, a time which happened to be particularly inconvenient for Isaac Golding. He had continued to ply his trade as a fish hawker just as he had done in Jagielnica, trudging from door to door through the streets of North Manchester, and Fridays were among his busiest times for customers. So instead of going to the station himself, he sent Annie's son, ten-year-old Isaac, with instructions to meet Lea and bring her back home. It is inconceivable to modern parents, not least my own daughters, that a father wouldn't be bursting with impatience to be there in person to be reunited with the child he had not seen for years. But priorities were different then, and whatever his family feeling might have been – and evidence is pretty light on whether he did in fact possess much – he could not afford to disappoint his regular customers on a Friday, when business was at its peak and housewives needed fish to prepare for the Sabbath meal.

Young Isaac Glaski, not entirely sure how he would recognise his new stepsister, made his way to the platform at Manchester Central station, now no longer in use but in 1899 the meeting point for the multitudes of bewildered migrants who were straight off the Grimsby boat. He waited amongst the crowds, watching out for a girl, a bit older than himself, who might be looking lost. He waited and waited but saw no one resembling her description. Then as the steam from the engines cleared, he saw her standing on the platform. As he moved forward, hesitantly calling out her name, she started to run, dropped her bundles, threw her arms around his neck and kissed him. It was at that moment, Isaac always said, that he fell head over heels in love. Ten years later they were married.

That is the romantic story of how my grandparents met, and it's the story that was regularly recounted to me as I was growing up. It was only after my mother's death that I came across some papers in my grandfather's handwriting, where he put paid to the myth that this crucial meeting took place on the station platform. His rather more prosaic version is that having gone to the station and waited for what seemed to him like hours, she never bothered to show up. Ultimately he gave up hanging around and went home alone, planning on going back the next day, presumably to see if she might still be there, like a piece of left luggage waiting to be collected. Early the following morning, however, when his stepfather was at synagogue, apparently unruffled by the absence of his missing offspring, there came a knock on the door. A girl stood there with one of the interpreters who had met the transport. In the process of dealing with the paperwork, when Lea told him her name and destination address, he realised that he knew Isaac Golding personally, and, as she was looking particularly forlorn, folded her under his wing. It was almost afternoon by the time he had finished his duties, and as he was anxious to be home in time for the start of the Sabbath, he took her to his own house to lodge overnight. He was now handing her over to her destination. It is still indisputable that she was so relieved to have finally made it that, in her typically impulsive style, the moment she saw her new stepbrother she flung her arms around him and kissed him, but I prefer *The Railway Children* station platform account myself.

My grandmother's is an unremarkable story for those remarkable times. Like all but the most privileged children of her generation, she learned to fend for herself from early on, and she quickly absorbed the lessons of resilience and common sense that combined with her innate exuberance to sustain her throughout her life. She was one of a multitude of children from all over Europe who were denied their childhoods as they were hustled into becoming independent adults well before the point at which modern children are allowed to board a bus on their own. Lea had arrived in Manchester on a Friday. On Monday, she set out to earn her living in a cap-making factory on Cheetham Hill Road, where she was employed putting the finishing touches to men's flat caps. She was a potential wage slave the moment she stepped off the boat.

The flat cap was the headwear of choice for working-class men during the early twentieth century. Cheap, warm and flexible enough to be rolled up and put in a pocket, it was usually made of wool and provided simple and effective covering against the elements. Manchester, already an international hub for the garment trade, was also one of the main centres for cap manufacture (the others were Stockport and Luton), churning out goods which were sold to shops not just across the North West but throughout the country. Most of the Manchester factories were Jewish-owned and rapidly expanding. Nathan Hope's Anchor Cap Works in Derby Street, and Mark Doniger's Carnarvon Street Cap Works, for example, both founded in Cheetham in the mid-nineteenth century, were forced to move to new, extended premises in the 1890s in order to cope with soaring trade as the cap became not just a denominator of social class but a significant fashion statement. Styles were modified in line with the latest trends, such as the shape of the peak or the number of panels forming the crown, to create continuous demand. In trying to meet this demand, the city accordingly developed an insatiable appetite for incoming unskilled labour, especially in the market for the small businesses that fed the escalating wholesale and retail industries. Whilst the large mills and factories continued to produce their bales of wool and cotton in ever-increasing quantities, hundreds of sweatshops also sprang up around the northern areas of the city with their huge migrant populations, where young girls and women were desperate to find employment at any price.

When Lea's older sister, Ada, had first started working there in 1893, the conditions in these sweatshops, many of which had Jewish proprietors, could be frightful. The rooms, which typically housed between ten and twenty workers in terraced houses or above small shops, were unbearably hot, overcrowded and airless. Women and children, some as young as nine, were crammed together at tables with just enough room to move their arms and the fabric they were working on, or they sat in shadowy corners of the rooms where the hand sewing was done. They were only ever taught one of the minor processes involved in cap-making, which meant there was little opportunity for promotion. It was mind-numbingly repetitive work, and the dim lighting and the need to peer closely at the fabric meant that many of them suffered from prematurely deteriorating eyesight, resulting in near blindness in early middle age. Ada wore thick-lensed spectacles from the time she was in her thirties, most likely a result of the strain on her sight when she was a girl.

Lea followed unquestioningly in her sister's footsteps. Throughout her teenage years she was at her machine from eight in the morning till eight at night. As well as the long hours, wages were pitifully low, and because the sweatshops were outside the scope of factory legislation, they rarely had any safety measures or protection in place for their workers. Still, as far as Lea was concerned, it was a definite improvement on selling fish in a market square in the depths of winter. Another advantage was that because both the boss and the entire staff were Jewish, the factory shut early on Friday evenings so that workers could get home in time for the Sabbath, and they all had time off for Jewish festivals. Several members of my family on both my mother and my father's side, including my grandmother, my paternal grandfather and great-grandfather and at least six of my great-aunts started out this way, as tailors, cap-makers or seamstresses, a somewhat surprising history given my own complete inability to produce a straight seam or even thread a needle accurately. At school I could be guaranteed to come bottom in sewing lessons, as the spindle on the sewing machine took on a life of its own however firmly I spoke to it, and the apron I stitched for domestic science, with its wonky hem and ties of different lengths, became a class joke.

My grandfather, Isaac Glaski, was a new generation of Jew, his lifestyle rooted in traditional observance whilst fully embracing the delights of the Western world. In 1894, when he was five, he began Hebrew classes at a local *cheder*, every day after school from half-past four to six o'clock as well as at weekends. He especially resented the Saturday afternoon class, which was added on to the synagogue services, plus a tutorial at home with his stepfather to whom he had to repeat the whole of that week's portion of the Law to prove that he had been paying attention. He needed to be word perfect for his bar mitzvah, which he performed immaculately, though his parents could never quite work out why his *cheder* headmaster failed to show up. They didn't know that Grandad had torn up the invitation, which he had been tasked with delivering, in revenge for a beating he had received a few weeks earlier.

The *cheder* itself was large compared with the one I went to twice a week as a child, where Mr Cohen would yell, "Donkey!" when someone gave the wrong answer to a question and would swear he had eyes in the back of his head whenever he turned to write on the blackboard. Grandad's establishment had six grades of classes with between thirty and forty children in each, and the syllabus included reading, translation from Hebrew into English, and Jewish history. This was on top of the hour a day, every day, of Hebrew and religious tuition that he received at the Jewish Free School, which catered entirely for Jewish pupils, 800 of them, paid for by public subscription.

Although virtually all the teachers were from Eastern Europe, the language of instruction was English. Indeed, the speaking of Yiddish was a punishable offence. The school wanted to prepare its pupils to play their full part in English society, not to perpetuate the life of the *shtetl*. As a head teacher of the time observed, "It was one great object with the school committee to inculcate at the earliest age in the minds of the children a pride in their English nationality." This policy was enthusiastically encouraged nationwide by the Jewish community leaders, who were keen to encourage integration in the hope that this would ward off a sinister tide of creeping anti-Semitism. Already there were rumblings in the British press that Jews were taking jobs away from Englishmen, feigning poverty to mask their rapacious dealings, and were in fact all secret millionaires. The push for assimilation was underlined by the *Jewish Chronicle*, which urged the provincial communities to "iron out the ghetto bend" and "turn Polish into English Jews".

Still, as the first or second generation of immigrants, schoolchildren were taught how to write Yiddish as well as Hebrew "because, you see," explained my grandfather patiently to me one day, "our people coming from a foreign land received letters regularly from Russia and if you could read them, you had some idea what it was all about." Then, as now, the children of refugees became interpreters for their parents, especially their mothers, many of whom were, like my grandmother, quite unable to decipher correspondence for themselves. As they picked up the gossip from Russia, Austria, Poland or the Ukraine, and conveyed the daily miseries and joys of life back home – who had moved in with neighbours because hooligans had vandalised their home, who was packing up to sail to New York, who was staying behind because Uncle Hymie was too sick to travel, and by the way Cousin Rochel's latest boyfriend is a total *schlemiel* – the intimacies of the *shtetl* infused the consciousness of this rising generation as an inextricable element in a living network of friends and relatives from the Pale, which wound itself around the roots of their hybrid identities.

Rapidly the neighbourhood where my grandparents grew up established itself as a centre of Jewish mercantile life. Immigrants launched small businesses based on the trades they had followed back home, often tailoring or carpentry, many of which rapidly grew into highly productive factories and, in a few cases, huge retail empires. The professions listed in the City Directories of the period reveal the enormous range of occupations associated with the rag trade, as entrepreneurial Jews began to specialise in waterproofing, silk or cotton spinning, dyeing, hosiery, millinery, cap-making and mantle making, and, a speciality of female workers, umbrella-making. As the industries expanded, so did the needs of the workforce and their families. They sought access to doctors and dentists. They wanted someone to manage their money and educate their children. They also needed food and drink from bakers, butchers, grocers, and most importantly for my family, fishmongers. Food was then and remains one of the great staples of ethnic life, binding together communities in a collective celebration of tradition and memories of home. It did not take long for my great-grandfather to become established in Cheetham Hill as a reliable fish merchant with fresh stock, and the family fortunes grew accordingly, although never to anything that could be described as riches. When Isaac Golding died in 1918, his entire estate amounted to £147, a respectable but not a huge sum by any stretch of the imagination.

My mother's parents flourished in this setting. It fed their zest for life and gave them a transformed and confident Jewish identity. Judaism was not so much a religion here as a way of life, and its practices were absorbed unthinkingly into daily routines. If anything, the clash of cultures was more noticeable between the different nationalities than between the Eastern Europeans and the English, with whom they rarely came into direct contact. My grandfather's mother, Annie, for instance, retained the style of the Pale in her dark workaday clothes, brightened by embroidery for festive occasions, and crowned by a high head dress reminiscent of Russian Orthodoxy. My great-grandfather Golding, on the other hand, proud of his "Austrian" heritage, which he considered a definite step up from the Poles and the Russians, accommodated himself much more easily to modern Western customs. A photograph taken around 1905 shows a distinguished-looking man, his dark suit, white shirt and carefully knotted narrow tie topped and tailed by a soft fedora hat and shiny polished shoes. Like his stepson after him, he aimed to be the model of a modern, alert and integrated Jew. No earlocks or kaftan for him. Cheetham Hill was a melting pot of races, languages, customs and traditions, where peoples from different walks of life were bound together by their religion and their immigrant status. Their shared history of persecution shaped their determination not just to survive but to succeed in a country that allowed them free reign to their enterprising spirit.

My grandfather, born and brought up in a Manchester that was fizzing with opportunity and activity, never thought of himself as anything but an English Jew. He was constantly enthused by the energy of his surroundings, where opportunities for entertainment seemed to be on tap. He had a beautiful tenor voice, and as a boy was a star of the synagogue male voice choir. In his teens, he performed in Gilbert and Sullivan operas as part of the Manchester Jewish Amateur Minstrels, and when I was a child, would often break spontaneously into song after meals, an odd medley of Hebraic songs and pre-First World War popular hits, such as "Won't You Come Home, Bill Bailey", as well as romantic ballads like "Shine On Harvest Moon". I used to get deeply embarrassed by this display as I'd always been taught that it was vulgar to show off but no one else seemed to mind at all. Social commentators have observed how the Jewish clubs that sprang up in this period played a crucial part in the cultural transformation of immigrants from the old world to the new. The Jewish Working Men's Club in particular provided billiards and table tennis but also presented musical soirees, brass bands and amateur dramatics, all of which my grandparents adored.

Grandad had been a great ballroom dancer in his youth, and even in his seventies would occasionally grab me by the waist and waltz me vigorously around my parents' lounge, a habit I found most disconcerting. From the time he was about fifteen, he and Lea, already an acknowledged couple, would go out on the town as often as they could. They frequented dance halls and went regularly to variety shows at the music hall and, a favourite excursion, to Belle Vue pleasure ground, which boasted a zoo, a circus and a magnificent funfair. Belle Vue had originally been opened in 1836 as a private bird sanctuary but by the turn of the century it was being advertised as an amusement park, "the showground of the world". Its attractions included rides that were guaranteed to give you the thrill of your life. In the 1920s these included The Bobs, a wooden roller coaster on a terrifyingly convoluted circuit, which was still in existence when Julian and I swooped our own way down it as children in the 1950s, screaming at the top of our voices.

My grandparents were keen racegoers and could be seen among the weekend crowds madly cheering on their favourites. All his life Isaac was a great gambler, whether it was horses or cards, though frequently the two were combined. As a nineteen-year-old he used to hang out with a bunch of other nifty young guys to go to the races, where they would lay bets, play brag and pontoon, and drink whisky. At one time he operated as an occasional turf accountant and was a regular fixture at the Castle Irwell racecourse, where he would take wagers and confidently expect to come away a clear winner. According to him races were habitually fixed, and standard punters had little chance of success. Jockeys and trainers collaborated in a crude cartel to predetermine who would win any particular race. Bookies were tipped off by the angle of the jockey's cap – worn backwards would indicate the winner – a pretty rudimentary scam which had to be managed with care as all but the most unsophisticated punters would have little difficulty in working it out for themselves. As he told it, my grandfather's friends all seemed to have nicknames like Sharp Ikey or Harry the Horse, and his description of their lives sounded to me like something out of a Damon Runyon story in *Guys and Dolls*. Both he and Lea never lost their love of gambling and after they were married, every year Grandad would take his young family to the St Leger race meeting at Doncaster, triggering in my otherwise highly decorous mother a totally unrestrained appetite for winning, whether it was horse-racing, cards or Scrabble.

My grandparents were mad about all this sort of thing. They loved treats of any kind, a predilection which extended itself indiscriminately to virtually every type of confectionery, including ice creams, cakes and chocolates. Once they had children of their own, and as soon as she was old enough to be trusted with hard cash, my Aunt Rita, a connoisseur of sugar from her youth, was assigned the serious responsibility of being sent out to the corner shop every Friday, with the instruction to buy "sweets for the weekend". She would come home laden with Barker and Dobson milk chocolates, chocolate limes and Everton mints – the factory was based in Liverpool – which were then stacked away in a cupboard to be doled out after meals or as a reward for good behaviour. The tradition was continued in my mother's household, where she kept a designated sweetie drawer, full of assorted candy, including boxes of Newberry Fruits, Cadbury's Dairy Milk chocolates, Aero, Mars Bars and Crunchies. It's hardly surprising that visits to the dentist were a recurrent and painful feature of my own post-war childhood. My grandparents' penchant for frivolity was encouraged in my mother's family, and became a standing joke between my parents, so much so that if my naturally reticent mother so much as arranged to meet a friend for morning coffee, my father would shake his head sorrowfully and mutter in his most lugubrious tone, "Pleasure mad".

Three

Abandoned Aunts: Manchester 1905

"Lions lie in wait for us round the corners of our past."
VITA SACKVILLE-WEST, *THE EDWARDIANS*

My grandparents' teenage years were spent alongside Ada, and Isaac's sister, Sarah, plus their little half-sisters, Millie and Katy. When I was growing up, I could never quite work out how it was that my grandparents' sisters were all from the same family. But if you think this is complicated, just wait until you get to my father's relations. Yet the Goldings were reasonably comfortable and there was space for luxuries. Fortunately for me, this included having studio portraits taken at least once a year in Goodman's photographic studio in Strangeways or at the more upmarket central studios, Davenports, in Piccadilly. This pictorial treasure trove forms a graphic record of the Golding sisters' changing fortunes and fashions from the mid-1890s onwards. In 1896, fifteen-year-old Ada already looks quite grown up with luxuriant curls heaped on top of her head, wearing a high-necked pleated gown and a black velvet bandeau around her neck, pearl drop earrings resting against her sculptured cheek bones. Four years or so later, she perches next to Lea, both girls almost engulfed by their lavishly flounced lacy blouses with deep frilled cuffs, their waists encircled by deep cummerbunds tied over long, pale skirts. Whilst they, especially Ada, look the picture of elegance, it was their stepsister, Sarah, who was the acknowledged beauty of the family, her expressive dark-eyed charm enhanced by full lips, which gave her the look of an ardent pre-Raphaelite heroine straight out of a Rossetti painting.

I am enthralled by these pictures, taken over a century go, which show the girls as fun-loving young things, especially when they are freed from the heavy, high-necked dresses with their boned bodices, and move into the flapper age. Ada and Sarah in particular, the oldest and the youngest of the original marriages, shine out from these portraits as if they are on the verge of a brilliant future. They are the true representatives of that heyday in the anglicisation of Manchester Jewry. By their twenties they had recovered from the drudgery of the factory and the aching hours bent over their treadle Singer sewing machines in airless rooms. They had become the bright young things living out the promise of the new century. Sadly, it was not to last.

Every family protects its victims, whose secrets are only referred to in hushed tones, or sometimes not at all. I never heard of Sarah's existence until after I was married. As for Ada, whom I saw throughout my childhood and teenage years as a sometimes twinkly and exceedingly wrinkly old lady in faded knitwear, it never crossed my mind that she could have been embroiled in a scandal of momentous proportions. When you are young, it's impossible to imagine that any of the antediluvian crones scattering cake crumbs at tea parties – and there seemed to be hordes of them at family gatherings – might ever have had a romantic past.

Everything had started out so well. On a remarkably clear and mild Boxing Day in 1905, at the age of twenty-four, Ada married her boss from the clothing factory where she worked. He was a desirable catch. She had grown into a striking young woman, her fashion sense more restrained and tasteful than in her adolescent years. It's all there in the photographs. Well-cut Edwardian coats and skirts shield delicate ruched shirts, while Ada's natural sense of extravagance is largely confined to a series of gorgeous hats adorned with massive feathers, balanced on her piled coiffure. As she became self-sufficient, her increased spending power is illustrated by an ever-expanding collection of costume jewellery, a cameo pendant, a gold locket, long ropes of amber beads, a gold pin and brooch, and a stunning pearl necklace. Her bridegroom, Herman Goldstone, was a Romanian immigrant a year younger than she was. He was good looking, charismatic and, like her, an extremely natty dresser, with an eye for the ladies that was to prove Ada's downfall. In the summer of 1905, however, when the couple got engaged, the bride-to-be was the envy of all her workmates.

At the time they began courting, Herman had already acquired a reputation as a modish ladies' coat retailer, and over the next few years he went on to build a successful business, opening stores in the centre of Sheffield as well as in Manchester. Ada was tall and striking with a fiercely independent spirit, and he adored her. He showered her with gifts of fine clothes and jewellery, including a magnificent double diamond, three-carat engagement ring. After Ada's death, the twin stones from this ring were divided, one bequeathed to my mother and one to her younger sister Rita. The one to my mother is now in my possession. Notwithstanding the fact that it is slightly flawed – did Herman perhaps acquire it on the black market? – it is a superb specimen, and a very precious (in all senses) link with my past. Herman was unfailingly generous and loved children. He was a hugely popular figure with his little nieces and nephews, to each of whom he slipped a munificent two-shilling piece whenever he saw them. In 1920, when my mother was five, this could buy a whole pound of Rowntrees Fruit Gums, normally sold by the quarter, or twelve Cadbury's Chocolate Pies at tuppence each. No wonder Ena and her sisters looked forward so eagerly to his visits.

As Herman's business continued to prosper, he and Ada moved from the rented rooms where they had begun married life and which they shared with another lodger, into a mock-Tudor detached house on New Hall Road in leafy Broughton Park. The house was Herman's wedding gift to his bride. I have fond memories of this lovely home where I would go and stay as a child. It was roomy and light, surrounded on three sides by a large, shady garden, perfect for stretching out on a wicker steamer chair or for taking tea on the veranda on golden summer afternoons. One of the bedrooms was set aside as a nursery. But when year after year no longed-for baby appeared, Ada was labelled a failure, somehow to blame for her infertility. The cracks in the marriage widened.

Childlessness was not the only source of their marital woes. Glamorous Herman was an inveterate womaniser, with lady friends and broken hearts scattered all over town, though it's unclear just how much of his philandering Ada suspected, at least in its early stages. It is hardly surprising that over the years the bond between husband and wife soured, and when it splintered beyond repair, Herman demanded a divorce. After countless short-term flings, he had fallen in love with his secretary, a young woman called Rachel Cohen. Ada was furious. Sticking to her righteous moral guns, she grimly refused to accept that the marriage was over. In the years just after the First World War, divorce was a social humiliation, and she could not bear to lose the respectability she so prized. Even I can remember how proud she was. Strong-willed and sure of her rights, she continued to refuse for the next thirty years, and as hopes of reconciliation grew more and more distant, she determined to erase all traces of Herman from her life. She ripped in half all the photographs that showed them together, so that my treasure trove of historic snapshots has a whole cache of torn pictures with jagged rents where once Herman's image would have been. Luckily, she missed a few, so I do still have some souvenirs of the vile seducer she once found so fascinating.

Under Jewish religious law it is technically possible for a man to divorce his wife without her consent. Indeed divorce is only sanctioned when the husband hands his wife a *get*, a physical document that states simply, "You are hereby permitted to all men". The brutal wording says it all. Their marriage is over, and she is released from her commitment, free to enjoy other relationships or marry again. Ultra-orthodox Jewish communities today still practise this archaic form of divorce, although it is not and never has been legally binding in the civil courts. Ada's refusal to accept the *get* meant that Herman could not have his way to marry his mistress unless he could find a hundred rabbis to agree that his wife's decision was unreasonable. Finding a hundred rabbis who can agree on anything is a pretty far-fetched concept under any circumstances, and as Ada was absolutely intent on thwarting his wishes, Herman quickly realised that he was not onto a winning streak. In any case, whatever the decision of the rabbinic court, Ada and Herman would have remained officially married in English law. Nonetheless, Herman moved Rachel into New Hall Road, where they set up residence on the first floor, while Ada was confined to quarters on the ground floor. A latter-day Cinderella, she spent most of her time in the kitchen, preparing meals for the adulterous pair, presumably one of Herman's conditions of keeping a roof over her head. However galling the situation, she had nowhere else to go. She was illiterate, unqualified, she had no bank account of her own and no source of income, having given up her job when she married.

How Ada could have put up with this set-up for even a single day is inconceivable to me, as she was never one to submit meekly to situations she found distasteful. Eventually the state of affairs became intolerable for all parties, including of course Rachel, who must have been terrified that every mouthful she ate, prepared by Ada, might be laced with juice from the deadly nightshade that flourished in the nearby hedgerows. At last, Herman, no doubt at his mistress's prompting, threw Ada out for good. Abandoned by her husband, she moved into lodgings consisting of a single, miserable attic room, a far cry from the comfortable residence she had assumed with some justification was hers for life. She fought for years to get her house back, and although she was eventually successful, it took over two decades of out-and-out warfare with the errant Herman. Meanwhile the faithless one and his Rachel went on to have three sons and a contented family life.

Predictably the affair became a local scandal. Like Ada, Herman was socially ostracised and his paramour considered nothing more than a scarlet woman, her name murmured behind locked doors. The sense of shame hung around for a long time and reverberated through the generations. Only a couple of years ago, when I asked my Aunt Rita about Herman, her mouth pursed in disapproval as she looked around the lounge of her London care home to make sure we could not be overheard, and whispered, *sotto voce*, that although he might have seemed very affable on the surface, this was nothing but a sham. He was not to be trusted as all the time they were married he had been "carrying on" with another woman behind Ada's back. She didn't know the half of it. According to Millie's daughter, Maureen, there were broken hearts and not a few illegitimate offspring scattered all over town.

It was only more than forty years after the marriage had started to fall apart that Ada finally capitulated to Herman's requests for divorce, persuaded by her nephew, Harry, by then a respected solicitor, that any settlement would almost certainly be to her financial advantage. This argument carried some weight. Ada swallowed her pride in favour of common sense, and the result had immediate benefits for both sides. In order to establish the grounds for divorce, she went to live with my grandparents, so that their home became her official address for the purposes of the petition. In October 1948, Ada and Herman were divorced in the Sheffield Courts on account of the respondent's adultery. A few days later, Herman married Rachel Cohen, spinster and the mother of his children, in a quiet registry office ceremony in Hemsworth, Yorkshire, discreetly tucked away from prying eyes.

Harry did a good job on his aunt's behalf. Ada got her financial security, including sole ownership of the property, where her sister Millie's family were now installed, and where the house became filled with the warmth and laughter I remember from the 1950s. She was also awarded the princely sum of £20 per week. But she remained with a powerful feeling of injustice that permanently coloured her attitude to life. She never forgave Herman for his treachery or the circumstances that had conspired against her to procure his defection. She may indeed, unknown to anyone, have had her revenge. A few years later, when two of Herman's three sons died relatively young, rumours went around amongst Rachel's friends that Herman's first wife had been a witch who had put a curse on the family. She was undoubtedly capable of it. While others fell around her, Ada lived on well into her nineties, feisty and indomitable, and much loved, if also slightly feared, by her nieces and nephews, who accorded her the role of honorary grandmother to their children.

During the period of separation from Herman, Ada had been taken in by Mr and Mrs Freeman, the kindly owners of a kosher hotel in Blackpool, frequented by the Glass and Golding families. Ada, an expert if traditional cook, was put to work in the hotel's kitchens, where she helped with the catering for the flow of guests who passed through the doors. She particularly excelled at strudel, an import from her Austrian childhood, which became a family legend for its flaky lightness. I would watch her as she stretched the pastry repeatedly over my grandmother's large kitchen table to an almost transparent thinness so that it almost touched the walls, before filling it with a mixture of apples, almonds, raisins and spices. For a number of years, kitchen work was her only source of income. The fine jewels and gowns of the early photographs disappeared as she sold off her valuables to support herself. The only thing she hung onto was her diamond engagement ring. Even Ada couldn't bear to part with this memento of earlier happiness. Or perhaps, canny as always, she knew its value would only increase in years to come.

In addition to her ring, Ada handed down her recipe for *eingemakhts*, a beetroot jam, which she would make regularly at Passover. It's an object lesson in creative cookery or how to produce something palatable out of nothing. In the low-income homes of the *shtetl* any small patch of land was an important culinary resource, and root vegetables became the mainstay of a poor household's diet.

Potatoes, carrots and beetroot all had their place in my family's collective alimentary memory. Potato *kugel*, carrot *tsimmes* and borscht, each dish relied on exceptionally slow cooking to make the tubers even halfway digestible. *Eingemakhts* was the crowning achievement. When a recipe starts with the instruction to "take 10lbs of beetroot", it gives some indication of the scale of the operation, and jars and jars of the stuff were produced each year to distribute as gifts among favoured relatives. All my family used to declare it delicious though it was not to my taste. If you want to try it, I still have Ada's recipe, saved in my mother's cookbook that she compiled from the year she got married. Maureen, who has a similar recipe, reminded me that the most important thing about this cookery is the pan, which needs to be sufficiently robust to withstand hours of boiling. The cooking instructions include a modern recommendation to wear disposable latex gloves. Otherwise your hands turn bright pink.

While Ada became a familiar presence in the homes of the next generation of nieces and nephews, none of us children ever knew anything about Great-aunt Sarah. She was an invisible spirit in a family where ties of birth were inviolate and parents, brothers and sisters were always on call. My mother for instance, born in 1915, never lived more than five minutes' drive from her birthplace in almost a century. When my grandparents moved the thirty miles across the Pennines from Manchester to Sheffield in 1912, it was considered a journey not dissimilar to that of the Voortrekkers making their perilous way into the South African interior. This tight-knit network, however, colluded in a conspiracy of silence and no one ever breathed a word to me about Sarah until shortly before her death, by which time I had children of my own.

Sarah was my grandfather's sister. She never knew her own father. She would have been about two when her mother remarried, and with the arrival of two more half-sisters, she grew up in the midst of an affectionate and fun-loving family. Like Ada and Lea, her stepsisters, she started work at the age of twelve, employed at a hat manufacturer on Cheetham Hill Road, where she put the finishing stitches to men's caps. The photographs show her to be by far the prettiest of the sisters, wide-eyed, full lips and a hint of a smile to a camera that normally showed its subjects as expressionless. Through these I can watch her progress from a lovely schoolgirl, her long, dark ringlets tied back with an outsized black-ribboned bow, to a fashionable young woman in sumptuous Edwardian evening dress. Exquisitely turned out, her long skirt is elaborately gathered, a lacy, pleated blouse reveals her creamy shoulders, gold chains hang round her neck, and her arms are encased in spotless white evening gloves which stretch up to her elbow. Suddenly though, the portraits stop. Their absence is more poignant than any words.

Gradually I pieced together her story. Sarah would have been in her early twenties when she fell in love with a young man from the North Manchester Jewish community, a highly suitable match. Like Herman's image, his name has been erased from family history. A wedding date was set, and, as was the custom for brides-to-be, Sarah spent hours preparing her trousseau by the light of a gas mantle. By this time she was a noted seamstress and a particularly skilled lace maker. Then, without warning, on the eve of the wedding her fiancé broke the engagement and vanished. The effect on Sarah was dramatic.

Depression can take many forms. Did she become hysterical? Suicidal? Suffer from delusions? Who knows? She is recorded in the 1911 census at the age of nineteen as still working as a cap finisher, but it's difficult to track the precise sequence of events after that. Although hospital records give some indication of her subsequent fate, patient information is limited by confidentiality so to rebuild her story I have to rely on a shared family memory, which is fast disappearing. In about 1920 Sarah was admitted to Prestwich Lunatic Asylum, where she was diagnosed as suffering from "disappointment in love", then a recognised mental disorder. Over the next few years she was discharged for trial periods into the care of her family, but these failed to revive her, and in the end, she was committed to the Asylum as a permanent resident. It became her home until she was carried out in her coffin.

Prestwich Asylum was considered a particularly progressive institution for its day. Founded in 1851 with 350 inmates, by 1913 it accommodated over 2,500 patients plus residential staff, both nurses and domestic workers, such as cooks, cleaners, laundresses and care attendants. Its population therefore by the time Sarah was admitted was about the same size as the village of Jagielnica during the years my grandmother and Ada had lived there. Indeed, the hospital was organised very like a village. In addition to the wards, where patients slept, there were kitchens, a bakehouse, a laundry, stables, gas and engine houses and workshops, and even a farm. Based on the principle that occupation was therapy for unbalanced minds, all but the most disturbed patients were found jobs looking after the estate once they were assessed as being relatively stable and no danger to other inmates. Women patients, such as Sarah, were expected to spend time mending and making clothes to be worn in the asylum. Others worked in the laundry or helped with the cleaning of the wards and other public areas. Sarah, herself, was resistant to all overtures.

The 1845 Lunacy Act had required all lunatic asylums to be monitored and regulated, and staff at Prestwich were trained in how to handle their charges and required to sign a copy of the Asylum's Rules, Regulations and Orders. These specified that staff could be fined or discharged for "acts of unkindness or violence to patients, for intemperance, for disobedience of orders" or for any action that might compromise the character of the institution. Although we hear a lot nowadays about the horrific treatment of the insane in late Victorian times, there is every indication that the regime in Prestwich was designed to help and cure the sick rather than punish them, as was the case earlier in the century. In the 1940s, by which time Sarah had been resident there for twenty-five years on and off, entertainments, including dances, concerts and sports days, were regularly laid on, and hobbies such as bird-keeping and playing music were encouraged. But in the 1920s, the hospital was going through a difficult period. Labour was in short supply following the First World

War when men were on military duty, and women either served as nurses and ambulance drivers or were required to take men's place in factories and on farms. This radical social shift was accompanied by a meteoric rise in cases of mental illness from post-war trauma in wounded or shell-shocked veterans, as well as in those wives and mothers who had lost husbands and sons, or who were unable to cope with the nightmares or disabilities of their returned heroes.

It's an effort for me to picture what it must have been like for this young woman, brought up in a modest home, to enter the doors of this huge establishment, however humane its policies. When he was in his eighties, my grandfather described how throughout the time they were growing up, he and his sister never came into contact with anyone from outside their immediate world. They went to Jewish schools, ate kosher food bought from Jewish shops, went to synagogue on Saturdays, visited the ritual baths and celebrated feast days together. Suddenly Sarah, already in a distraught state of mind, was not only torn from her family but found herself confined with drunks, whores and criminals "of doubtful character" as well as epileptics and erratic personalities. Admissions records for Prestwich reveal that many inmates arrived in a dire state. Unwashed vagrants and slum dwellers crawling with head and body lice were undernourished and suffering from contagious diseases, including the dreaded typhus.

In 1921 a book about Prestwich Asylum, *The Experiences of an Asylum Doctor*, caused a public outcry. Its author was Dr Montague Lomax, who had been assistant medical officer at Prestwich during 1917 and 1918, shortly after I reckon that Sarah was first admitted, and who had been shocked by the conditions he found there. *The Experiences of an Asylum Doctor* depicted a regime where neglect, confinement and cruelty were common, where patients' meals were virtually inedible and their clothes "inappropriate". Even as late as the 1950s inspectors reported that when they visited, they did not see a single woman resident who was wearing a bra, and new staff were shocked to discover that patients were being bathed in batches, herded together and often exposed to the unclean water from the previous group. Lomax reported that both nursing staff and management lacked professional training and their irresponsible attitude to patients led to abuse, which went unchecked. Restraints were used on both men and women to calm them down and those patients who refused to settle were forced to wear unusually heavy clothing to prevent them from moving easily. Although Montague Lomax's account ultimately led to a Royal Commission, which resulted in sweeping changes in the treatment of psychiatric patients nationally, the conditions he described were those that my abandoned aunt encountered when she was first incarcerated there.

Once those studded doors had clanged behind her, Sarah was in an alien routine. The atmosphere was gloomy, the dilapidated accommodation resembled a barracks, and despite good intentions, there was little for inmates to help lift their spirits. I could find no indication that Sarah was suffering from anything other than a bout of clinical depression but in the early years of the twentieth century, psychiatric medicine was in its infancy and there was no real treatment for dealing with emotional trauma apart from an improved diet, sleep or sedatives. Sarah, locked away in this massive Victorian edifice, was heavily drugged in order to quieten her hysterical symptoms. Purging was also a regularly prescribed treatment.

Visitors were generally discouraged in the belief that they brought with them too many unhappy reminders of the world outside the hospital walls. On one occasion when my grandfather went to see her, Sarah tried to throw herself out of a second-floor window. As she struggled and attempted to smash the glass, he grabbed her legs to pull her back into the room. She was strong and determined, and he had to hang on with all his might until nurses arrived to drag her to safety. After that, he was advised not to go anymore because his visits were too distressing, though whether this distress was worse for him or the patient is difficult to say.

As the years passed, Sarah became increasingly institutionalised and increasingly ill-equipped to handle life outside the hospital walls.

Despite attempts by staff to engage her interest, she remained passive. Even sewing was beyond her, though her hands moved constantly, restlessly on her lap as if she were making lace, the skill for which she had once been renowned. By the time the country was settling down after the Second World War, and psychiatry had become more advanced, it was judged unwise to release Sarah from the secure hospital environment into a world of traffic and telephones, a world that had altered beyond her recognition. Although Ada continued to visit, she refused to tell anyone the purpose of her expedition. "Where are you going, Aunty?" Maureen would ask as Ada left the house on Saturday afternoons to catch the bus. There was never any answer. Sarah's name remained unspoken and her story remained, like her, conveniently out of sight. She died in 1976. Returning from her graveside, my mother composed some verses about her, which capture the imagined life of inner isolation.

In all her numbered years to eighty-three
She knew no husband, children,
Home was long forgot,
More distant than some ancient oubliette.
Only cold walls, nurses, barred windows, tranquillizing tablets.
Now in tranquillity she lies at rest
The turmoil of her girlish years suppressed.
I would have liked Aunt Sarah to have had a larger headstone.

Once she was young. Skipped, played, went to school,
Brown flowing hair, schoolgirl brushed,
Held by broad butterfly wings of black petersham ribbon.
Had skills. Her lace-making was a byword.
Had dreams, fell in love, was jilted. That was the beginning.
The end, a meagre cortege of niece and nephew she had never seen
The headstone stood forlornly bleak in the thin sun,
The bare inscription saying just "Sarah...", date of birth and death.

They say she never smiled again. Just sat for sixty years, staring,
Her hands fondling a lace invisible.
A silent, pale young woman, then middle-aged and matronly.
At the last, shrunken, bent like a squirrel, with clipped white hair.
Unloved, uncherished, unbefriended.
The dumb dull stone says nothing.
Yet flanked on all sides by handsome monumental marble
Its insignificance tells all.
I would dearly have liked Aunt Sarah to have had a larger headstone.

In 1996 the Asylum, now re-designated the Mental Health Services of Salford, closed its final residential long-stay ward, my great-aunt's home for so many years. A Tesco superstore and a smart hotel now occupy the site. As today's customers stand at the checkout with special offers, bottles of gin and tins of baked beans, how can they know that they are treading on a village of forgotten souls, where the sane were closeted with the demented to wither away their lives? From being the beloved beauty at the heart of the family, Sarah was consigned to the periphery, punished for an excess of passion and her faith in a young man's promises. She was not the last of my relatives to be broken by her dreams.

Four

Montgomery Road: Sheffield 1910

"Memory is always a montage of disparate fragments. In order to put these fragments into some kind of sequence, I need to set [their] memories now side by side with the fuller versions I remember from childhood and my own youth."

LISA APPIGNANESI, *LOSING THE DEAD*

My grandmother never went to school. Although she quickly learned to speak English with barely a trace of a foreign accent, her conversation was peppered with Yiddish terms, the language she had grown up with. By the time she married, she had also learned to read because my grandfather was determined to teach her, and once she got the knack of it, she devoured whatever books and magazines came her way. She was completely uninterested in romances but had a particular fondness for Westerns with their exploits of cowboys and Indians on the American prairie, a place she knew only through the flickering screen of silent cinema reels. Perhaps she found some resonance with her own history in these tales of pioneers in a barren landscape, forging a new life in the frontier settlements of Iowa,

Kansas and Montana. Who knows? Apparently, stories of Native Americans continue to have an almost canonical status in some sections of Eastern Europe today. Yet despite her love of books, which she borrowed from the local lending library in big print, the art of writing remained permanently beyond her reach, and whenever I received birthday cards from my grandparents they would always be signed by Grandad. On their marriage certificate, the bride's signature, Leah Goldberg, is distinctly shaky. Someone is evidently guiding her hand. The registrar had also adopted the anglicised version of her name from the King James Bible, and that was how everyone spelled it for the rest of her life.

Her sister, Ada, on the other hand, never learned either to read or write English. When she visited my parents' house, where small talk was in short supply and it was considered almost *de rigueur* to settle down after supper with the *Jewish Chronicle*, a library book or, in my father's case, the latest edition of *Bridge World*, Ada would sit erect and gaze in front of her. In 1953 when television became widely available in British homes, timed just right for the Queen's coronation, my uncles and aunts clubbed together and bought a twelve-inch screen TV for my grandparents but there was never any thought that we might have one in our own living room. A set eventually arrived in the late 1960s after I had graduated from university. So without Eamonn Andrews or even Archie Andrews to entertain her, Ada occupied herself by doing the washing up after meals. Once, as she was sitting patiently, hands clasped on her lap, I offered her the newspaper, and was told off by my mother for being rude. But how could it have crossed my mind that a grown-up wouldn't be able to read?

Deprived of books, and without the modern resources of TV or the internet, both Leah and Ada became expert games players. They were authorities on solitaire, and a large polished oak solitaire set with inlaid holes for the marble balls sat permanently on my grandmother's dining table. They also knew endless different versions of patience, the supreme card game for keeping boredom at bay, and would sit for hours absorbed in the problem of how to get all the cards "out" in any particular arrangement. I learned spider patience, clock patience and pyramid patience under their tutelage, as well as the more competitive "pisha-pasha", a version of patience for two players, although I found it hard to resist the almost overwhelming temptation to cheat, as virtually all the games ultimately relied on chance rather than skill and in the end seemed rather pointless to me. My grandmother, however, was a child of fortune and liked nothing better than to feel that luck was determining her future, as indeed had proved spectacularly to be the case. She and Ada played a particularly esoteric game for two, known as *sechsundsechzig* (sixty-six). Apparently this was the national card game of Austria amongst the uneducated classes, and I eventually became quite adept, although never in Ada's league, and learned to call the court cards by their Yiddish names, such as *Malke* for queen and *Yossel* for jack.

My grandmother also spent afternoons playing canasta with friends, and evenings playing whist, kalookie or bridge. She had a natural instinct for card play although her bidding was completely erratic, based on impulse rather than judgement. She and my grandfather would regularly come to play bridge at my parents' house on winter Saturdays, evenings that must have been absolute torture for my father, who was a professional bridge writer. He bore it well, however, and on occasion used my grandmother's mistakes as comic subject matter for his articles, including one famous incident where, having vaguely recalled a rule of thumb that the person sitting second should play a low card, she failed to put the ace of trumps on her opponent's king, normally not a recommended strategy but on this occasion a masterly stroke that happened to be the only possible way to defeat the contract. Quite apart from anything else, I learned the very important art of shutting up as I watched the play. *Kibbitzing* was absolutely *verboten*.

Stepsister and stepbrother, Leah and Isaac, were married in March 1910, just four months before their first child, Harry, was born on 8 July that year, an unfortunate concurrence that was kept hidden from their offspring and that I encountered with some surprise when scrutinising the family records. In retrospect perhaps such an event was predictable given that the couple had been living together under the same roof prior to their marriage. My grandfather had left school at the relatively advanced age of thirteen and immediately found a job as an office boy at a small finance house in Manchester at a salary of five shillings a week. He was quickly promoted to the rank of commercial clerk and his wages were raised to two pounds a week when he married, although as he cheerfully admitted later, he fiddled more than that by claiming "booking fees for the client". In 1911 he was asked to manage the Sheffield office on behalf of his employer, Mr Bennet, thirty miles across the Pennines. So Isaac Glaski changed his name to Glass, took his doubled weekly income of four pounds, and went off to Pinstone Street in Sheffield city centre, where he spent a considerable part of each day drinking coffee and playing billiards in a nearby snooker parlour at a stake of ten shillings a game. Despite his innate idleness, he enjoyed considerable success in these early days, his natural friendliness and laid-back manner instantly endearing him to clients, who were innocently happy to put their trust in him.

He always described his profession as financier, a traditional Jewish occupation, partly because it was one of the few professions that Jews were not barred from in nineteenth-century Europe, and consequently turned to by default. It is of course the source of the great Jewish banking empires, such as the Rothschild and Oppenheim dynasties, but Grandad was nowhere near that league. He had a small, dark office in the heart of Sheffield's commercial district, where he went every day, working well into his eighties. His office sign figures prominently in a 1970s painting of Pinstone Street by a well-known local artist, George Cunningham, and was featured in several Sheffield art exhibitions as well as on popular postcards. The business itself consisted of lending money to individuals who needed cash quickly and who felt intimidated by the grandeur and off-putting formality of the large banking institutions. Isaac, with his soft Northern accent, his relaxed smile and his general air of approachability was much more user friendly. Typically, his clients were young couples who required funds for a down payment on their first home or to buy a bed, table and chairs to fill it. In the days before credit cards, online loans or even hire purchase agreements, small money lenders were often the only means many people had of access to ready money.

Arriving in Sheffield was a severe culture shock for Grandad. Sheffield, with approximately 800 Jews in comparison to Manchester's 30,000, was not only a smaller but a much more integrated Jewish community than he was used to. Instead of streets of flourishing mercantile action, where businesses were Jewish-owned and Yiddish was spoken on a daily basis, he found a handful of Jewish shops, a single Hebrew school and a small congregation of varying degrees of piety. In contrast to the hubbub of Cheetham, where every house was occupied by Jewish and mostly recently arrived immigrant families, in Sheffield his neighbours and the workmates in his shared office building were not just English but from determinedly Yorkshire stock with blunt manners and ways that were foreign to him. It took a while to realise that he had to adapt to this new habitat, and at first he continued to follow the customs of the deeply observant Jews as they had been practised in Manchester, including walking to the synagogue on Saturday mornings to take part in the Sabbath service.

Because of acrimonious rifts in the community dating back decades, Sheffield in 1910 possessed two rival synagogues, the Sheffield Hebrew Congregation in North Church Street and the Central Hebrew Congregation at West Bar, both tucked away in a warren close to the city centre. So although it was nothing like Manchester, where houses of prayer were virtually elbowing each other out of the way, my grandfather still had the luxury of choice, as goes the old Jewish saying, of deciding which *shul* not to go to. He joined North Church Street as being the most prominent. On a particularly festive Saturday when the Sabbath coincided with a Jewish holiday, young Isaac Glass dressed in his best silk top hat and frock coat as was the Manchester custom, and to make a point that he was a man of means. As he walked down the Moor, one of the main Sheffield shopping streets, he was taken aback to discover that he had attracted a large crowd of children, who followed him all the way through town, hanging onto his coat tails, cat-calling and dancing around him as if he were a side show. This was how he learned about Long Sammy, a clown who used to parade the inner city with advertising sandwich boards, dressed in almost identical if rather more tattered gear. When he entered the synagogue and saw the rest of the congregation wearing sober dark suits and soft fedora hats or discreet skull caps, he became aware of the full extent of his mistake. He took good care to dress down in future.

Nonetheless, he felt he had a position to establish, and paid the top price subscription of two shillings and ninepence a week to guarantee the best seat in the house. Jewish communities have habitually raised funds on this subscription basis and continue to do so today. The synagogue hierarchy was a hornets' nest of internal political divisions, and my grandfather soon became drawn into the heart of these and played his full part in the squabbles and plots that form the life blood of Jewish communal activity. While still in his early twenties, he was elected to the synagogue governing council, and remained a member until he gracefully bowed out at the age of eighty. In an unpublished fragment of memoir, written shortly before he died, he offered some insight into the internal wrangling that formed the catalyst for council meetings, and the strategies that younger members adopted to circumvent time-honoured process.

"After I had been in North Church Street a little while," wrote Grandad, "Mr Friend approached me and told me there was some disagreement among the members owing to the fact that the lower paying members, who were called seat-holders and were paying 1/- or less a week, were not allowed to have a vote. As a large number of members were related to him, and not on the Council, he suggested we call an extraordinary meeting of members and he would muster his family and we would pass a resolution for all members to have a vote. Otherwise the Council, who all voted for one another, would be re-elected. This we duly did and a special meeting was arranged for everyone to attend and we elected a new Council." Reading this,

I am seriously impressed by Grandad's talent for tactical planning. He clearly missed his vocation as a political agent. Following this democratic turn of events, he became the honorary auditor for the congregation jointly along with a Mr Spiegel, and remained in this position until the Government decided they required a chartered accountant to audit the books, a qualification in which he was notably lacking.

I love the references to "Mister" Friend and "Mister" Spiegel in my grandfather's account. My grandparents always used titles rather than using first names when speaking about people they knew, however close the relationship. This habit persisted in company even when they were referring to one another. "Mr Glass likes to smoke a cigar after his dinner," my grandmother would tell her friends, or conversely, "Mrs Glass, it's your turn to bid," my grandfather might say at the card table with barely a touch of irritation. I never once heard them call one another Leah or Isaac.

When his luck was in and business was good, Grandad could afford luxuries that many of his friends could only dream of. In 1919, he bought a car at enormous expense and employed a chauffeur to drive it. He readily acknowledged that he was far too lazy to bother with driving lessons. The chauffeur was a young man called Eddy Sutherland, who went on to become the largest manufacturer of cooked and potted meats in the North of England, creating a vast business empire that made him hugely wealthy. In 1921, however, he was driving my grandparents around Sheffield or on holiday to Blackpool, and in 1924, 160 miles to the Cup Final at Wembley, when Sheffield United beat Cardiff 1–0. In fact, Grandma and Grandad nearly missed this triumphant moment as the car had five punctures on the journey, each of which required Eddy to get out and repair the tyre at the side of the road, while they stood by enjoying a leisurely cigarette, watching him work. As a result of these mishaps they were late for the game and didn't arrive in the stands until ten minutes after the 3.00pm kick off. Fortunately for them, the single winning goal, as reports of the match verify, was scored at precisely eleven minutes past three.

Going in a car was still something of a novelty, and as he was both gregarious and generous, Grandad took enormous pleasure in giving rides to all his friends. There were times when he owned two cars, an unheard-of extravagance, and would hire one of them out. By the 1920s he was making forty pounds a week, a massive sum easily equivalent to an annual six-figure salary now but with even greater spending power for a man without a mortgage. He loved to entertain and to give his family treats, usually limited to a fortnight twice a year at Freeman and Bowman's, a small Blackpool private hotel that was strictly kosher. He also had considerable costs when over the next two decades, he put three of his children through university or college in the days before student loans or grants, none of whom started earning until the mid-1930s. The luxuries gradually disappeared. His decline was accelerated by the introduction of the Moneylenders Act in 1927, which restricted the amount of interest any individual or bank could charge, and then further by the Second World War, when borrowing was the last thing on anyone's mind. After the war, once the nation began to find its feet again, the increasing popularity of hire purchase agreements put paid to any business interests such as Grandad's. He was left without any reliable source of income and had to fall back on his savings, which rapidly evaporated. Certainly, by the time I came along, there was never much money around, and my grandparents lived extremely modestly.

Grandma was small and when I knew her quite stout. She could never be called elegant but she loved stylish clothes, even if her idea of chic never advanced much further than her personal apogee of the 1930s. I was particularly entranced by the double fox fur she used to wear around her neck, with the foxes' beady little glass eyes peeping out at me over her shoulders. She tottered about on high-heeled shoes, wore a lot of red lipstick, and chain smoked, lighting one cigarette from the butt of the one she was just finishing. Her ample bosom was permanently thick with ash. She was only ever seen without a cigarette on the Jewish Sabbath. Smoking was strictly forbidden on Shabbat because it involved lighting fire, which was categorised by rabbinic law as work, and as Grandma was an observant Jew, she put down her cigarette at dusk every Friday evening and didn't light up again until the Sabbath was over at dusk on Saturday. I've no idea how she managed it as the rest of the time she was totally addicted. She was jolly and sociable, chattered and gossiped, and had a natural gift for making other people laugh. After her final illness, the family received a letter from a woman who had been a patient in the same hospital as Grandma, and who, not realising that she had died, had written to thank her for having cheered up the whole ward with her infectious sense of humour and buoyant spirit.

In 1921, Grandad bought a spacious semi-detached stone house on Montgomery Road at what was then the colossal price of £1,650. The average property price in Sheffield that year was around £150. Montgomery Road was a tree-lined street with large, solid houses, into which more prosperous Jews were moving as they relocated away from the terraces around North Church Street. Number 49 was where my grandparents brought up their five children. Harry, known in the family as Sonny, was the eldest, born in 1910. Then there was Rae, 1912, followed by my mother, Ena, in 1915. The two little sisters, Rita and Nancy, were born in 1918 and 1921 respectively. All the names were deliberately short and simple and none of the children had middle names. My grandfather claimed not to believe in excess, and in any case found that it was sufficient effort to think of first names without troubling with extras. When they had first come to Sheffield, my grandparents had rented a much smaller house, just around the corner, on Raven Road and it was here that my mother was born. The family moved to Montgomery Road when she was five. Unfortunately, they forgot to tell her. Ena toddled off to school quite happily one morning and came home that afternoon only to find that the house was empty of people and that the furniture had disappeared as well. Being a highly intelligent as well as a resourceful child, she didn't waste any time on self-pity but set off walking on her own in the general direction of the new house. Thank goodness that child-catchers were rare on Sheffield streets back then.

Two years after they had moved in, my Uncle Harry turned thirteen. His bar mitzvah was celebrated in splendid style with a party at home following the synagogue ceremony. A marquee was erected in the garden and sixty guests, twenty of whom came over from Manchester, were invited for dinner. Workmen put down a temporary floor for dancing and a three-piece band was hired. According to my grandfather, champagne flowed like water, there was a stall serving ices, which in a period when there were no domestic refrigerators was something of a feat, and both the chauffeur and the charwoman got drunk.

The house on Montgomery Road had a living room that stretched the length of the building, much of which was taken up with a long dining table, where, when I was a little girl, the whole family would gather for lunch at weekends and on Jewish festivals. Menus were traditional and *heimische* with chopped liver, golden chicken soup with *lockshen* and *kneidlach* (matzo balls) and tiny embryonic eggs from inside the fowl, followed by roast chicken and *tsimmes*, a carrot dish which had been baking all night in the oven. Grandma then served up to cries of delight a dessert of *lockshen* pudding, a great wodge of baked noodles, heavy with sugar and raisins, which sat indigestibly in the stomachs of anyone brave enough to sample it. There were also stewed prunes for the fainthearted, presumably intended to counteract the effects of the pudding.

Next to the living room was a rather gloomy, square morning room, furnished with dark leather armchairs and a leather sofa. This was Grandad's sanctum but it was where I liked to curl up in private with a book, completely unbothered by the sound of Grandad snoring in a post-prandial stupor across the hearth. There was no danger of either of us being disturbed, as my brother and younger cousins played, and my uncles chatted in the much lighter and more cheerful main living room, whilst my aunts gathered in the scullery to help Grandma with the dishes. I especially appreciated the, admittedly fairly limited, selection of reading matter left behind by my Aunt Nancy, who as a girl had been a devoted fan of school stories. There

I immersed myself in the adventures of the *Girls' Crystal Annual* and the works of Angela Brazil, even though half the time I didn't have much of a clue what was going on. Nonetheless it was the work of an instant to become utterly engrossed in the passionate friendships and the equally passionate jealousies and feuds played out in the enclosed world of girls that the books depicted. The banter occasionally defeated me. The word "brick", as in the phrase, "Ooh, Philippa, you are a brick!", was a particular teaser.

But the best room in the house was the big kitchen, with its black cast-iron range and glowing fire at one end and a rocking chair in which a black furry cat snuggled against cushions with their bright crocheted covers and pom-poms. There were shelves along one wall with pots and pans above, and cupboards beneath in which Grandma kept her sewing things, which I was allowed to play with, arranging buttons in order of size and making patterns with coloured silks. The kitchen led into a wash house with a massive copper tub, where wet clothes would be stirred with a wooden dolly, and then wrung out by squeezing them through a mangle. At the other end of the kitchen, hanging up on the wall just near the cellar head as you went into the room was a threatening-looking strap, an old razor strop, which we were warned was used by Grandad to beat naughty children. As my grandfather seemed to spend most of his time eating, sleeping or playing cards, it was difficult to take this warning seriously but nonetheless we used to sidle our way past it just in case.

The upstairs of the house was more sinister. In order to use the bathroom, we had to navigate our way past an evil-looking wall cupboard, which housed the flue and was liable to spring open without warning, exposing its cavernous interior. The bathroom itself sported an impressive array of brass pipes over the cast-iron bath on its curled claw feet. This was in fact a sophisticated shower attachment, installed in the 1920s and at that time the last word in contemporary plumbing technology as water sprayed out of holes in the pipes as well as from the shower head. The real item of interest, however, was in Grandma's bedroom, which had a whole black bearskin rug on the floorboards at the foot of the bed – I could sit on the bear's head, grasp its ears and ride away to somewhere far more exciting than here. The two other bedrooms on the first floor were where my aunts and uncle had slept as children. Harry as the only boy had the luxury of a room all to himself. The four girls were together, with Rae in a small truckle bed, and the other three squeezed up cosily in a big double. My mother found this intimacy somewhat overpowering – sharing a bed was stretching family affection a bit too far – and at the age of ten she decided to move out. She retreated to the attic on the top floor, a bare, chilly room, used for storing old toys, and where she could be secure in the knowledge that no one else wanted to sleep up there as it was colder and more isolated than the rest of the house, precisely why she liked it. She carried this inborn asceticism into adulthood, and the houses that she inhabited were always kept at what felt like sub-zero temperatures. I made sure I put on extra layers whenever I visited her.

Opposite my grandparents' house lived the Isaacs family with their four children, Zara May (Maisie), Phyllis, Edward (Teddy) and Edna, who all formed lifelong intimacies with my mother and her siblings. Julius Isaacs was a successful jeweller, and the family lived in grand style with a veneer of cultivation that eluded my own grandparents. The façade of civilised living, however, masked two tragic episodes. Mrs Isaacs suffered from a psychiatric disorder and as her condition deteriorated, it became clear that she was unfit to manage the household or bring up children. Mental illness in those days carried associations of syphilis or other hereditary weakness and was never openly alluded to. The stigma of madness was thought to pollute the whole family, and in the Isaacs' case was kept concealed even from her own grandchildren, one of whom, now in her seventies, was only enlightened when I started writing this memoir. Rather than have his wife incarcerated permanently in an asylum, Julius Isaacs employed a nurse to care for her at home, where she lived in a hut in the garden. Fans of *Jane Eyre* will quickly recognise the fictional scenario of the banished madwoman concealed safely out of sight, guarded closely by her keeper, and only occasionally permitted to enter the main part of the property. But this was no fiction. When Mrs Isaacs did venture out, it was just as frightening as Jane's glimpse of the monstrous Bertha Mason through the curtains of her bed in Thornfield Hall. My mother never forgot walking up the Isaacs' driveway one day, to ask Edna to come and play, and being confronted by a wild-eyed face at the window of an unkempt woman, who glared menacingly at her and shook her fist. This was Mrs Isaacs, let briefly out of confinement. Ena, aged nine, turned and fled.

As a result of their mother's illness, the younger children were looked after by the second sister, Phyllis, who, from the time she was a teenager, ran the household with great efficiency. She was both loving and competent, and by all accounts a devoted substitute mother. One day in 1928 as she finished clearing the dining room table after lunch, she held up the tablecloth to shake the remaining crumbs into the fireplace. Horrifically, the cotton fabric caught a flame and set alight. The down draught from the fire blew the tablecloth into a billowing sail, which wrapped itself around the helpless Phyllis, who was fatally burnt, lingering for months in agony before she died. She was twenty-two.

Harry and Teddy Isaacs were inseparable from boyhood and lived within walking distance of one another for over eighty years. Their friendship was cemented even more firmly when, in early 1939, Harry married Teddy's oldest sister, Maisie, a union that came as a blow to my grandmother. As the only son, Harry was the golden hope of the Glass family, with a bright future ahead of him and his pick of pretty, young, marriageable girls. Maisie was eight years his senior, a stern and forthright bluestocking, who cared little for her appearance and made no concessions to femininity. Rita, as a naïve sixteen-year-old, was understandably bemused when she walked into a room one day to find her perched on Harry's knee. Maisie was a remarkable woman with a doctorate in literature and an independent professional life. In the 1920s she travelled to Egypt as a journalist and throughout her life retained a fervent interest in theatre. As an undergraduate, she was elected the first female Vice President of the

Sheffield Students' Union, and in 1926 completed a PhD thesis on Renaissance drama. For many years she was on the Board of the local repertory theatre, the Playhouse, later to become the Crucible, and in her seventies, became the official archivist for Sheffield Theatres. During a distinguished career as a JP, she served as Chair of the Yorkshire Magistrates Association. In 1990, together with my Uncle Harry, she received an Honorary Doctorate from the University of Sheffield for her services to the theatre and to academia.

Her impressive intellectual virtues, however, were not particularly wifely credentials as far as my grandmother was concerned. She was horror-struck at the match, and she and Maisie never found common ground. The fact that Maisie made it clear that she had no interest in family life didn't help, and the marriage, to my grandmother's eternal disappointment, was childless. It was also, despite the knee-sitting incident, almost certainly celibate, an arrangement that Maisie had apparently made clear to Harry in advance, and that according to family gossip, suited him well. Reflecting Maisie's lack of interest in domesticity and creature comforts, their home remained in a time warp from the day of their marriage, making few allowances for modern conveniences other than always being equipped with a state-of-the-art gramophone and the latest classical recordings. At the time of their deaths at the end of the century, its furniture, ornaments and kitchen utensils dating from the 1930s, many of them received as wedding presents, a few still unpacked, could have been used to reconstruct a social history of the period. The set of eight heavy, buttercup-yellow pottery storage jars, graduated in size, each with their clear designation, "Sugar", "Tea", "Currants", "Salt", etc. and virtually untouched in Maisie's day, now sits proudly on the shelf in my own daughter's retro country kitchen in Kent, a perfect example of inter-generational recycling.

Five

The Stranger: Barrow-in-Furness 1915

"I am a stranger in this country. I have no property here, no connexions."

ALEXANDER HAMILTON, LETTER TO COLONEL JOHN LAURENS, 8TH JANUARY 1780

On a cold December morning in 1915, a small boy stood holding his older sister's hand on the platform of the crowded railway station in Barrow-in-Furness on the western edge of the English Lake District. The station was thronged with young men, many in uniform. Some were soldiers who had been home on leave and were returning to the trenches of the British Expeditionary Force in France. Rather more were excited new recruits, off to fight for their country. Fresh from training and in high spirits, they called across to one another through the clouds of steam as if they were old friends. In fact most of them were. A recruitment and training station was centred in Barrow, drawing young men from the neighbouring towns of Whitehaven and Workington. As the initial surge of enthusiasm for the war waned during 1915, a campaign to recruit whole brigades from the same district was deliberately mounted to encourage men to enlist with their "pals". "Join the Fifth and fight with local lads", read a recruiting poster in Barrow that year, in a campaign for the county's own company, the Fifth Cumberland Battalion Border Regiment.

Men were warned that if they postponed joining up, they might later be sent to train in another county with "strange officers and men". In August the Cumbrian cost had been shelled by the Germans (casualties: one dog, no children), an event that was seized on by the authorities as an opportunity to drum up volunteers from the area; conscription was not introduced until the following year. The flaw in such a plan was that while it promoted local companionship, it also meant that under heavy fire, an entire neighbourhood of fathers, brothers and sons could be wiped out at once. On the Western Front, 1915 was the year that the British army, in retaliation against the German offensive, began to use poison gas, a deadly weapon that was often blown back by strong winds into the faces of their own forces. Few of those who boarded that train would ever return.

The small boy was undersized even for his age – he was six – and he too was leaving home for an unknown future. An orphan, he knew only that he was being punished for being naughty, so naughty that his stepmother was sending him away. He did not cry. He had only the vaguest idea of what he must have done to deserve it. Refusing to go to bed when he was told to? Running off to play when he should have been indoors? Asking too many questions? The train's twenty-one carriages were jammed to overflowing. Although records show that the young men from Barrow were relatively puny in comparison to the majority of their countrymen, to him they were giants as they sprawled across benches and leaned against the coaches, their cigarette smoke mingling with engine fumes. As he peered through the open doors of the compartments to find a corner to sit in, he suddenly felt strong arms sweep him off his feet and swing him up almost as high as the roof. He spent the next few hours perched in the luggage rack of the troop train until it steamed into Sheffield's Victoria station. The small boy was my father, David Brown, and his sister's farewell hug was one of the last gestures of affection he would receive for ten years.

This experience seared itself into my father's DNA. It shaped his attitude to life and his fiercely protective stance to his own family. He never forgot the camaraderie of the soldiers going off gaily to their deaths nor his own feeling of being abandoned as he travelled away from his infancy towards the next phase in a rough and tumble existence. He also never fully came to terms with the knowledge that he was unwanted. He was only conscious that he had been ejected from the place he called home, and was going to a household full of strangers, where he would have to be brave and take care not to get in anyone's way. But who would give him supper? How would he know where to find his bed? Would the strangers notice whether he was there or not? These, and similar anxieties, haunted him all his life.

Trying to visualise the events that led to my father, not yet seven years old, swaying precariously in his rope nest on that train, his legs dangling above the heads of those exuberant recruits, forces me back over a century to reflect on the erratic, roller-coaster existence of his early childhood. How different from when I was growing up. My parents were always there to kiss me goodnight, supper appeared on the table without fail every evening at six o'clock, and the living room furniture stayed in the same position for years. "May you live in interesting times", cautions the ancient Chinese curse. As a small boy, my father was subject to the full force of this malediction, dragged from place to place to at least five different homes in as many different towns. He was almost always hungry, and he never knew the luxury of a bed of his own. Just as his family seemed to have found their feet in a mean couple of rooms above a modest shop front, his life was blown apart and he found himself without either mother or father, being moved on yet again, unsure what would be waiting for him when he arrived. It is unsurprising that in later life stability was the quality he valued above all others.

My father is one of the heroes of my story, surviving not just his own ill-fated start in life but rescuing other waifs and strays along the way, lost souls for whom he became a saviour and a prop on whom they could rely. At the point at which his tale begins, however, in the dreadful winter of 1915, the woman who was in fact his aunt as well as his stepmother could no longer afford to keep him. As I ponder on this, my father's history begins to sound more and more like the opening of a Grimm's fairy-tale or a scenario from a blockbuster novel. Certainly, his own account of his early years, with which he used to regale me and my brother in spare moments, usually to remind us how lucky we were not to be him, was just as heart-rending as the sentimental Victorian fictions I devoured as a teenager, and could be guaranteed to reduce me to tears in a Pavlovian instant.

Now, whilst my emotions may be more under control, my curiosity is sparked by the circumstances that brought him to this moment. For a start, what on earth was my father doing up in Barrow-in-Furness in the first place? At the end of a godforsaken peninsula reached only by means of a tortuous road even today, Barrow was not an obvious destination of choice. As I tried to map the tales my father told me onto the facts, such as they are, from the extant materials, I came up against a series of blanks. I never knew my grandfather, and the section that should contain his image is the most tenuous of all with hardly any clues to help to flesh out his hazy personality. So the next part of the picture took me months of detective work. It signals the shiftless, uncertain existence that so many of these migrants faced in their first years in a new country. As I combed through the records, searching for details that corresponded with one another, I gradually uncovered a buried story of loss, defeat and personal anguish that not even my father had been aware of. He would certainly have told us about it if he had. Like me, he relished melodrama.

My father's family history is more convoluted than my mother's, and on his father's side at least its origins more shrouded in mystery. His father, Max or Marks Brown, son of one Shepsell Brown, was born in Russia around 1873 and arrived in England just before the turn of the century, his escape route from forced conscription into the Czarist military forces. From 1875 up until the First World War, Jews faced a heavy annual quota of approximately 3,000 recruits, so that there were more Jews than non-Jews in the Russian army in proportion to the general population. Heads of households and professional men could claim exemption, and the draft requirement passed on to less fortunate younger brothers or sons. Not only was the call-up rigorously enforced but it was a route to almost certain death as Jewish conscripts were habitually placed in the front line of battle. The attempt to avoid military service was one of the major factors in the high incidence of single, young, uneducated men among those emigrating from the Russian territories.

The earliest reliable contemporary sighting of Max is by a compatriot, Morris Sirkin, a draper and dealer, who went on to become a prosperous furrier in Leicester, and coincidentally a friend of my future parents-in-law. Morris and Max were from the same Russian *shtetl* and travelled together on the same immigrant ship. There are no hints as to which village they came from. Morris regularly spoke of his childhood in Russia and how in winter, as a boy, he would gaze at the river for hours as massive logs were rolled downstream by the icy currents from the forests to the timber yards. But this could apply to any number of spots on the reaches of the lower Volga, from the Ukraine to southern Siberia. Nor are there any clues as to my grandfather's original Russian name. The surname Brown, acquired after he landed in England, was either conferred on him by the immigration authorities because his own name was too difficult to spell or because he couldn't make himself understood or because subsequently he changed it to ease the process of assimilation. The only possessions he brought with him were a spare shirt, *tephillin*, needles and thread and a chased silver goblet, used for the Sabbath and Jewish festivals. That cup, made from non-hallmarked Russian silver, and now slightly dented, sits on my own sideboard, ready to be filled with wine on Friday evenings.

Max Brown was small and slim with a trim dark beard and twinkling eyes. My father remembered his loving manner and gentle, wheezy voice, a relic of the privations he had suffered. No photographs of him survive, if indeed there ever were any. Family folklore had given me the impression that he was a genial but feckless wastrel, who lacked any sense of responsibility and couldn't even provide for his wife and children. My researches reveal instead a victim of serial misfortunes, who fought to look after those he loved. Each time he surfaced from one catastrophe, disaster struck again. In total, he fathered eight children, and in 1901 he was living near his old friend Morris Sirkin, with a drapery stall in Leicester market, peddling his wares around the outlying districts, using his home at 59 Nichols Street as a stockroom. In 1898 he had married Dora Cohen, another Russian refugee. Their wedding just predated the opening of the Leicester synagogue later that year, one of the first provincial buildings to be designated for the purpose. At the time there were just over sixty Jewish families living in Leicester, a fourfold increase from the sixteen registered there in mid-century. Life looked promising, and in January 1900, Dora gave birth to a son, Hezekiah.

The year 1902 was characterised by miserable weather. It hardly stopped raining throughout the first half of the year, and chill north-easterly winds persisted for most of June and July. Two-year-old Hezekiah developed a nasty cough, which refused to mend. He lost his appetite, grew listless and complained of pains in his head, arms and legs. Dr Beecroft, the physician who attended the little boy, diagnosed tuberculosis. TB was one of the most dreaded diseases of the early twentieth century, and one of the major causes of infant mortality. Hezekiah had contracted tubercular meningitis, a common killer of children under the age of four, especially if they were living in the sort of environment that provided a fertile breeding ground for the deadly bacilli. Dora, who was expecting her second baby in September could do nothing but watch helplessly as the summer drew on and Hezekiah's condition deteriorated. Suddenly his temperature shot up alarmingly, he started vomiting and his small body was shaken with rapid seizures. On 4 August, he died at home in his father's arms. On the day of his funeral, over 21mm of rain fell in Leicester, reducing the soil of the newly consecrated Gilroes Jewish cemetery on the outskirts of the city to a muddy swamp.

Today, on a visit to Leicester, I conjure up a mental picture of the mourners in the bleak cemetery, following the tiny coffin to the graveside. Young parents murmuring prayers over the loss of their first child, their tears staining the pages of the prayer book. Neighbours bringing soup and bread, urging the distraught mother to keep up her strength in preparation for her imminent confinement. Dora, with her swollen belly, unable to get comfortable in either body or spirit. Just four weeks after the funeral, on 1st September, her daughter, Bessie, was born. The anxieties of trying to ensure the baby survived her first few weeks were stressful enough for new mothers trying to recover from their ordeal but to do so while mourning a darling son must have been indescribably harrowing.

The couple coped with the twin shockwaves of bereavement and birth as best they could and it was not long before Dora became pregnant again. Another daughter, Sarah, known as Sadie, was born in the spring of 1904. This time the birth was less straightforward, and Dora, physically and emotionally drained, fell victim to puerperal fever, a frightening illness triggered by infection if the new mother was touched by dirty hands or if her dressings were not properly clean. It is estimated that in the early 1900s approximately one in every hundred births resulted in death from this cause. A debate on the sources and prevention of puerperal fever was conducted in 1910 in the pages of the *British Medical Journal*, with a letter from a Dr F. C. Bottomley suggesting that it was an especial hazard for those who gave birth at home rather than in lying-in hospitals, and who did not have access to antiseptic materials or a sterile environment. Dora had neither. She contracted a vaginal infection, which turned to septic peritonitis. After three days of agony, doctors operated but too late, and she died in hospital on 28 April 1904, before she had time to nurse her baby. She was buried at Gilroes, close to the mass grave in which lay the body of Hezekiah along with ten other babies' remains. Among the causes of death, her death certificate lists post-operative shock.

At this point Max was not quite thirty years old. After the loss, first of his son and then his wife, he now found himself left in care of a toddler and a new-born. A childless couple from nearby Nottingham, Ruben and Fanny Woolfe, came to his rescue and agreed to act as foster parents for the two girls. Both Russian immigrants, it is possible that Max had known them from *shtetl* days. Although the 1911 census states that the children were adopted, I can find no record of any formal adoption process, and it is likely that the term was loosely applied. Sadie was to remain in Nottingham for the rest of her life. Bessie, however, never really settled. She remained on and off with the Woolfes for the next few years but regularly returned to visit her real father, and ultimately made a different home for herself in Sheffield.

By 1906, his two motherless little girls safe with their substitute family, Max had started to rebuild his life. He left the rooms in Erskine Street, where Dora had died, and moved to nearby Gladstone Street, his fourth move in as many years. This was more cramped accommodation than the previous home, and it seems likely that his circumstances were considerably reduced, possibly because he was paying the Woolfes for the upkeep of his daughters. A man of considerable charm, he had also become betrothed to Annie Woolman from Sheffield. My grandparents, Max and Annie, were married at North Church Street synagogue, Sheffield, on 11 September 1906 in a ceremony attended by the bride's numerous relatives. The newly-weds moved into Max's humble lodgings in Leicester, where their daughter, Rachel, soon shortened to Ray, was born the following July. Another move quickly followed, this time to 3 Upper Kent Street, where on 30 March 1909 Annie gave birth to a son, David. The labour was complicated, the baby was weak and looked at first as if he might not live. Max, who seems to have had scant respect for bureaucracy, failed to notify anyone about David's arrival until 7 June, more than two months after the event. As this was way beyond the forty-two-day statutory period allowed for registering the birth of a child, when he did ultimately get around to dealing with the official details, he entered the birthdate as 30 April, a month later than the true one. A consequence of this cunning ploy, originally designed to prevent Max getting into trouble with the authorities, was that for years afterwards we celebrated my father's birthday on the April anniversary until, in his fifties, he decided to revert to the correct date. Presumably he felt he had no longer anything to fear from the registrar.

In the months following David's appearance in the world, awful summer weather once again seemed to conspire against the family. It is remarkable that my father survived at all. The meteorological office for June that year records that "from beginning to end there was not a day of real summer heat" throughout the month, and July saw "very inclement conditions" and abnormally low daytime temperatures. Nonetheless, Annie, with the resilience that marked all the Woolman women, got up from the bed where she had just given birth, and bustled around as usual. She appears to have acted as a part-time social worker and nurse, tending to friends and neighbours – her next-door neighbour when she was growing up had been a "monthly nurse" – and in July she was called to Sheffield to tend to a sick relative. It was here that she contracted the acute bronchitis that would kill her, and at the beginning of August, when my father was four months old, she died at the age of twenty-seven. Her gravestone can be found stacked up against a wall at the far end of the Gilroes Jewish cemetery, alongside a handful of other chipped and crumbling tombstones, where it was pushed some time during the 1950s, along with her bones, in order to make room for the more recent dead.

As Annie lay dying in that cold summer of 1909, her younger sister, Julia, came to take charge of the household. After the death, she stayed on to nurse the little ones and restore some sort of order to the small family. She also comforted Max, who must have been wretched, having lost two young wives and had three children taken from him in the last four years. He was not it would seem completely inconsolable, and Julia's comfort exceeded its remit to such an extent that by the autumn of that year, she found that she too was expecting a child. My uncle Alex (no one ever called him by his given name of Alexander) was born in August 1910. A mere two months (two months!) later, Julia was once again in the family way, and it is here that details in my timeline become hazy. For, in April 1911, six months pregnant and still using her maiden name of Woolman, she was back living in her parents' home in Sheffield. Had the couple been evicted? Did she find the prospect of looking after four children in poky rooms in Leicester too dismaying to contemplate or was she just desperate to escape from the poisoned atmosphere of the city in which her beloved sister had died?

Rooting around in a tin box filled with old family papers, I came across a *ketubah*, a Jewish marriage certificate. It's an odd document. At first glance it looks like standard fare with its heavily inked Hebrew script on one side of the paper and an English translation on the other. It states that a marriage was solemnised on 28th March 1910, four months before Alex's birth, and clearly relates to his parents' union. I look again. On closer examination I can see that the paperwork is incomplete. The bride's name, Julia Woolman, is inscribed together with the names of two witnesses, Lazarus Schweitzer and Isaac Ferk, both Sheffield residents. But where is the groom? The space where his name should be is blank. I double check. The Sheffield synagogue marriage records have nothing to indicate that this marriage ever took place, and there is nothing in the civil marriage register either. Clearly the marriage was planned and a date set. Did Max take flight?

I was taken aback by this discovery. My grandfather and Julia were always referred to as a married couple, and their children and my father never suspected otherwise. Julia's death certificate gives her name as Julia Brown, and she later described herself as a widow on all official documents. Yet there is no evidence that they went through any form of ceremony. Until 1907, when the Deceased Wife's Sister Act had been passed, it was in fact illegal for a widower to marry his sister-in-law, and less than three years later, taboos against such a marriage were still prevalent and subject to the discretion of individual clergymen. Additionally, Jewish law stated categorically that a man was not allowed to marry any woman with whom he had had "relations while in their unmarried state". Given Julia's very visible pregnancy that spring, there was no denying that "relations" had definitely occurred. Did the rabbi, on seeing the bride, refuse to conduct this planned wedding? Or did my grandfather, Max, get an attack of the nerves? His track record with wives was none too successful after all.

When I think about how my father's family prided themselves on their respectability, it jolts me into sharp awareness of just how scandalous Julia's situation would have been. Even in the late 1950s, when I was a teenager, a single mother was a thing of shame. A girl at my school was expelled when she became pregnant. Her name was whispered in corridors. She was sent away to a hostel for unmarried mothers and her baby was taken away for adoption. In 1910, for decent, modest Julia Woolman to give birth out of wedlock must have been unthinkable, especially in a closed provincial Jewish community. The Woolmans, however, were nothing if not practical. They gathered around their black sheep daughter and offered her and Annie's children a temporary home. It would have been out of the question for her to return permanently to Sheffield, the community where her sister's wedding to Max had been celebrated so recently. They needed to find a place where no one knew her, and where she and Max could pass themselves off convincingly as a married couple.

Max disappeared for a time, who knows where. He may have been on the road seeking a safe haven. He may have been hiding from the irate Woolman clan. Or perhaps, given his habitual diffidence, he was just fearful of giving his name to anyone who smacked of the establishment, for curiously there's no trace of him in the 1911 census. He resurfaces in the records when his third son, Joe, was born in July that year. I can trace his route up the west coast, as with Julia and the children, he stopped in Workington, Joe's birthplace, and in Cockermouth, where Harry, the youngest boy, arrived in the world in 1913. Max joined the band of itinerant pedlars on the edge of the Lake District before alighting on Barrow-in-Furness, the family's last halt, where he set up a market stall selling sewing equipment, needles, scissors and rolls of fabric. This stall was later to form the basis of my Uncle Alex's much more substantial store, Brown's the Busy Bee, on Dalton Road, one of the town's main shopping thoroughfares.

Here, in the 1950s, he sold Ladybird children's clothes and Chilprufe underwear, hosiery and skeins of knitting wool, all folded away in transparent cellophane packages, and stored in neatly labelled, blond wooden drawers, with metal handles that pulled out smoothly on runners. If a customer bought anything, the money was rolled up in a plastic bag, and packed in a small, metal cylinder that flew around the shop ceiling on a magical system of ropes and pulleys that then returned it gratifyingly with exactly the right amount of change. As a child, I was quite transfixed by this contraption and could watch it for hours. After all, we were starved of drama in those post-war days. But this was forty years after my father and his brothers had moved into their cramped couple of rooms above shop premises in Crellin Street near the centre of town. Here, on winter mornings, when the family woke up, one of the children, usually David or Alex, was deputed to go into the living area to light the gas mantle in the age long before homes were fitted with electric light. As the gas flame began to flicker, bringing the dark room to life, the floor appeared to sway, a sight which always unnerved them. The movement was from the hundreds of black beetles, which had covered the bare floorboards like a carpet during the night and were now scurrying for safety back into their holes behind the wainscoting.

During the years when my father was a child in Barrow, the town was a hive of industrial activity, specialising in the production of iron and steel, and in shipbuilding. Only sixty years earlier it had been a rural hamlet with a mere 700 inhabitants but by the early 1900s it had capitalised on its natural resources of local iron ore and on its prime position on Morecambe Bay to develop not just the ironworks but an entire system of dockyards together with their associated industries. The vast shipyards, with their own engineering works and foundry, provided employment for an enormous range of trades, including carpentry and sail-making as well as engineering, and the population of Barrow swelled accordingly with families who also required housing, feeding and clothing. In 1912, the shipyard alone employed 14,000 men. After war was declared in 1914, the industrial production intensified with the demand for warships, submarines and armaments, and factories and cranes dominated the skyline, pumping out noxious fumes that suffused the lungs and stunted the growth of the local lads.

In the first years of the century, the Barrow population contained just a handful of practising Jews. A synagogue had been built in 1901 on Abbey Road but as their minister pointed out in a letter to *The Jewish Chronicle* in June that year, the newly formed congregation consisted mainly of working-class members and was "sorely in need of extraneous assistance" to equip it. By 1914 the congregation had grown sufficiently to advertise for a general factotum who could perform a range of duties, including carrying out circumcisions, slaughtering kosher meat, and taking charge of religious instruction. The appointment was delayed because of arguments about exactly what sort of paragon the community could afford. Still there were obviously enough children by that stage – my grandfather alone had contributed a fair proportion – to warrant Hebrew classes. As the President, Mr I Stoller, acknowledged, "When a community is small, it is impossible to expect anyone to undertake the control of a congregation… who must be a married man, a young man with a good appearance, and a model to the town as a Jewish minister, with an average salary of 30s. per week."

Alex was to become bosom friends with Philly, the son of this Mr Stoller, a friendship that lasted until they were both in their eighties. The Stollers had started out as carpenters and cabinet makers. By mid-century they had built up a highly successful business in the furniture trade with a large retail store, which stood a few doors away from Browns the Busy Bee, and which ultimately provided jobs for a hundred or more local workers. They were well-known benefactors to the Barrow community and made generous donations to charity. In the 1960s, Philly Stoller bought a disused and deconsecrated church to function as a warehouse for his surplus stock. As wardrobes, sideboards, sofas and dining tables piled up in the echoing spaces where the pews and altar had once stood, locals became accustomed to the furniture vans loading and unloading inside the no longer sacred walls. The family's name was prominently displayed on the parish notice board at the front of the building, more conventionally used to display the times of services, with the result that the church became a celebrated Barrow landmark, widely known as St Ollers.

November 1915 was one of the coldest on record in the North of England, with persistent rain and gale force winds. Max had by this time established himself as a Master Draper but his professional status was no longer any use to him. Of slight frame and worn out with continually moving from place to place, he developed phthisis, a form of wasting tuberculosis that proved fatal. He died on the 30th November at the age of forty or, as his death certificate states, forty-two, depending on which birthdate one chooses to believe. He was difficult to pin down right up to the end.

The previous year Julia had taken the children to a photography studio. The resulting portrait shows the four boys all dressed in identical button-down jackets with white handkerchiefs folded neatly in the top pocket, and extravagant cream lace collars, possibly items from stock later to be sold. Harry is seated on a miniature chair at Julia's side, holding tightly to the arms so he doesn't fall off, and steadied by his mother's guiding hand. Joe, on a stool, leans against her knee. Ray and Bessie stare gravely into the lens, Bessie at the age of twelve already showing signs of the corpulence that dogged her adult life. David stands slightly apart from the rest, gazing wistfully ahead and clearly wishing he were somewhere else. Very soon he would be.

This then is the course of events that led directly to my father standing on that crowded station platform in Barrow in the year of the Battle of Loos. Julia must have been at her wits end, a self-styled widow in her twenties, with no social security and six children on her hands, the youngest of whom was not yet two. David was a particular trial, far and away the liveliest, forever getting under her feet and bothering her with incessant chatter – and not even her own child. Ever resourceful, she decided to pack him off to Sheffield, where he could be brought up in the bosom of her (and his dead mother's) family. Years later, Alex would say that David was the lucky one – he got away – but at the time and for a long time after David thought himself anything but lucky.

Six

Arrival: Sheffield 1885

"Everything is imprinted for ever with what it once was."
JEANETTE WINTERSON, *THE STONE GODS*

The relics of the past populate my home. Brass candlesticks, a tapestry fire screen, an ivory-topped cane, willow pattern china with its story of lovers frozen in time. Each of these objects once was new in someone else's house. Through them I can revisit those houses and meet their owners. They are the building blocks that give colour and depth to my jigsaw history. The solid brass candlesticks for instance, weighted in three sections, which unscrew for cleaning, were once polished to a lustre by my grandmother, Annie Woolman, who at the age of twenty-four became Max Brown's second wife. She was born in 1882 in the small town of Serey (Seirijai), about seventy miles west of Vilnius in southern Lithuania, and in the 1880s under Russian rule.

About 400 Jewish families lived in Serey, which was governed by the enlightened Napoleonic code that since 1815 had granted equality to all its citizens, with the exception of course of Jews, who had no civil rights whatsoever. Despite this, the town's Jews were exceptionally well educated, with a dedicated *cheder* in its own building surrounded by a garden, the gift of a local philanthropist. Here, under the supervision of four teachers, children learned maths and Russian alongside religious and Yiddish studies. Specially gifted youngsters had access to secular books from the Society for Spreading Knowledge among the Jews. As part of its extra-curricular activity, the school had a professional arm, where after normal lessons children were taught crafts to prepare them for a future career. Consequently there were far more talented artisans and middle-class Jews in Serey, among them businessmen, doctors, shopkeepers and factory owners, than in many Lithuanian towns and villages of the time.

Today there are no survivors of this once thriving community. On September 11, 1941, 229 Jewish men were stripped naked and led through the town to a forest grove near the lake, where they had once fished and bathed. They were forced to lie down in the ditches that they had dug under orders a few days earlier and were summarily shot from above, not by German soldiers but by their Lithuanian compatriots. The remaining 384 women and 340 children were taken the following day. Local householders, whose families for centuries had lived alongside the victims, acted as guards to drive the groups of Jews to their place of execution. Under the command of the former city council head, the town's notables, including schoolteachers and other cultured folk, were "invited" to watch the shootings, after which they all went off to drink in the Serey brewery.

It was during the tidal wave of immigration in the mid-1880s that Annie became one of the first and, at three years old, the youngest of my family to move to England. Following the assassination of the Czar Alexander in 1881, rumours circulated that Jews were to blame for his death, instigating a wave of savage pogroms, which swept through the region. Troops and local farmers alike were incited to mount vicious attacks on Jewish homes, burning villages and plundering property without fear of recrimination. My great-grandfather, Mark (originally Mordecai) Woolman, owned a small tailoring business in Serey, and it is likely that his was one of the premises destroyed in these barbaric rampages. While there exist hair-raising descriptions of whole communities being wiped out, senseless murder, assault and looting casting their shadow of fear over daily life, my family never spoke of these horrors. Brutality and discrimination might have forced my predecessors out of their homeland, but they were also the sparks that ignited their transition into the modern world, and changed their lives forever, offering them brick-built homes, education and dignity.

It is estimated that in the final decades of the nineteenth century the Lithuanian regions lost almost a quarter of their population through the mass exodus of its citizens, many of them Jews. Unlike Isaac Golding, my mother's grandfather, and other young men from the remote *shtetls* and small towns, Mark Woolman, Annie's father, did not travel alone to England to seek work, hoping to send for his family later. Perhaps he saw how this sort of parting often resulted in permanent separation, and, given how seriously he took his role as paterfamilias later in life, I am convinced that he would have done everything to ensure that the family stayed together. Immigration archives hold affecting letters from wives who were left behind, begging to be reunited with their errant husbands, who had enthusiastically embraced both their new opportunities and more often than not another woman at the same time. Thirty-two-year-old Mark, on the other hand, brought not just his wife, Fanny and little Annie, but, unusually, his widowed mother Rachael, then over sixty, and his seventeen-year-old sister, Sophia. His younger brother, Myer, had left a few years earlier, had acquired a wife and two children since his departure, and was now settled in Leeds. This then was their destination.

Their journey followed a rather different route from that of my other grandmother, Lea. The Woolmans were among the first to reap the benefit of the network of railway lines that had been constructed throughout Lithuania during the 1860s and 1870s, criss-crossing the country and opening up access between the major cities. From Vilnius, travellers could catch a train to the border with East Prussia 150 miles away, and from there to Hamburg for onward travel to the

West. This was not nearly as straightforward as it sounds. For a start, Jews were forbidden to leave the Pale, and the Woolman group, which so obviously contained different generations of the same family, would have been suspect figures, moving conspicuously through places where they clearly did not belong. Secondly, they did not possess passports or exit visas, and had no means of acquiring any via official channels, which were in any case clogged up in a maze of bureaucracy. Even for legitimate travellers, it could take six months from application to issue, with stamps and duplicates required at each stage of the process. One frustrated voyager reported that he had to go through eight separate administrative procedures before he was successful, as documents kept getting lost in the system, and offices would deny all knowledge of them.

The first major stop for Mark, his wife, his baby daughter, his sister and his mother was Vilnius, a bustling city with thunderous noise levels and ceaseless commotion. As another young girl recalled about her own journey from the *shtetl* en route to America in 1891, "I grow dizzy even now when I think of our whirling through that city. Strange sights, splendid buildings, shops, people and animals all mingled in one great confused mass." Instead of a friendly group of co-religionists, who shared their way of life and customs, and would provide them with a haven, the Woolmans found a metropolitan society of 40,000 Jewish residents, forty-five per cent of the population. Nothing was familiar and they could rely on nothing.

Their first task in this disorienting landscape was to secure tickets and papers for their onward journey. These could be purchased, for a price, from undercover agents, mostly Jews themselves, who by the mid-1880s were conducting a booming trade in illegal human cargo. As well as providing exit permits, the traffickers were licensed by the two main German shipping companies, Norddeutsche Lloyd and the Hamburg America Line, to sell vouchers for steamship tickets. By 1885 transporting migrants had become serious business. As few Jews had sufficient funds to cover all their expenses for the whole journey, many travellers found temporary work in Vilnius to earn enough to pay for the onward tickets and a group passport. Individual ones were expensive and unnecessary, and it was not unusual to find complete strangers lumped together on a passport as if they were natural travelling companions. It is not impossible that the Woolmans travelled with the Neuman family from their hometown, one of whom later became Sophia's husband. After days, maybe even weeks of nervous waiting and some heavy bargaining, their next step was to board a night train at Vilnius station. Night-time travel was both cheaper and carried less danger of being searched but was no guarantee of unimpeded passage. At the border with Prussia, forbidding-looking Russian soldiers in military uniform were on constant patrol, scrutinising travellers' paperwork, and quite prepared to turn back dubious-looking passengers.

Badly paid and undernourished, these troops were also notoriously corrupt. Knowing they were easy targets, it was common practice for travellers to keep their valuables close. Women would sew jewellery into the hems of skirts or the lining of a dress to evade thieving guards, who quickly grew wise to the ruse. In 1965, my friend, Vera Russell, née Poliakoff, told me how her wealthy parents with children in tow determined to hide their treasures somewhere the soldiers would never dream of searching. They kneaded the family diamonds into dough, which was then baked into loaves and packed in a basket of seemingly innocent provisions. But when they reached the border, the guards who confronted them were starving. The expensive silver plate was of no interest to them. Instead they fell ravenously on the basket of food as they despatched the helpless travellers on their way. Mark Woolman's party had heard the tales, and there must have been some heart-stopping moments while they bribed a guard to issue them with the precious legitimation tickets, which allowed them to cross from Russian territory into Prussia.

Quick to recognise the commercial potential of refugee traffic, in 1885 the German government had removed all restrictions on Russian migrants so that they had free passage through the country once they were within its borders. This liberality did not extend to granting citizenship, and a new concurrent policy of deportation in the year my family arrived and left in quick succession meant that even if they'd wanted to, they were not entitled to settle there. The Woolmans' itinerary took them to the border town of Tilsit, subsequently integrated into Soviet Russia, where they could rest for a few days and buy provisions for the next gruelling stage of the transit, nearly 500 miles by train. Like Hamburg, Tilsit was making the most of this apparently unending stream of Jews from Lithuania, Latvia and White Russia, who throughout the mid-1880s and 1890s spilled into its streets and overcrowded lodging houses. A designated quarantined area housed a medical centre, where they were held for health checks before they were allowed to continue.

It was summer 1885 when the Woolmans disembarked at the Victoria Dock in Hull just at the time when the British authorities were gearing up to cope with the hordes pouring in from Eastern Europe to the English ports. There were trains laid on to take migrants to the correct station platform, recently constructed waiting rooms set aside for them, separate washrooms for men and women, and interpreters who could advise them. Mark and Fanny spoke Yiddish and Russian plus a little Polish and the one English word they had learned, "England". Armed with this and not much else, they made their way to Leeds and Mark's brother, Myer, a fixed compass point in an unsettled journey. The crossing from Serey to Leeds, which now takes just under three hours by plane from Vilnius, had lasted weeks, possibly even months. But the discomforts and the frights the family had endured were quickly forgotten as they prepared for their new life.

It was in Leeds that my great-aunt Julia, who was later to evict my father from the family home in Barrow, was born in 1887. But any plans for a lengthy stay there did not work out. Mark, who according to the reputation handed down through the generations had a hasty temper, might have discovered that brotherly love did not extend to living at too close quarters. In any case, Myer was making plans to emigrate to South Africa. Mark moved to Salford, Manchester, where two more children were born at 45 Charlotte Street, Broughton: Wolf in 1888, who anglicised his name to Wilfred when he was in his teens, and Rosie in 1891, who, over half a century later, was to preside as the *grande dame* of all Woolman comings and goings, and who became one of my all-time favourite relatives. Mark and Fanny and their four children are all present and correct in the 1891 census (apart from the fact that Julia's name is mistakenly inscribed as Judith) but by the time their next child arrived, Mark had uprooted his family once again. This time they landed firmly on their feet.

In 1889, Mark's sister Sophia had married Morris Newman (previously Marcelia Neuman), also from Serey, and the couple were now based in Sheffield. My great-great-grandmother Rachael had moved in with them to a tall, three-storied house at no 50 Ecclesall Road just south of the city centre. Morris, who in the 1891 census is listed as tailor, had a shrewd business brain, and within the next decade had upgraded his status to shopkeeper/employer. That business was eventually inherited by his son, and "Isidore Newman" became a byword for high-class tailoring in Sheffield for well over half a century. Mark followed in their footsteps. He and Fanny settled into a small terraced house at 54 Bellefield Street in Netherthorpe, a working-class area of the city, nowadays devoted mainly to student accommodation, and only a couple of miles from the Newmans. The two families remained close all their lives. Mark set up his own independent tailoring establishment, and embarked on what was clearly his true vocation, integration into a small and imperfectly formed Jewish community in which he could play a leading role as mover and shaker. According to reports, his main passions in life were political meetings, producing babies and shouting at his wife, not necessarily in that order. Bellefield Street was perfectly positioned for him to pursue them all.

It was a move that was decisive in shaping my own fortunes. In comparison to the provincial bases of Leeds and Manchester, the Jewish population of Sheffield has always been a poor relation, dwarfed by its northern neighbours. The *Jewish Year Book* for 1903 puts the total at about 800 souls, even after the surge of immigration in the final decade of the nineteenth century. The traditional heavy industry core of the city did not form a natural magnet for Jewish migrants, whose skills were more often found in the artisan garment or carpentry trades or as merchants. Although Sheffield provided opportunities for silversmithing, fine jewellery and watchmaking, immigrant Jews more traditionally gravitated towards the centres where the talents they had brought from their former lives, in tailoring, retail or cabinetry, could be best deployed. But with Sophia, Morris and his mother, Rachael, as the main attractions, the small-town mentality of Jewish life in Sheffield was just what Mark was looking for.

The published history of the development of Anglo Jewry has largely been confined to the rise of the major centres of Jewish life in London, Manchester and Leeds. Far less attention has been paid to smaller enclaves such as Sheffield, where Jews formed a distinctive but tiny minority element, and where a sense of corporate Jewish identity was volatile to say the least. When I was growing up in the city in the years after the Second World War, the community numbered not much more than 1,500 people. The *cheder*, which I trotted off to meekly every Sunday morning, counted 150 children on the roll between the ages of five and thirteen. Yet the sense of Jewish life was all-consuming. There were at least thirty different societies, offering a lively programme of sporting, charitable or quasi-religious activities. Their work is thoroughly documented in the pages of the *Sheffield Jewish Journal*, the local magazine published three times a year, which forms an invaluable record of the communal energy that characterised this period. This was the zenith of Sheffield Jewish life, and as a child I was completely engulfed by the security of its tight embrace as well as blinkered by its insularity. It has never been as populous since, and for the past forty years has been in steady decline. In another forty, I doubt whether it will exist at all. Although there are records of Jewish families in Sheffield during the eighteenth century, the basis of the modern community where I grew up was only really established in the early years of Victoria's reign. Jews were still something of a rarity in the city – my grandfather Isaac Glass's pilgrimage down the Moor in 1911, followed by a crowd of sniggering urchins, is testament to that. The outlandish clothes and foreign foods were bound to arouse suspicion. In 1851 a Sunday funeral at the Jewish cemetery in Bowden Street attracted a decidedly unruly crowd of onlookers. The funeral procession happened to be unusually large that day because the deceased was the local rabbi, who had suffered a fatal heart attack the previous afternoon after the exertion of conducting the Sabbath service. When the sombre funeral gathering was augmented by this cast of unwanted extras, the resulting furore became so raucous that the following week it featured in *The Sheffield Times*, which noted sadly that there was "a large concourse of spectators, the conduct of some of whom we are sorry to say was rude and disgraceful." Jews were news.

Yet the Jewish community punched above its weight, and over the years a huge number of its members took on prominent civic positions, including two Lord Mayors, Presidents of the Chamber of Commerce, two High Sheriffs and chairmen of countless charitable and commercial bodies, not least the kosher butcher, Abe Silver, who to everybody's amusement became President of the Sheffield Pork Butchers' Association in the 1950s, an embarrassment that his son, Harvey, who was in my *cheder* class, tried unsuccessfully to live down. Less surprisingly there were lots of business successes, many of whose founders were keen to assimilate into secular life. One that stands out from these early years is Harris Brown, a watch repairer in the Lower Don Valley, who opened a shop in 1861, which gradually metamorphosed into the city's most upmarket specialist jewellery store. He was the son of a contractor to the Russian government handling Sheffield-made tools, and left Warsaw during a pogrom in 1860. It is said that he started in the jewellery business by selling watches to his workmates in the steel firm, which was the springboard for his Sheffield career. Determined to blend his heritage with his patriotic love for his new country, he joined the Hallamshire Rifles before he could understand the English words of command. On the occasion of Queen Victoria's Jubilee, he passed along in the procession in his carriage and pair, from where he could admire floating in front of his shop the blue and silver silken banner bearing the words "God Save the Queen" – in Hebraic lettering. H. L. Brown has remained in family hands ever since, with Harris's great-grandson its current chairman, and his great-great-grandson now Managing Director, the fifth generation to be engaged in the firm.

But the most spectacular success story was that of the fifteen-year-old Lithuanian immigrant, Moshe Osinsky, who arrived in England a few years after Mark Woolman with nothing more than ambition and a keen sense of opportunity. Starting as a pedlar in Chesterfield, selling accessories door to door, he spotted a gap in the retail market for cheap clothing for the working man. In 1906 he borrowed £100 to open shops in Mansfield and Sheffield, bought a range of ready-made suits from a wholesaler in Leeds, marked up the price by thirty per cent and sold them on. He moved to Sheffield, changed his name to Montague Burton and expanded his business to sell both ready-to-wear and made-to-measure tailoring at bargain prices. His big break came in 1914 with the outbreak of war, when production changed from civilian mufti to uniforms for the armed forces. When Burton died in 1952, his empire covered 600 shops and fourteen factories and was estimated to be clothing a quarter of the British male population. Now based in Leeds, the company trades under the name of Arcadia, the largest privately owned retail operation in the world.

But the story that most fascinated me was that of Horatio Bright, a leading figure in the nineteenth-century steel industry. Bright's wife was the daughter of a well-heeled steel manufacturer, Thomas Turton, and the union gave Bright both the means and the entrees to set up his own company of Turton, Bright & Co, which manufactured high-quality dies for the Royal Mint. In 1891, around the time Mark Woolman was planning his move to Sheffield, Bright suffered a personal tragedy when both his wife and only son, Sam, died within the space of a few months. Struck down with grief, and resentful of the community elders' hostility to his marriage, he refused to allow the

Jewish burial society to come anywhere near the bodies and insisted on carrying out the last rites himself. He personally prepared the corpses for burial and interred them in a private stone mausoleum, which he had constructed in isolated splendour in woodland he owned at Hollow Meadows, Moscar, with ornamental gardens laid out with mosaics overlooking the crags of the dramatic moorland landscape. He furnished the interior luxuriously and had glass panels inserted into the lead coffins so that he could sit and gaze upon the faces of his loved ones. He arranged for an organ to be installed and would ride out in a coach and four across the moors to spend evenings playing mournful dirges to their remains, while his groom quietly got on with dusting the coffins. For some reason, my father thought this desolate and rather creepy place provided the perfect Sunday afternoon outing to entertain a little girl.

Bright's outpourings of grief became the talk of the town, but they did not last. Four years after the deaths, he married again, this time to a young actress who bore him a son as a seventieth birthday present. In 1906, he too was buried in the mausoleum, which became something of a tourist spot for day trippers. In the current climate of dark tourism, it is easy to see the attraction. The place is high Gothic in its isolation, the stone building, cordoned off by iron railings, hidden in a copse of trees, whose gloomy, intertwined branches give it an added air of mystery. In the 1980s the mausoleum was vandalised and the coffins smashed open by thieves who had most likely hoped to find buried treasures, as if Moscar somehow resembled a latter-day Valley of the Kings. They were disappointed. Only bones and desiccated cloth were waiting for them amongst the bird droppings and other debris. The bodies were subsequently re-interred in the present-day Jewish cemetery at Ecclesfield, and Horatio Bright was returned to his faith. The land at Moscar is now overgrown and the buildings derelict but the original coffins are still on display as exhibits at the Kelham Island Museum in Sheffield, less than a mile from where Bright's factory once stood.

These events were all in the future when my great-grandfather set up his own humble concern in Netherthorpe, eventually relocating to 10 Paradise Square, a cobbled Georgian enclave in the Sheffield Jewish heartland, which is where the business is registered in 1905. He was no Horatio Bright or Montague Burton. Lacking their entrepreneurial flair, he was just glad to have found a place where he could put down roots amongst a group who asked nothing of him other than unpretentious fellowship and love of a healthy argument. There were certainly plenty of these. His own home was a chaotic place, dominated by fighting, swearing and utter disorder. One of my father's most miserable memories was of lying cowering on the kitchen floor while his fourteen-year-old aunt, Cissie, kicked him for some perceived misdemeanour, and the adults carried on unconcernedly about their business. But if violent behaviour was the norm in that household, it merely reflected the anarchic state of the surrounding community, which even I remember as riddled with divisions, a handful of overbearing personalities guaranteeing their continuation for years to come.

Far from finding the squabbles off-putting, Mark seems to have thrown himself enthusiastically into their midst and done his best to sort them out. Despite his temper, he was a man of integrity and people respected him. In 1897 he was elected to the synagogue committee, and became a prominent member, playing his full part in communal life, and encouraging his children to do the same. The Sheffield Hebrew Congregation had moved by this time from Figtree Lane to the more imposing building on North Church Street, where my grandparents, Annie and Max, were married. As he became more respectable, Mark also became a member of the Royal Antiquarian Order of Buffalos, a non-Jewish quasi-masonic body, where he was photographed in full Buffalo regalia with apron and an impressive gold chain. The Sheffield Directory for 1908 lists almost sixty different meeting venues for the "Buffs", mostly pubs around the centre of Sheffield within easy walking distance of Mark's home. The Order, dating from 1822, was primarily a fraternal organisation, whose principal aims were friendship, charitable works, social activity, mutual support and care. These values were ingrained in the family, and my father, who had a profound mistrust of pomposity, and steadfastly refused to join a masonic lodge, nonetheless made charity and concern for others a central tenet of his life.

A few years after arriving in Sheffield, the Woolman family moved into slightly more capacious accommodation at 14 Broomhall Street, now demolished to make way for a modern estate. The area was not far from the industrial heart of the city, which at that time contained some of the worst slums in Sheffield. In fact, the problems of overcrowding and poor sanitation grew to such an extent that in 1900 a slum clearance scheme was planned and then abandoned because it was proving too expensive. Number fourteen was typical of many Victorian terraces built to accommodate the working class. Two small rooms, one of them a kitchen and one a bay-windowed sitting room, took up the ground floor, with two bedrooms above. There was an attic on the top floor and a cellar in the basement where coal was kept for the kitchen range, coal fires being the only form of heating. There was no bathroom or any other washing facilities apart from an outside tap. A privy in a shed situated in a narrow yard behind the house was one of a row shared with the other families who occupied the terrace. This frequently froze in cold weather, and for the rest of his life my father continued to have nightmares about the piles of stinking faeces that would greet him on winter evenings when he was a boy. Just about adequate for a family of four or five, by 1911, 14 Broomhall Street housed thirteen people.

From the time they arrived in England, Fanny Woolman produced a baby virtually every year until in 1902 at the age of forty-four she gave birth to Celia, her youngest daughter, whose name was always reduced to Cissie. Given the conditions in which they were living and the primitive medical services of the period – all twelve children were born at home – it is a wonder that so many lasted not just to enjoy adulthood but well into their eighties, and several were to become formative figures in my own life. In addition to Cissie, my great-uncles and aunts born in Sheffield were in descending order: Harry (1892), who, having survived the trenches, subsequently made his life in Leeds and lost contact with the family; Joseph (1894), who became a research chemist and head of the laboratories at Firth Brown, one of Sheffield's major steel manufacturers; Abram (1895), known as Abey, who at the age of nineteen in a fit of the patriotism that swept the country joined up to fight for king and country in the Great War; Lillie (1896), who ran her own secretarial agency in London, and who, most glamorously, worked for a while as a secretary in Hong Kong, memorably bringing me, aged three, a silk kimono which had a beautiful golden dragon breathing out flames embroidered on the back; Raphael (1897) who died at the age of six months; Maud (1898), who enjoyed a forty-year career as a primary school teacher at Hunters Bar School in Sheffield; and Minnie (1900), who died when she was just four. These eight supplemented the four older living children, Annie, Julia, Wilf and Rosie. The majority of this colourful cast of characters enlivened my childhood and popped in and out of my father's life with varying degrees of influence from the moment he stepped off the train in the winter of 1915. For Broomhall Street was to be home to the Woolmans for quarter of a century, and it was to this shabby, overcrowded, tumultuous but spirited household that my father was headed on his momentous journey from Barrow-in-Furness in the middle of the First World War.

Seven

The Woolmans: Sheffield 1915

"The past is never dead. It isn't even past."
WILLIAM FAULKNER, *REQUIEM FOR A NUN*

I never thought of my family as being particularly ill-fated though it certainly had its share of troubles, most of which I knew about from an early age. It didn't occur to me that this was particularly unusual, and even now I don't think that its toll of unfortunates was so different from that of other families during this period. They accepted hardship as a way of life and met their misfortunes with a degree of fortitude that is unusual nowadays, when vulnerability has been elevated to an art form. By and large the Woolman family bore their heartbreaks with remarkable fortitude and looked after their casualties as best they could. Yet my father without any shadow of a doubt felt that the pains of his childhood loomed over him with all the force of Dickensian myth. When he told us stories of his past, he made his upbringing sound like a blend of Oliver Twist's less jolly times in the workhouse and David Copperfield's trickier encounters with the Murdstones. Without mother or father, banished from home as if he were a criminal, he spent hours of internal reflection trying to establish what exactly it was that he had done wrong to be exiled in this way.

The winter of 1915–16 was bitterly cold. In November, the Sheffield canal froze for the first time in living memory, and young people flocked from all over town to skate over its solid surface. Their delight in this impromptu ice-rink turned to horror when the crowd of skaters became so dense that the ice cracked under their weight and six people were drowned. The tragedy generated headlines in the local press, rivalling the daily toll of fatalities from France in its shock effect if not in its numbers. It was a grim atmosphere that greeted young David when he clambered down from the troop train onto the dingy platform at Victoria station. Like Barrow, Sheffield had built its wealth on iron and steel, and foundries belched out foul-smelling smoke that polluted the air. Each morning when he woke up in 14 Broomhall Street, his eyes were gummed up with what he termed "sleep", a crusty discharge produced by the grime in the atmosphere. It took him several moments to prise open his eyelids as he stumbled, half blinded, out of bed to dress shivering in the unheated attic. Unlike my mother, he always hated the cold.

He had been dropped into a household already full to overflowing with eleven people officially in residence, including his grandparents, Mark and Fanny, and a mob of youthful uncles and aunts ranging in age from thirteen to twenty-four. It was a house full of disputes conducted at high decibel range, where people were constantly rushing, absorbed in their own affairs, where they fought for space, for a hook to hang their clothes, and for a place at the table. It was a house where you quickly learned to stand up for yourself. David became merely the youngest in the crowd of squabbling teens and young adults, whose rowdiness he found overpowering. The vitality and mischievous spirit that had so exasperated his stepmother had been replaced by an overwhelming shyness as he tried to edge unnoticed into a corner. There was no counselling available then for disturbed children nor any suggestion that being wrenched from your home at the age of six might prove harmful. Yet the experience was profoundly traumatic and never left him. From time to time, when my brother and I were growing up, he would look round the dinner table at the four of us and murmur, "Hello family", to remind himself of the stability that he had never known as a child, and which Julian and I took for granted.

Fanny Woolman had little time to spare for this insignificant grandson who had landed on her doorstep. He was another mouth to feed and a body to clothe in a house where money was chronically tight. In her youth she had been a dressmaker for the Russian court, and her own children were always immaculately turned out. Goodness knows how, as she managed on a shoestring. By the time David arrived, however, she was tired. His clothes were cast offs, handed down from his uncles or picked up from jumble sales and then altered to fit. A photograph taken when he was ten shows him swamped by an oversized jacket, his socks falling down and his short trousers sagging to his knees. His fingers are just visible, poking out from beneath long sleeves that flop over his wrists, and he is wearing a shirt with an uncomfortable paper collar in an attempt to make him look halfway respectable. As an adult, my father was always impeccably groomed, his spotless white shirt, with collar attached, starched and pressed to perfection. It helped to compensate for the fact that as a child he never owned a white shirt nor had the luxury of new clothes. Going through his wardrobe after he died, I recognised his innate dandyism in the drawers of shirts beautifully folded, many still unworn, and a selection of neatly rolled ties, still in their pristine cellophane wrappers. On the back of that century-old photo, rather dog-eared now, is a scrawled note to his stepmother, Julia, "A present for my dear Mother from your loving son, David", with a telling and characteristically self-deprecating postscript, "PS. Please excuse the face – it is my fault".

In common with virtually every family in the country, the Woolmans' lives had been overturned by the war. Fanny waited anxiously for news of her sons in the forces, and, like all mothers during those years, treasured the too-brief visits when they were granted leave. Wilfred, the eldest, who was a talented musician and gifted flautist, had left home in 1910 for a career as a schoolmaster in the Royal Navy. In 1914, Wilf, service number M1865, was serving on HMS *Dido*, a 5,600-ton warship, armed with twenty-seven guns and equipped with ten torpedoes. This impressive military might was never put into action. *Dido* was based in Portsmouth as a depot ship for a cruiser squadron, processing crew reinforcements and replacements as well as providing material support to its dependent cruisers. In 1916 Wilf moved to HMS *Ganges* in Shotley, the last sailing ship of the Navy to serve as a flagship and the base of the training establishment for boys during the war. Thankfully he was out of harm's way for the duration. Subsequently, he kept a journal of his time on HMS *Repulse* during the Empire Cruise of the Special Service Squadron in 1923–24. Known as the World Cruise or more familiarly by its men as the World Booze, this monster public relations voyage covered a total of 38,152 miles and made ports of call in all the countries which had served in the Great War, starting with Sierra Leone. In addition to official meetings with foreign dignitaries, royalty and various governor generals, there were gun salutes, formal marches on shore, cricket matches and in Newfoundland a Miss World beauty contest was hosted on board, won by Miss Honolulu. The journal is now lodged in the Royal Naval Museum. Following service on HMS *Hood*, Wilf rose to the rank of Headmaster Lieutenant at the Royal Naval College in Portsmouth. He died of illness on board HMS *Victory* on 25 March 1945, six weeks before peace was declared at the end of the Second World War, and just before I appeared on the scene.

Younger brother Joe, who was studying Chemistry at Sheffield University when war broke out, went to work in munitions manufacture, and so was also spared active service in France. Harry and Abey on the other hand were both in the thick of the action, although apart from a single photograph of Harry in army uniform, taken in Newark, I cannot unearth any substantial evidence of his military career. Newark was the base for the Royal Engineers Technical

Centre, which carried out basic recruit training, and it is likely that he was stationed there for a while. Trained as a cabinet maker, he appears in the Military Records as a sapper artisan in the Royal Engineers with the regimental number 187994 and was awarded the Victory Campaign medal. After that he vanishes from view. It is possible he was invalided out of the army for in 1917 he married Rachel Dora Goodson at North Street synagogue in Sheffield. They moved to Leeds and had a daughter, Shirley, whose photo as a curly-haired two-year-old I came across in a box of Woolman remnants. A rift of some kind occurred during the 1920s, as from that moment Harry cut off all contact with the family, a connection only resurrected a few months ago when I managed to track down his grandchildren, Amanda and Hugh. All they had been told about their missing grandfather was that in 1924 he had walked out on his (admittedly difficult) wife and had never been heard of again. His death is recorded in the Leeds database as 1977 but this registers the year of entry and not necessarily the date of his actual demise.

Abey's movements can be traced more accurately. Private no 21290 was posted to France with the 15th battalion of the Durham Light Infantry and landed at Boulogne in September 1915. He arrived as part of the reinforcements for the Big Push at the Battle of Loos, the first major British offensive of the war, where the deadly chlorine gas was released for the first time, and where German ammunition decimated the exhausted British forces. In October he too was awarded the Victory medal for campaign service, and during the subsequent gruelling months, along with thousands of other teenagers, he marched in boots that didn't fit, followed instructions that didn't make sense, and toiled mindlessly in the trenches and behind the lines. In the middle of the following June, the 15th battalion received their orders to proceed to the front line, and in July, Abey's regiment was sent over the top on that infamous first day of the Battle of the Somme. With 58,000 casualties in a few hours, July 1st 1916 still stands as the worst day in the history of the British army and the greatest loss of life in a single day for Britain. Young men saw their friends cut down in front of their eyes, and body parts flung through the air, impeding their progress as they stumbled into the blanket of smoke that was No Man's Land. As one of Abey's comrades in the Durham Light Infantry noted in his diary, "the sights I saw are too terrible to write about… I saw dead and wounded lying side by side. Some were moaning and others had so far lost there (*sic*) reason that they were laughing and singing." Throughout the following months of continuous bombardment, as rain gradually turned the battlefield into an impassable sea of mud, Abey miserably managed to stay alive for another ten weeks before being caught in the onslaught of shelling and machine gun fire. He fell on 16 September 1916, aged twenty-one. Blown to bits, his body was never recovered.

Now his name is inscribed on the Lutyens arch of the Thiepval Memorial to the Missing in northern France, along with those of 72,194 others, officers and men with no known grave. His only remaining relics are two photographs, which he had sent as souvenirs to his parents before he experienced active service. One shows him proudly posing in military dress holding a swagger stick. The other is taken in company with members of his platoon, formally seated for the camera in a clearing in a French wood. Abey, shorter than the others, standing with his hand resting on the shoulder of the man in front, looks much younger than his twenty years. The poignancy of the image stems from both the innocence of his expression and the fact that he is wearing a uniform that appears to have been made for a much larger man. Six months after his death, the army grandly presented his mother with two pounds fifteen shillings, the amount he was owed in back pay, being the total sum of his effects. Finally, on 23 September 1919, almost exactly three years after the family had received the telegram that every family dreaded, Fanny was sent a further eight pounds ten shillings as a war gratuity, the sum paid by the British Government to the next of kin of men killed in action. In total her son's life had been valued at just over ten pounds sterling.

The shockwaves of his death ravaged Broomhall Street. David, aged seven, was deeply shaken by the air of hopelessness that suffused the household, which had previously been bursting with activity. Sunk in gloom, the family gathered to observe the Jewish mourning rites as faithfully as if they had an actual body to bury. For seven days, they sat on low stools, lit candles in Abey's memory and said prayers each evening in the company of the rabbi. Friends crowded in to pay their respects, bringing food and comfort to the weeping mourners. David, forgotten by everyone, watched from his corner in silence. He had seen all this before. The ghastly memories he had been struggling to suppress of his father's death less than a year earlier came flooding back, with their nightmarish images of the wasted corpse lying in the Barrow flat, candles at head and feet. Had this too been his fault? Was he going to be sent away again?

With his grandmother preoccupied by grief, he sought out the one person who was unfailingly kind to him, and tried his best to remain invisible, especially keeping away from Cissie, whose place as the baby of the family had been usurped by this little interloper. His saviour was Maud, ten years older than her nephew, and with a natural empathy for children. In 1916, she had just begun her career as a trainee schoolteacher, managing a class of seven-year-olds, as she did for the rest of her professional life. Warm-hearted and practical, she was more attuned than anyone else to the little boy's loneliness. She made sure he had clean clothes and a washed face in the morning, that he got up in time for school, and that there was some breakfast for him to eat, even if just a slice of bread. Jam, as my father would regularly remind us, was a luxury beyond their means. Out of them all, bound up with their own burgeoning lives and fortunes, she was the one who during the months that followed kept an eye on his welfare, and to whom he could turn when his misery needed an outlet. She was also the one whose insistence on order made the domestic mayhem bearable. Together with Rose, who had by now abandoned the childish designation, Rosie, and was a naturally commanding figure at the age of twenty-four, they kept David on an even keel.

Yet he pined for Barrow. He missed his little brothers, his sister and Julia, the only mother figure he had ever known. He ached for companionship and a home where a small boy was not made to feel like an intruder. At night, when no one could hear, he cried himself to sleep. Patiently he waited, longing for the school holidays, when twice a year he was released from Sheffield to go back to what he still thought of as his real family. The annual summer weeks in Barrow were the highlight of his young life. There on fine days, he would go off with Alex and Joe – Harry was left in the care of big sister, Ray – to the beaches of Walney Island, a small spur of land eleven miles long that was connected to mainland Barrow by a bridge. They caught the tram to Biggar Bank, a popular seaside recreation area, took sandwiches and fishing nets, not that they ever caught anything worthwhile, and stayed out all day. They ran around in the tufts of coarse grass that grew among the sand dunes, played roly-poly down the grassy banks, rolled up their trouser legs and stuffed their socks in their pockets to go paddling in the waves. They chased one another and had fights with the neighbourhood lads. Occasionally they were given a penny to buy ice cream cornets from the stall with its striped blue and white awning, the colours of the local football team. This was freedom. This was bliss. Walney remained a favourite spot for my father and Alex until their deaths. On a clear day, as they never tired of telling me, you could see the Isle of Man from its headland.

But it was Broomhall Street that gave my father a base and a set of traditional Jewish values that were to determine his direction in life, and that he went on to implant in his own children. His grandmother, Fanny, had been a bride of sixteen when she first met her husband under the marriage canopy. She was fifty-seven when David landed on her doorstep, and pretty much a fixture in the kitchen, where, with the ingenuity of those who were always hard-up, she managed to dragoon every edible morsel into service. She stuffed necks of chickens, boiled sheep's intestines, and transformed calves' feet into a nourishing jelly known as *verschnoggie*. Hardboiled eggs were chopped with onions and mixed with rendered chicken fat to make them stretch further, and cheap pieces of fish were macerated through an iron mincer that clamped onto the side of the kitchen table, before being blended with onions and flour for *gefilte fish*. Fanny baked all her own bread and boasted that in her entire life she never resorted to a bakery. In the winter, a cast-iron pickling pan bubbled away on the stove, containing a huge speckled ox tongue, which was then pressed between heavy metal plates, loaded down with weights, ultimately reappearing in wafer thin slices to be eaten with pickled cucumbers and coarse black bread. In the summer, muslin bags full of sour milk dripped from hooks over the scullery sink, the rancid odour cloying the atmosphere, to produce *smetna* and *kes*, a form of cottage cheese. My father subsequently transferred these culinary delights to my own childhood home. Grudgingly, I can still recall the reek of that simmering tongue and the whiff of the dribbling curdled milk, smells that even now are guaranteed to make me heave with nausea.

In the kitchen, greyish kosher meat lay on a special wooden board, punched with holes, to allow blood to drain away before salting. Fanny made expeditions to the Jewish shops around Paradise Square. At the beginning of the twentieth century Paradise Square, cobbled, lit by gaslight and framed by its eighteenth-century buildings, was the focus of Jewish life. Situated between town and ghetto, it was where the customs of Eastern European cuisine flourished alongside the gossip at Silver's kosher butcher, at Gabbitas the fish man, at Davison's and Gotlib's grocers and at Berman's the bakers (though my great-grandmother swore she never set foot in the place). Sugarman's fish and chip shop served a special "family parcel" for threepence, and at Grindlegate, Mr Alexander would kill a chicken to order for any Jewish housewife who popped by. The Woolmans may have been needy but they certainly weren't prepared to starve.

A child's wretchedness doesn't last forever. David quickly got to know the neighbourhood urchins and built up a tight knit band of Jewish friends. Together they spent hours on the streets, sitting on the kerbstones flicking cherrywobs into the paths of horses. "I became a little ruffian," said my father, recalling those days. "I had to fight every playtime and after school as well. Fighting *was* the game." The far end of Broomhall Street backed onto the wide avenues around Collegiate

Crescent, and at the other led directly into the city. A favourite trick was to run after the horse-drawn hansom cabs and jump on the ledge at the back while the cab was moving. This risked being flicked with the cabman's whip or being dropped in the gutter if the horse reared without warning but it didn't detract from the sense of adventure. If anything, it added to the thrill. Besides, if you were successful you got a free ride into town or out towards Fulwood or Ecclesall, now upmarket suburbs, but then green villages backing on to the Peak District. It was many years before Sheffield lost its image of being a dirty city in a beautiful frame. The gaseous fumes and stench of the steel manufacturing plants hung over people's homes, especially powerful in districts such as Attercliffe or near to the cutlery works in Kelham Island, and pervaded skin and nostrils. It was only after the Clean Air Act of 1956 had established smokeless zones in certain areas of the city, followed in 1972 when this was extended to the entire conurbation, that you could breathe freely in Sheffield. Before that, throughout my childhood, if you blew your nose, your handkerchief would turn black.

Although she didn't live with the Woolmans, being no blood relation, Bessie, my father's older half-sister, was a regular visitor to Broomhall Street. The 1911 census shows her still based in Nottingham with her foster parents, Ruben and Fanny Woolfe, but a couple of years later she left their guardianship and became apprenticed to a Sheffield dressmaker, Kate Saxon, who took care of her future education. It says much for Mark and Fanny's big-heartedness that they continued to watch over Bessie's welfare. When I was a child, it took me a while to work out who was and who wasn't an aunt or cousin in my father's byzantine familial network, so when I would be taken to visit Kate Saxon, her actual relationship to the Woolmans eluded me. I just knew my mother disapproved of her.

Kate was a larger than life character, both physically and in personality, who automatically dominated any company she was in. When she died in 1960, her obituary in the *Sheffield Jewish Journal* described her as having been as strong as a horse and mentally alert as a Geiger counter, with language as uninhibited as her judgement was unerring. From modest beginnings as a cutter for ladies' dresses, she built up a couture fashion house that by the 1950s was known as the place to go for beautifully cut designer garments. These were often end-of-line last season's catwalk models, which she had schmoozed or bargained for at knock-down prices from her impressive network of industry contacts. Kate became notorious in the city for her bluntness with customers when they tried on clothes in her shop, and she specialised in a nice line in insults. If a clearly outsize client came looking for a little black dress, the ultimate in modishness, the redoubtable Mrs Saxon would chide her, "A little black dress indeed? A bloody big black dress is what you should be looking for." An alternative strategy was to insist. If a customer complained when trying on a garment that it made them look fat, she'd disagree outright. "But just look at me sideways," her somewhat subdued client would plead, only to meet with the brisk rejoinder, "Then don't stand sideways." Strangely neither of these tactics appeared to have the slightest effect on consumer loyalty and Mrs Saxon's business boomed. Women never needed to ask if their bums looked big in that outfit, Kate told them – it was all part of the service. On her deathbed, she paid her doctor, ordered her clothes to be sent for cleaning so that they could be given to the poor, and laid bets with her nurse as to the date of her expiry, although there is no record as to how she intended to collect the loot if she won.

Bessie thrived under the care of this feisty character, and went on to become an equally plain-spoken saleswoman, who developed a genius for peddling curtain materials from a stall in Sheffield market. Boisterous and expansive, as a girl, she came in useful as a child-minder for David, and at weekends could be bribed to take him out of the house and from under his grandparents' feet. David, trailing along despondently behind Bessie and her chums as they window-shopped one Saturday, only brightened up when they stopped for tea in Fargate, the main Sheffield shopping street. When a tiered stand, piled high with enough cakes for five, was placed on the table, the girls failed to notice that an unusually quiet David was gradually munching his way through the lot. Only when the bill arrived did Bessie see the empty plate and realise that cakes were individually priced.

David did well at school and was the star of the local *cheder*, which was run with impeccable discipline by the imposing S.H. Finklestone, headmaster and scholar, who was himself a Russian immigrant. A photograph of the boys' class of 1911 shows thirty lads, with Mr Finklestone at their side, resplendent in a frock coat and shiny top hat, a marked contrast to the ragged pupils in their cloth caps staring glumly ahead. In that coronation year, every child had received a medal to recognise the accession of the new king, George V and Mary, his queen, and they all have them pinned on.

In January 1916, when David entered as a new boy, Mr Finklestone was in his prime, and the arch practitioner of a simple educational methodology. This consisted of walking up and down the classroom between the rows of desks, his arms behind his back Duke of Edinburgh style, clasping a cane. As he repeated his favourite phrase, "Again der same. Again der same," in a thick Yiddish accent, the children recited in unison the lesson that had been dinned into them. Anyone who wasn't paying attention received a sharp prod with the cane, though on one occasion one of the older boys objected to this treatment and had a stand-up fistfight with a junior teacher, an acolyte of the Finklestone method, whose prodding had become rather too enthusiastic. The rote learning appeared to work, however, and by the time students reached bar mitzvah age, they were word perfect in Hebrew, able to read any and every portion of the scrolls of the Law. Apart from the trusty cane, the main hazard in attending *cheder* was having to run the gauntlet of the neighbourhood gangs, who would stand in the shadows of Paradise Square each evening, armed with bricks ready to throw at the "Jewboys" as they left at half-past eight on the dot.

A particularly unfortunate target of these missiles was the fat boy of the school, Aaron Chester, a luckless classmate of my father's. Aaron's mother was convinced that her naturally plump son could earn the family a fortune by acquiring fame as the fattest boy in the world, who could then be displayed as a freak at travelling fairs or circuses. She had been reliably informed that bananas were a guaranteed way of putting on weight, and she consequently fed her son on a calorific diet of which bananas formed the main constituent. She also refused to cut his hair and cultivated his curls so that they flowed to his shoulders. To complete this dire picture, she insisted on dressing him in a blue velvet Little Lord Fauntleroy suit with a lace collar and hauled him around fairgrounds to see if there was any interest in hiring him out. Aaron merely grew fatter and unhappier as she stuffed him on the banana-heavy diet but not a single circus showed any interest and he never achieved the celebrity his mother dreamed of.

On Sunday mornings, members of the Hebrew Education Board with nothing better to do had a habit of dropping in at the classes for ten minutes or so to conduct random spot tests to see if the teachers were doing their job properly – the pupils thought *they* were the ones being tested. The secretary, Mr Levi Abrahams, sat at a desk, waiting to be paid as the children arrived at 10.00am. The price of tuition was a shilling a week, although some of the more penurious youngsters were allowed, humiliatingly, to pay a reduced rate of sixpence. The majority of teachers were recent migrants, many of them almost destitute, their knowledge of Hebrew and Scriptures their only marketable asset. With their limited language skills, they inevitably relied on the cane to keep order but their general air of being down at heel made them ripe targets for schoolboy cruelty. One especially irascible individual, Mr Davison, tied up his trousers with a handkerchief instead of a belt. On a memorable Sunday, gesticulating in despair at his pupils' general inattention, he waved his arms around so energetically that the handkerchief came undone and his trousers fell down. The children thought this was the funniest thing that had happened all year, and the incident worked its way into *cheder* folklore.

Because he was top of his class and, once he'd got over his diffidence, a skilled communicator, David earned pocket money by giving Hebrew lessons to the children of wealthier families. He was

Ena, David, Julian and Judy, 1950   *Judy and Julian, 1951*

The Market Square, Jagielnica

Great grandmother
Rachel Goldberg

Lea Goldberg, the teenager

Isaac Glass, man-about-town

Lea and Ada

*Great grandmother Annie Golding
with Katy*

*Great grandfather Isaac Golding
with Ada and Herman*

*Ada in her torn photo
with Herman removed*

*Julia Woolman with L to R, Ray,
Harry, Bessie, Joe, David, 1914*

Great-aunt Sarah Glaski

Browns the Busy Bee 1948

*Mark Woolman in his
Buffalo Regalia*

Wilfred Woolman

Harry Woolman

Abey Woolman

Joe Woolman in graduation gown

David Brown aged 10

Joe, David and Alex at Walney Island

The Cheder Class of 1911
with Mr Finklestone standing R

Maude Woolman

Rose Woolman

David Brown for hire
1936

Hetty Feinhols

Ena and David 1943

Illa Wolfsfeld, Berlin c.1935

Ena, Harry and Rae Glass, 1916

Harry Glass in uniform, 1940

*Ena: the photo my children
can't believe*

*Nancy, Rae, Ena, Rita Glass
at the fairytale wedding*

*Great-aunt Fanny
Woolman, her
engagement photo*

*Harry Lowit and Zelda
wedding*

*Sadie Brown and Fanny
Woolf c1915*

Ray Brown with a feline friend

*Harry, Alex and Joe Brown with their mother
Julia. Ray in the background*

overawed by the grand houses of some of his pupils, who lived in the posh Broomhill area of Sheffield, celebrated by John Betjeman as the prettiest suburb in England, where "winding tree-shaded roads house handsome, gabled black stone mansions". He saved up his earnings from these lessons for weeks in order to buy books – there were none at Broomhall Street. He especially coveted a copy of *Encyclopaedia Britannica*, which he was convinced was the key to all knowledge, and one weekend was overjoyed to discover the complete volume set at a knock-down price at a local jumble sale. He rushed home, counted out his savings – he had just enough – and bought the lot. Back home, he put the books in his secret hiding place and went out to play. When he returned at tea-time, he ran upstairs to pore over his treasures only to find that they'd vanished. Maud, who had been using her day off to tidy up the accumulated mess, had found them stashed under the bed and generously donated them to the jumble sale around the corner, the very place he'd bought them. "We've got enough rubbish cluttering up this house," she snapped.

Nonetheless, even without the help of *Encyclopaedia Britannica*, David excelled not just at *cheder* but at school as well. In those days children stayed at elementary school until they had reached the statutory school leaving age, which in 1918 had been raised from twelve to fourteen. Unless that is they had aspirations to go further. At the age of eleven, David, proudly accompanied by Maud, went to Sheffield Town Hall to receive his prize for coming top in the whole of the city in the scholarship examination. Secondary education beckoned, and he was on his way up.

Eight

Hero?: Sheffield 1920

"Whether I shall turn out to be the hero of my own life, or whether that station will be held by anybody else, these pages must show."
CHARLES DICKENS, *DAVID COPPERFIELD*

In 1920 David entered the Central Secondary School for Boys in Leopold Street, housed in a building that subsequently became the Sheffield Education Offices, and is now a boutique hotel. It was a struggle for the Woolmans to buy uniform, even hand-me-downs, and pupils were also expected to supply their own textbooks. The cost of these could mount as high as five pounds, two and a half times the average weekly wage for a working man, although there was a thriving second-hand trade in used schoolbooks at Cadman's Bookshop or at a couple of the stalls in Sheffield market. In common with all secondary education of the time, the Central School was highly regimented. Its curriculum included Mathematics, Chemistry, Physics, English, French, Latin, German, Scripture, History, Geography, Music and Art. Boys were also required to take classes in woodworking and metalwork, although my father's attention must have been elsewhere during these lessons as his DIY skills were famously complete rubbish. For sports, the boys had to share playing fields with a girls' school, but sessions were rigidly timetabled so that the sexes never ever overlapped or even caught sight of one another in their sporting gear. This was the case even thirty years later when I was at school, and naughty boys would climb up and peep over the wall just for the thrill of seeing us in our navy blue, serge gym knickers.

The Central School offered a range of clubs and societies. Its Shakespeare Society acquired such a reputation for its annual productions that it was invited to Stratford each year on Shakespeare's birthday to lay a wreath on the poet's grave. Sadly, rehearsals were held after school on Fridays during the autumn term, when the nights were drawing in. This meant that David was automatically excluded, there being a three-line whip at Broomhall Street on Friday evening for the Sabbath meal. This was a shame as he was a talented performer. In the early 1930s he appeared semi-professionally in repertory on the stage of the Sheffield Playhouse, where the cast included Bernard Miles, who as a celebrated actor and director was knighted for his services to theatre, and subsequently elevated to the House of Lords, one of the first theatrical peers after Laurence Olivier. David also played a leading role in school debates, which proved a fruitful training ground for him to develop his powers of argument and his keen sense of social justice. "An idea – particularly an injustice – can obsess me," he noted later in his diary. "I want to hit out and fight." This urge combined most tellingly with more polished oratory a decade after he had left school when he took to the floor in various public forums to debate the "refugee problem", where he compellingly argued the case why Britain should provide shelter to Jews fleeing Nazi persecution.

In retrospect, I can see that he had always championed the underdog. At school this tendency combined with his strong streak of individualism to make him something of a ringleader. In my stash of memorabilia is a crumpled letter, which has been torn roughly into pieces and painstakingly stuck back together again. It is addressed to the fearsome Miss Payne, who was a legendary fixture in the Central

School, and my father's form mistress when he was fourteen. "Mr Burgess has threatened to pile upon our already overloaded shoulders the terriffic (*sic*) burden of a second lot of chemistry Homework per week," moan the twenty-six signatories to this letter, pointing out the unfairness of such an action. "Against this offence we protest as a form and we hope you will take steps to have the burden removed. Mr Burgess, to carry out his threat, gave us extra homework on the 8th Inst and we understand he will do this until further notice. Please see that this notice is given forthwith." It is not recorded whether this petition had any effect but its tatty appearance indicates that it was rescued from the waste paper basket to which Miss Payne had presumably consigned it, and the fact that my father kept it safe all those years suggests that he took particular pride in its composition.

Despite – or perhaps because of – the extra homework, David sailed through school. At the end of his first year there, he was placed a miserable 124th out of 125. By the time he had reached the fifth form, however, he was in the top three every year with the result that in 1926, his headmaster decided to enter him for a scholarship to Cambridge to read Natural Sciences. Oxford and Cambridge had their own entrance exams, which could only be taken on site at the university. At first David feared he wouldn't be able to go at all. The rail fare from Sheffield to Cambridge cost seven pounds, a sum way beyond the family pocket. Help was at hand in the shape of his Uncle Joe, who purchased David's ticket out of his own slim earnings. My father never forgot this act of benevolence, and in Joe's old age paid him numerous little acts of kindness as recompense, hiring taxis to take him on holiday door to door from Sheffield to the Lake District, once his driving days were over.

Arriving in Cambridge to sit the exam was a daunting experience. My seventeen-year-old father, thin and undernourished despite the stuffed chicken necks and *verschnoggie*, and still wearing the ill-fitting clothes that dogged him all the way through adolescence, was overwhelmed both by the grandeur of the pale limestone architecture, a stark contrast to the blackened grit of Sheffield, and the aristocratic tones of the undergraduates. These young men in their immaculately cut trousers and with the self-assurance that comes from being constantly well-fed and admired, were creatures from another world. Finding his way on foot to the imposing porters' lodge, David was shown to a college room to stay overnight before taking the exams the following day. He was confused by the system, by the fact there was a uniformed servant who called him "Sir", and most of all by the other candidates, each of whom appeared to be an archetypal English public schoolboy straight out of the pages of *Tom Brown's Schooldays* or Frank Richards' *Greyfriars* stories, and who all spoke with the cut-glass accents of Eton, Rugby or Winchester. Their poise drained every bit of his own already shaky self-confidence.

His worst moment came in the morning when, after a sleepless night worrying about both the examination ordeal and his shabby clothes, he had to find a bathroom and make his way to breakfast. Every other boy he met on the staircase was wearing a dressing gown. My father had never seen a dressing gown before, let alone possessed one. Instead he put on his scruffy gabardine mackintosh over his shirt and pyjama trousers. No one spoke to him. By the time he walked dejectedly into the examination hall, he knew he was doomed to failure. He always claimed later that if he'd only had a dressing gown, he'd have passed the papers with flying colours. A Cambridge education would have made all the difference, not least to his self-esteem. In the end he won a full scholarship to the University of Sheffield. With his scholarship money he bought a new overcoat to celebrate, and on his first day as an undergraduate it was stolen.

There was of course no need for dressing gowns at Broomhall Street. There was no bathroom or indoor plumbing. The water closet housed in the yard was shared with other dwellings in the terrace. Family members washed discreetly in the privacy of their bedrooms. Although there was a tin bath, kept hanging outside on a peg on the wall, it was rarely used. Fanny Woolman frequented the *mikveh*, the ritual bath in the synagogue reserved for married and post-pubertal women. My father, however, used the public baths. Glossop Road

Baths, now a trendy spa for the upwardly mobile, offering Glowing Beauty treatments, is the oldest Turkish baths in the country. It had been built in 1836 originally as a medical facility to provide sanitised bathing for the general public at the height of the cholera epidemic in which 402 Sheffield people died. In the 1870s a plunge pool was added, and the building was fitted out in grand style as a leisure facility with two new swimming pools at ground floor level and a Turkish bath suite in the basement below, complete with steam rooms and scrub down areas, serviced by attendants. Shortly after it opened in 1877, the architectural publication, *Building News*, ran a feature on Glossop Road which advertised, "New Turkish Baths, considered the finest in the kingdom, have just been opened in Victoria Street… The interior is lavishly fitted with tessellated pavements, white and coloured glazed brick walls, arched and decorated ceilings, with easy chairs, marble and felt covered seats." There were 50,000 glazed bricks in red, yellow, green and cream, and a bespoke fleur-de-lys motif was designed for the mosaic floor.

This magnificent construction was largely a male sanctum that became a haven of indulgence for my father. At first, he was taken along once a week by Uncle Joe, purely for the purpose of getting clean. Soap and towels were included as part of the entrance fee. Later on, as a young man, he would go regularly with a group of pals every Saturday and spend the whole afternoon there. It was a warm place to gather on winter weekends when their own modest homes were invariably so icy that you could see your breath misting in the air unless you were lucky enough to be right in front of the kitchen range. Glossop Road Baths acted as an informal clubhouse, where young men would congregate, sitting naked in the steam with towels wrapped around their waists, putting the world to rights, refreshing themselves from time to time with bracing dips in the plunge pool, or lying on warmed wooden benches being pummelled by strapping attendants. In 1933, when my father was twenty-four, it cost only one shilling and sixpence to take a Turkish bath, and this included "a choice of four attendants to scour your body with scrubbing brushes before packing you off for a thumping massage" and then returning to the dry hot rooms, effectively a modern sauna, which were maintained at a temperature of between 185–195°F.

David's first exposure to the comforts of luxury living were when he used to accompany Maud and Rose on visits to their well-to-do relatives, the Feinhols, who owned a large furniture store on the Moor. The Feinhols lived in a rambling house in a spacious tree-lined road in Endcliffe, an affluent Sheffield suburb, a world apart from Broomhall Street. Sholly Feinhols established his claim to distinction partly because of his reputation as a munificent philanthropist but more substantially because his stomach grew so enormous that he apparently never saw his toes after the age of forty-five. Given this, it's no surprise that he had great difficulty tying his shoes and for the last thirty years of his life he was forced to enlist help. His wife, Hetty, a similarly rotund figure, was my grandmother's first cousin – her mother was Sophia, who as a seventeen-year-old had accompanied Mark Woolman on the trek from Serey thirty years earlier. Hetty was a plainspoken and exceptionally kind-hearted woman, with a penetrating intellect and an immensely charitable nature. For David, their house resembled a palace, where you sank into padded armchairs on carpeted floors, and where there was never any shortage of cake, served on fine blue and white willow pattern plates, edged in gold.

In the late 1980s, a few years after my father's death, I was dawdling around a country antique fair one weekend when I spotted a vintage dinner service laid out in full on a stall. I snapped it up. It was only afterwards that I discovered that Booths Real Old Willow, the make of this china, out of innumerable versions of the willow pattern design, was identical to the one my father had so prized at Hetty's house. Booths went out of production in the 1930s, and today sells at ridiculously inflated prices on eBay. The service gives me immense pleasure to use, especially now I realise that my find was pure serendipity. In 2008, Hetty's daughter, Barbara, at the age of ninety, decided to move out of the Endcliffe Road house, by this stage divided into flats. Despite having downsized considerably since the old days, the place was still stuffed with Hetty's possessions, mostly stored in the vast cellars, which ran the length of the property. As Barbara was packing up, she called me and escorted me down to this subterranean Ali Baba's cave. As a parting gift she gave me the complete set of willow pattern china that had belonged to her mother, its gold edging still lustrous. I can now stage a forty-person banquet if I only knew forty people to invite. I've always regretted that my father never saw these pretty plates in daily use by his own family more than a century after he first admired them.

Hetty was part of the web of Woolman kin in which I was entangled as a child, and her house with its heavy polished furniture and blue velvet armchairs always seemed impossibly grand. A famous Lady Bountiful, she had been an indomitable supporter of young people, and was responsible for giving David glimpses of a world beyond his own. Born in Sheffield to Sophia and Morris Newman, marriage to the wealthy Sholly Feinhols in the summer of 1911 meant that she had the wherewithal as well as the desire to spread her largesse, especially where she felt it could do some good. Her elder son, Carl, was sent to board at the Perse School, Cambridge, which had a Jewish house, making my father green with envy. Not only was this a classy boarding establishment but its advantages appeared to be completely wasted on Carl as far as David could see. It certainly had no demonstrable effect on raising his aspirations and on leaving school, Carl went straight into the furniture trade, ultimately inheriting his father's business, a stroke of good fortune that my father always felt slightly aggrieved about.

Hetty was a strong proponent of gender equality, and she made sure that her daughter Barbara also enjoyed the benefits of private education. This turned out to be much more worthwhile. Barbara became a psychiatric social worker and a leading light in the Soroptimists Association. Inaugurated in 1921, Soroptimists was and still is a volunteer organisation for professional women, whose members are committed to improving the lives of women and girls in local communities and, nowadays, throughout the world. For many years, Barbara was President of the Sheffield branch, and was indefatigable in her work to widen career opportunities for disadvantaged young women. Sadly, for a family who were such champions of education, Hetty's younger son, Stevie, was born brain-damaged, diagnosed with what was known in those non-PC days as "retarded". After his mother's death, he became the focus of Barbara's life. Her career in mental health was primarily inspired by her brother's condition and she gave up all chances of having a family of her own, including breaking her engagement to an up-and-coming young solicitor, so that she could devote herself to Stevie's care. For years he was a familiar figure to local shoppers, an almost permanent fixture at the foot of the Moor. He spent his days hanging around outside the Feinhols' store in all weathers with a vacant expression on his face, greeting passers-by with his unvaryingly cheerful, lopsided smile.

In 1921, Hetty had started a girls' club that was intended to help turn young women into responsible citizens and prepare them for adult life. The Sheffield Jewish Girls Association was originally envisaged as a counterpart to the Jewish Lads Brigade, a popular national movement of the time, which used the discipline of the parade ground to instil principles of order and moral rectitude in working-class boys. All the Woolman lads had been members of the JLB, and it was probably answerable for instilling the patriotic spirit in Abey that led to his fervour for an early and inglorious death in the First World War. Launched in 1891 and the UK's oldest Jewish youth movement, the Jewish Lads Brigade was established initially to provide for the children of the countless poor immigrant families in the East End of London, but its summer camps and athletic activities soon spread to the provinces. Hetty felt keenly that there should be something similar for girls, where they could learn social as well as domestic skills and which would encourage public-spiritedness.

Hetty was the first and only Chairman of this association. Its stated aims were to provide recreation and to encourage any occupation whereby girls may benefit. Members had to pledge to abide by a

Code of Honour, which is reminiscent of the Brownie motto my own children can still recite word perfect, although with a few subtle differences. Its first three principles are familiar to anyone who has had any truck with the Girl Guide movement, namely that a girl on her honour may be trusted, that every girl will do her duty before anything else even though she gives up her own pleasure and comfort, and that members must help each other when called upon to do so. The Code also includes a telling reminder that "no member must be a snob", helpfully explaining that a "snob is a person who looks down on another because she is poorer, or being poor resents another because she is rich", and furthermore that "the endeavour of every girl be to keep herself pure, clean-minded and womanly".

The session fee of two shillings and sixpence entitled all members to come free to social functions, "boy friends" to pay a nominal charge. The first meeting, attended by sixty girls, was a dance, held at the Cemetery Road Vestry Hall and was a great success. As the months went on, classes were started in physical training and swimming, and there were play-readings and discussions. A class in sweetmaking at Mrs Pearson's house attracted sixty-one young ladies but a lecture by Rabbi Cohen had to be cancelled owing to lack of an audience. The Chairman found herself continually having to make apologies to speakers of a more cerebral type and issued strong reproofs to members for persistent absenteeism. In 1924 a Carnival Dance held at the Abbeydale drew record numbers but among the waltzes and the old-fashioned dances such as the Veleta and the Dashing White Sergeant, Hetty had sneaked in an edifying talk from Rabbi Cohen (again) regarding attendance at Hebrew classes. This did not completely undermine the enjoyment of the evening with its novelty dances, a tombola and spot prizes, one of which was won by lucky Nancy Newman for keeping her balloon intact. From reading the account of these entertainments, no one would ever dream that this was the age of nightclubs and the Charleston, when racy dances such as the foxtrot and the tango were all the rage in more sophisticated venues. Hetty, her values firmly rooted in the Victorian age, went in for simpler pleasures, and insisted that the young did too. It was what I was brought up to believe in. At a push, I can probably still do the Veleta.

Hetty also hosted cultural evenings for students at her palatial home, at which David was a regular guest, one of the main attractions being the buffet. Food always featured centrally in my father's life, probably a throwback to the days when he never had enough to eat. His diaries make constant reference to the meals he ate, whether at home or in other people's houses or in the occasional restaurant, where he invariably baulked at the price. Phrases such as "there was a terrific spread" make him sound like Billy Bunter, eyeing the groaning table. The Feinhols' evenings were famous for their hospitality and for bringing young people of all social classes together. Hetty was a great leveller. They consisted of musical soirees, quizzes and brains trusts as well as invited external speakers, who gave informed lectures on politics or science. There were dramatic entertainments, play readings and virtuoso performances by visiting artistes or by the students themselves. When they were invited to present literary extracts, David chose "The Ballad of Reading Gaol", only realising halfway through his performance just how long it was and that apart from him, no one had heard of Oscar Wilde or his sentiments, and cared even less. "I sweated and squirmed," he said afterwards, "and probably so did the audience."

Given that he always relished opportunities for dressing up and being silly, David's party pieces were more usually comic songs of the period. Most painfully when I think about it now, as a child I was taught a number of these routines and memorised all the verses of "The ladies of the harem of the court of King Caractacus", though I thankfully never appreciated what a harem actually was, let alone a eunuch. "King Caractacus" was one of those serial memory-game songs, with gradual additions to each seemingly interminable verse. Its denouement, "If you want to take some pictures of those fascinating witches who put the scintillating stitches in the britches of the boys who put the powder on the noses of the faces of the ladies of the harem of the court of King Caractarus" (deep breath)… "You're too late!" gives some indication of the intellectual highpoint of my father's sense of humour. The song can now be viewed on YouTube in a version, appropriately perhaps, recorded by Rolf Harris, who popularised it for a new generation of youngsters. Another favourite, which my father declaimed as a child, and later camped up outrageously as a young adult was a sentimental cautionary rhyme that was much easier to remember than Caractacus, and was always accompanied by suitably exaggerated actions: "Mother told Jack not to go/Near the brook where rushes grow./ But he went and tumbled in/ Wet he got, right to his chin./Now he has to stay in bed/ Such a cold is in his head/ Sneezing makes his cheeks quite red/ Tishoo! Tishoo! Tishoo!" Take my word for it, it doesn't improve much in performance.

Despite these distractions, in July 1931 David graduated from the University of Sheffield with Honours in Physics. In those days, any student awarded Honours was automatically entitled to a Master's degree on the payment of a fee. This was how my mother acquired her apparently postgraduate qualification six years later. Sadly there was no way David could afford the ten pounds required to purchase the additional letters after his name, and as a result he remained in his wife's academic shadow for the rest of his life. In 1979, I wrote to the University of Sheffield asking if I could belatedly buy the degree certificate as a seventieth birthday present for my father who had after all earned it a half century earlier. After months of waiting for a reply, I eventually received a sniffy letter from the university registrar, clearly an individual with a limited sense of humour and less foresight, who curtly informed me that the practice of buying degree awards had long been defunct, and there was no way they could consider my request. How short-sighted. Now, when begging letters arrive on the door mat, inviting me to make a donation to help fill the university coffers, they find their way smartly to the round file I keep under the desk.

Armed with his brand-new degree, David set about applying for jobs, sending around a photograph of himself to prospective employers. No one looking at this photograph now would ever think of hiring its subject. In various shades of grey, a pathetic looking young man in an ill-fitting jacket, with carefully crimped hair and a hangdog expression stares out of the picture frame. It reminds me of the images of lost animals that pet charities used to send around, asking if anyone wanted to adopt abandoned puppies or cats who had been ill-treated. Unsurprisingly, it didn't stimulate much interest. Help was at hand, however, once again in the shape of Uncle Joe, by then in a senior position in the research laboratories of his steel firm. He had connections across the city and managed to secure David an interview at steel manufacturer, Jessops. Despite his timidity in unfamiliar situations, David must have done something right, for he was hired on the spot and engaged to start the following week. He went home jubilant, his self-confidence restored and managed to convince everyone that their worries for his future were totally unnecessary as this was bound to be the start of an illustrious and highly lucrative career. He was wrong on both counts.

The evening before he was due to turn up for his first day at Jessops, he could be found in his normal habitat at the bridge table, in the company of three young men he had known since boyhood: his partner, Maurice Lewis, an old school pal, Morris Stanford, who had just qualified as a teacher, and a junior doctor, Hyman Brody, in his first year as a houseman at Sheffield Royal Infirmary. David had learned to play bridge while he was still at school, and it soon become apparent that he had a rare aptitude for the game. It brought out many of his best qualities, his mathematical brain and powers of logical thinking, his love of problems and his ability to find inventive solutions. Bridge is also a deeply social game, capable of arousing intense feelings, and some of David's most long-lasting friendships were formed at the bridge table. The Brown-Lewis partnership is still remembered as one of the most formidable that the city has ever seen, and their names remain emblazoned in gold lettering on the roll of honour at Sheffield Bridge Club. There is also a photograph of them on display, under the title "Sheffield Bridge Club Celebrities", taken in the early 1930s at a tournament where they triumphed over a visiting team of top international players. On this particular evening, however, the four became so riveted by the cards that they lost all sense of time. It was a shock when they saw that dawn was already quite advanced, and they had played through the night. My father just had time to race home, shave and hurriedly change. At each tram standard, he paused and put his ear to the posts to which the cables were connected in case he could hear a tramcar approaching, gauge its distance and catch a ride.

David was resolved to make a good impression at Jessops. That morning he was shown around the plant by the foreman, who explained the different processes involved in steel manufacture. Halfway through the tour, as they were standing by a furnace, the foreman was called away, leaving David to wait for his return before moving on. Puddling, the process whereby boiling iron is stirred and cooled, requires exceptionally careful management. David had watched the procedure with interest as the metal bubbled away, and after a while decided he would help matters along. Unfortunately he had failed to observe that the dipper used to stir the liquid pig iron needed to be bone dry before it made contact with the molten metal. As he plunged the ladle, which had been cooling in water, into the vat, the reaction was literally explosive. On his first day at work, my father managed to blow up the factory, or at least a significant proportion of it. Thankfully there were no fatalities, but David, as the person at the heart of the blast, was naturally the one who had suffered the severest burns. An ambulance was called, and he was rushed unconscious to hospital.

As he opened his eyes in the accident and emergency unit, his dim vision gradually merging with a dismayed awareness of where he was, the first face he saw bending over him was that of the duty doctor called to attend his injuries. This nightmare become reality was a bleary-eyed Hyman Brody, whom he had last seen two hours earlier staggering away from a hard night of smoking, drinking and card-playing. He had just enough presence of mind to protest feebly,

"Don't let that man near me. He's drunk," before mercifully fainting away once again. Hyman went on to become Sheffield's leading consultant physician, Dean of Graduate Students and advisor to Sheffield University Hospitals.

For some unknown reason, Jessops were still keen to employ my father – perhaps they appreciated his initiative – and he was able to return to work a few weeks later, much to his colleagues' hilarity, though for months to come he had to put up with being the butt of their jokes. He ultimately found his true metier as Sales Director at Lewis Rose, a small cutlery firm that specialised in high-quality tableware, and in 1953 he was admitted as a Freeman of the Cutlers Company. Sales Director was a role that allowed David to exploit his gift for client relations, underpinned by his knowledge of materials and stainless steel manufacture, thankfully somewhat matured after his initial uncomfortable experience. Lewis Rose was the factory that my brother and I became familiar with as children in the days before the new technology invaded modern production. Its clanking and grinding noises and the distinctive smells of heavy machinery, blade oil and coal dust come bounding back every time I am in the vicinity of Bowling Green Street. Along with almost every other cutlery factory, it no longer exists. It was absorbed into the much larger tools manufacturer, Spear and Jackson, in the late 1960s, and then was hit by the crash of the 1970s, when cheap knives and forks made in Japan or Korea flooded the market. Lewis Rose just couldn't compete. But our childhood had long disappeared by then.

Nine

The Secret Marriage: Sheffield 1941

*"But it's no use going back to yesterday because
I was a different person then."*
LEWIS CARROLL, *ALICE IN WONDERLAND*

One Friday lunchtime in the summer of 1941, a young woman in a thin cotton dress caught the tram from the office where she worked as a translator and made her way to Sheffield Town Hall. The weather was glorious, a perfect June day. She was wearing a large-brimmed hat, perhaps to shield her face from the sun or, more likely, to hide her nervousness. The hat brim may have tilted slightly lower than usual but apart from this, there would have been nothing to suggest that the day was any different from an ordinary weekday. She had set off promptly that morning at her normal time of eight o'clock from her family home to the offices of Henry Boot Ltd, a large construction company on Ecclesall Road, which at that time was concentrated on wartime requirements. She told no one where she was going that day, not even her sisters. My mother was notoriously secretive.

My parents were married on 29th November 1942 in Wilson Road synagogue, Sheffield. Their *ketubah* was kept with our birth certificates and their wills in a locked box in my mother's bedroom. Although he had never given my mother an engagement ring, as he became more established in life, my normally undemonstrative father regularly marked their anniversary with a gift of jewellery that disclosed his inner romantic. A glowing spray of kingfisher-blue opals, a midnight dark enamel circle set with tiny starry diamonds, a delicate silver filigree bracelet from Florence, woven into a wiry string of knotted daisies – my mother treasured these all her life. And every November without fail, he presented her with flowers, usually the sooty-centred, purple and white anemones she had carried in her bridal posy, a tradition I subsequently kept up for the thirty years of my mother's widowhood. Lies and secrets. Secrets and lies. My parents, in every other respect upright and scrupulously honest in all their dealings, kept their own secret immaculately.

For as my parents arrived at Wilson Road synagogue to be joined in matrimony on a predictably dreary November afternoon, Ena coming direct from Montgomery Road, and David from his aunts' house, no one knew that they had in fact been man and wife for the last year and a half. They stood underneath the embroidered canopy before God and their relatives and went through the Jewish marriage ritual as if they were innocents. The nuptial scroll, inscribed in Hebrew and in English and witnessed by the synagogue officials, was then painstakingly filed away along with other important family papers, It was not until seventy years later, after my mother's death, that I was to discover another record, slipped inside a brown foolscap envelope with the banal inscription, "marriage cert", scribbled in pencil on the outside. This unassuming piece of paper testifies to the fact that Ena Glass, aged twenty-six, and David Brown, thirty-two, were officially married "by licence" in Sheffield Registry office on 27 June 1941. They had successfully carried their secret with them to their graves.

The only people who knew about this clandestine marriage, which had been quietly organised and scrupulously concealed from even their closest friends, were Eva Yaneske and James White, two characters who never appear again in this history and who were total strangers to the rest of the family. I looked them up. Eva Yaneske was the daughter of a Jewish-Polish immigrant father, Paul Yaneske, who had arrived in England at about the same time as my own great-grandfather and is listed in the 1891 census of Sheffield residents. Eva's mother, Minnie Wragg, was neither Jewish nor married to her father. The twin stigmas of illegitimacy and mixed faith parentage would have ensured that Eva remained at a safe distance from any Jewish community connections who might have known my parents. There's even less to learn about the other witness, James White. Perhaps he was a business colleague of my father's? Or one of his employees? Or a passer-by whom they yanked in from the street? The only James White I can track down who fits into the right age bracket and location is a young man in the Yorkshire Regiment, who was killed in Burma in 1944. The evidence, admittedly slim, suggests that both Eva and James might have been paid witnesses.

But on that June evening of 1941, after signing the marriage registry and presumably having their own private celebration somewhere, my mother and father each went back to their respective families and never breathed a word to a soul. Even Ena's sisters remained in complete ignorance until I unearthed the certificate and confronted my Aunt Rita with it. "Oh, she never told us anything!" was her exasperated reaction, wearily irritated that she hadn't been let into the secret earlier. "Ena was always odd."

Why did they do it? I can only speculate on the reasons. It was wartime after all and young people everywhere were following their passions. My mother was twenty-four when war broke out. Harry and Rae were both married but the rest of the family were still living at home. Rita was working as a secretary, and Nancy just starting as a trainee schoolteacher. On Thursday evening, 12th December 1940, Ena was on her way to visit friends. She had just turned the corner of the road when planes overhead began dropping incendiary bombs. She hesitated several minutes before she turned back, a wise decision.

The cellar at Montgomery Road had been reinforced in preparation for bombardment, and she found the entire household huddled down there, including a fifteen-year-old girl who had started work as a resident skivvy for the family earlier that day. Soon more substantial bombs began falling thick and fast. That ominous whistle and then the crash. "When we heard the crash we knew we were safe," said my mother, "– until the next one." My grandfather went upstairs on reconnaissance, and each time came back dishevelled and coated in dust. When silence eventually fell, the family emerged to find the street on fire, soot and ash everywhere, but the property miraculously unscathed. They collapsed into bed at six in the morning, until, an hour later, Special Police appeared with loudhailers, shouting for everyone to evacuate the area. The fledgling maid, boasting one of the shortest employment records in history, raced gratefully back to the arms of her family, and never returned. One night in a cellar with the Glass clan was enough.

The others walked the three miles to Ringinglow on the outskirts of the city, which was untouched by the bombs. There, together with the Isaacs family from across the road, they sought shelter in Harry's new house, sleeping three to a bed. Once they were safely installed, Harry set off to see for himself what was happening in town. Rita, suffering pangs of conscience, asked him to take a message to her office explaining why she would be late for work. When Harry reached the Moor, the so-called office was just smoking rubble in the midst of tangled metal and smouldering carcasses of buildings. The Luftwaffe's main target had been the steel mills, now transformed into centres for armaments manufacture. Even though they failed to halt or even reduce the rate of weapons production, the Sheffield Blitz resulted in the utter devastation of whole swathes of the city. Nearly 700 people were killed in those December air raids, and 1,500 were injured.78,000 Sheffield homes were damaged, either from a direct hit or as a result of the ensuing fires from incendiaries, and 40,000 people were made homeless.

During the weeks that followed, Ena and David walked past ruined buildings where once shops and houses had stood. They stepped over the piles of stones and bricks that cluttered up the uneven pavements, and skirted their way gingerly past craters, exposed gas mains and over spiky shards of broken glass from blown-out windows. The entire city centre was in ruins. Much of the debris remained in situ for years, so that even when I was a child the tattered wallpaper still blew in the wind from the shells of those destroyed homes, with their intriguing glimpses of cast-iron bathtubs and twisted pipes hanging perilously from the wreckage. As I try to think myself back into my parents' feelings, I envisage a time when life seemed even more fragile than usual and the future even more uncertain. During the day my father was engaged in classified war work, turning out weapons where once he had been responsible for beautifully crafted silver. At night he was out on the city streets, firefighting. It is hardly surprising that in this climate of insecurity lovers wanted to grasp moments together when they could. My mother was high-principled, and probably needed the moral fortification of a marriage certificate before she would spend the night with her intended. For me, the mystery is how they managed to keep their skeleton hidden in the cupboard not just for the eighteen months after the marriage but for the next seven decades. People, even (or perhaps especially) those closest to you, are full of surprises.

It was autumn 1942 when both my mother and her sister Rita formally announced they were engaged. Their weddings, a fortnight apart, were hastily arranged, Ena's at just two weeks' notice. Perhaps it was Rita's decision that gave her the impetus. My grandmother was dismayed at the thought of the sort of unadorned, simple ceremony my mother wanted, to say nothing of its speed. She would have been even more horrified had she known that Ena was already married. My grandfather also had reservations about the groom, who had a reputation for general unsteadiness. Rita was later to tell me that "everyone" knew that David's only enduring passion was for contract bridge together with all its associations of late-night drinking and gambling – he was also an expert poker player. Virtually every spare hour he had was spent at the bridge club on Thornsett Road, of which he was a founder member. When he wasn't there, his weekends involved travelling around the country, representing the city at national congresses. Her parents were convinced that Ena would be a bridge widow, neglected, lonely and unloved. My mother was made of sterner stuff.

The engagement came as a bolt from the blue. "Having just recovered consciousness I hasten to send you heartiest congratulations", ran a telegram from Ben Pomerance, one of my father's best pals, on hearing the news. He typified the general reaction, not least from Ena's sisters, who couldn't quite credit the fact that she had been quietly conducting a romantic intrigue all the time they had privately put her, at the age of twenty-seven, firmly on the shelf. Still, the Glass family was getting used to bombshells (an unexploded one had been found in their garden earlier that year), and arrangements for the ceremony were hastily put in motion. So on that dank November day, my parents stood composedly side by side while Rabbi Cohen performed the marriage rites, and David slipped a gold ring onto the forefinger of Ena's right hand in accordance with Jewish ritual. And my mother's name was duly recorded in the register, falsely, as Ena Glass, spinster. At last I have the explanation of the two wedding rings in my mother's jewellery case, which had so mystified me. The first ring I knew she had put away because her fingers had swollen so that it no longer fitted. But the other had been a conundrum, until now. Though when I think about it, virtually everything about this wedding was covered with a veil, apart from the bride. The day itself was so misty that the only photograph of the happy couple, a snapshot taken by Alex with a cheap Brownie box camera, shows them almost entirely obscured by drizzling fog. My father, with the understatement that he always employed at moments of deep emotion, subsequently appended a note to this picture, labelling it as "the only photograph of David Brown in a hat". The term "wedding" is never mentioned.

It was an "extremely shabby wedding" as Jane Austen's Mrs Elton would have had it. "Very little white satin, very few lace veils; a most pitiful business!" Instead of drifting down the aisle adorned in silk and lace like her sisters, the bride wore a sombre, two-piece costume, acquired from the Rosa Woolman boutique, an outfit which my mother always complained never suited her. On her head she wore a dark felt hat, and she carried the anemones, flowers that, like her, were unshowy and with mysterious, hidden depths. David's brother Alex was best man. His younger siblings, Joe and Harry, were away on active service. Ena categorically refused to have any bridesmaids and there was definitely to be no "fuss". These decisions disappointed not just my grandmother, who after all had another daughter's wedding to enjoy two weeks later, but most especially Maud and Rose, who, even considering the wartime privations, felt they had been cheated of the jamboree they deserved. They were also perplexed by David's choice of bride, so different from the alluring young things they were used to seeing in his company. Ena, naturally reserved and intellectual, with her love of the outdoors and solitary walks, was the antithesis of those bubbly girls. Still at least she was Jewish. As a wedding present they gave the couple an electric sweeper, a non-too subtle hint for the new wife, whom they suspected, quite correctly, was deeply undomesticated.

In spite of the sparse nature of the event, Ena and David were showered with greetings from well-wishers, to say nothing of gifts from relatives and friends of my grandparents as well as their own. At the bottom of the locked chest, next to the "marriage cert", I unearthed a list of wedding presents, scrupulously typed on what I recognise as my mother's ancient black Royal typewriter, which she used for another thirty years until it was replaced by an electric Smith Corona. As I read through it, each gift numbered and with the donor's name beside it plus a pencilled tick to show that she had sent a note of thanks, I am at once surrounded by the phantoms of my childhood. Their names invoke a graphic group sketch of that previous generation with a clarity far more intense than modern wedding photos, which show guests massed around bride and groom, waving at the camera, the finished print so packed that faces are often indistinguishable. Is that Aunty Freda half hidden by the fascinator in front? Can't be sure. Memory, however, is a more reliable strongbox, where pictures do not fade, especially when prompted. The catalogue of articles reconstructs my childhood home with its Pyrex dishes, tea trolley and silver candlesticks. I can see again the heavy glass flower bowl from Edna and Robert Halle and the onyx book ends given by Max and Miriam Waldenberg. The electric clock from Teddy Isaacs sat on my mother's mantelpiece for forty years and the silver tea set and tray from Lewis Rose remained in use for even longer.

Ena and David received a total of ninety-six wedding gifts, an extraordinary tally in a country beset by shortages and rationing, especially when most of the donors weren't invited to the reception. There were glass ashtrays and a cigarette box (my father, like the King, was at that time a heavy smoker), a hearth brush (vital in an age of crackling fires and cinders), a wireless set (an essential when everyone was glued to the latest bulletins) and a bread board (no ready-sliced in those days), all of which reveal the habits of the time. The list also itemised what the young couple most needed in starting out on married life, hard cash, amounting in all to £269- 9s, the odd number is accounted for by the fact that several cheques were made out in guineas, including two munificent ones of fifty guineas each. One of these, as might perhaps have been expected, was from David's employer, Isidore Lewis, later to become Lord Mayor of Sheffield. The other, astonishingly, was from his fly-by-night but open-handed brother, Joe, a Warrant Officer in the RAF. An inveterate gambler, he must have amassed some staggering winnings on the horses on his last leave. As the purchase price for Ena and David's new home on Dobcroft Road was a mere £700, this was riches indeed.

The ceremony was followed by a reception, with a strict limit on invitations – family only. My grandparents' decision to invite Rita's future mother-in-law, Rose Simons, on the basis that she would soon count as a relative by association, was to have dire consequences. This mean-spirited hag, who always wanted to be the centre of any family gathering, was enraged to discover that when they sat down for tea in the synagogue hall, her chair was rather too near the door, in her eyes a deeply insulting placement. In high dudgeon (never a phrase I thought I'd have opportunity to use), she stormed out – she didn't of course have too far to walk to the exit – dragging her mild-mannered husband in her wake and resolving never to speak to any member of the Glass family again. The upshot was that twenty-five years later, when I became engaged to her grandson, David, she refused to attend the wedding. With unerring tactical foresight, she left this revelation to the very eve of the ceremony for maximum impact. This effectively redirected the attention of the Simons' supporters towards her and away from the bride and groom and inserted a spoiler into the otherwise joyful mood of our festivities. Her timing was flawless. Revenge, as they say, is always a dish best eaten cold. After quarter of a century it must have been practically frozen solid.

Paradoxically, it was Hitler who had brought my parents together. In January 1933, seventeen-year-old Ena had gone on a school trip to Berlin to improve her spoken language skills before sitting her Higher School Certificate. It was her second visit, the first being an exchange when she was fourteen. She had an aptitude for languages and went on to study languages at university. The 1933 visit, however, was unlike any other, for she was in Berlin when the news came through that Adolf Hitler had been appointed Chancellor. She never forgot the chilling sights and sounds of that day and for years was haunted by thoughts of the ultimate fate of the Jewish family who had hosted her, and the girlfriend she had met. In the evening, Stormtroopers carrying flaming torches paraded through the Brandenburg Gate, singing the Horst Wessel song and cheered by thousands of ordinary people. Many of the crowd were wearing swastika armbands, including the police, who only a few days before had been treating the Nazis like troublemakers. In a matter of hours, they had performed a startling volte-face. When Hitler finally showed himself to the populace, appearing at a window illuminated by the beam of a spotlight, he was greeted with the sort of adulation now reserved for rock stars. Carefully staged by Goebbels, and accompanied by slow drumbeats, it was a not dissimilar spectacle. "It is almost like a dream – a fairytale. The new Reich has been born," Josef Goebbels wrote in his diary that night. For Ena, already politically aware, and for the nine and a half million European Jews, it was of course not a dream but the start of a nightmare.

A couple of months later, a raft of official policies was issued, legitimising the anti-Semitic dogma of Nazi ideology, reinforced in 1935 by the now notorious Nuremberg Laws, which labelled Jews a separate, inferior race, denied them German citizenship and made "inter-racial" marriage a crime. In the resulting violence, Jews were regularly beaten up by Stormtroopers and left lying in the street, while Jewish homes and businesses were looted. News of these happenings resonated with sickening familiarity for Anglo-Jewish families, whose parents had themselves escaped from the brutality of the pogroms just one generation earlier. They became supremely conscious of the fragility of their own position as well as that of their Continental counterparts, many of whom were, like them, deeply embedded in and accepted by their homelands. By 1938, Jewish community leaders in the UK, stricken by what was materialising, promised the government that they would bear all expenses relating to any refugees "whether in respect of temporary or permanent accommodation and maintenance... without ultimate charge to the State". It was only through this collective undertaking that so many fugitives were able to find a haven in this country. But it was not always easy to keep to this pledge.

As British Jews began to receive increasingly desperate requests for help during the late 1930s, my father was at the forefront of the action. Many of the writers of these letters addressed identical copies to dozens of communities throughout England and the non-occupied countries. David was Secretary of the Jewish Aid Committee, though he couldn't recall there ever being a meeting and he worked virtually single-handed, personally reading every letter out of the thousands that arrived in Sheffield. His almost unendurable task was to determine whether there was a genuine case for support – there always was – and, more importantly, if and how help could be provided. It was heart-breaking and seemingly hopeless work. It was not until late in

1938 that the world publicity given to the plight of refugees made its way into the Sheffield headlines, and on 15th December that year a meeting, at David's instigation, was held at Sheffield's Victoria Hall, which resulted in the formation of the Sheffield Refugee Council. This was chaired by Arnold Freeman, warden of the Education Settlement, with Rabbi Barnet Cohen and the archdeacon of Sheffield as Vice Presidents. My father's nominal role was Treasurer, but he was in fact the prime mover behind not just the Jewish community's response to the crisis but the wider community as well. A half-century later, when my daughter, Victoria, solicited information about the refugee crisis for her A Level History project, she received a letter from a colleague of David's during that period, who told her uncompromisingly that "there was only ONE person who masterminded the local work – your grandfather!... the man who inspired and urged and was the unquestioning overseer."

As part of the extended rescue operation, during 1938 and 1939 my father traipsed solitary miles on foot through Sheffield and its outlying districts, trying to find sanctuaries for displaced persons or homes for children, whose despairing parents were frantically trying to get them to safety, knowing in their hearts that they might never see them again. He raised funds to rent a house on Priory Road, Netheredge, just around the corner from Montgomery Road, which could serve as a hostel with enough room to accommodate sixteen disturbed refugee boys. Working closely with Rebecca Fish, the dynamic wife of another of Sheffield's rabbis, they appointed a warden, Hugh Roberton, who as a conscientious objector was exempt from military service. Hugh and his wife looked after the children throughout the war, while my father set up and chaired a management committee, which foraged food, clothing, bedding, school places and even jobs with local employers for some of the older ones. In December 1940, during the Blitz, the hostel received a direct hit and emergency arrangements had to be made for the boys, who had been sheltering in the cellar, and who were then temporarily housed in the synagogue hall while new accommodation was found. These children, both from the hostel and those who had been placed in foster-homes around the city, owed their lives to my father, and many retained contact with him after the war.

All through my childhood, young adults who had managed to escape the terror through my father's exertions would drop in for a cup of tea or a chat if they were visiting Sheffield. They included Hana and Hans Kohn, dark-eyed twins from Czechoslovakia, who were ten when they boarded the Kindertransport on the eve of war, leaving behind their parents and older sister to perish in Auschwitz. On arrival at Sheffield's Midland station, they were separated, as no family could be found who were prepared to take in not just one but two little foreign waifs. Hana went to the Crookes family, who already had three boys of their own and were not at all sure they could cope with the expense of another child. But at their first sight of Hana with her large label and number around her neck, Mrs Crookes cried, "She's ours!" Hana later became a teacher in Liverpool and her witness testimony is now part of the Holocaust display in the London Jewish Museum in Camden. Hans, who was formally adopted by a Rotherham family of extraordinary compassion, changed his name to John Mulroy, and became a GP. He also became one of my father's regular bridge partners in the 1960s, and the two subsequently went on to win several tournaments together.

Many of the letters that arrived on David's desk in 1938 were of course written in German, and despite his many admirable qualities, my father was no languages expert. Ena Glass, by this time a fluent German speaker, came to his aid. Having witnessed the crowd hysteria on the night of Hitler's election five years earlier, she had also got to know well several refugees who had managed to get to England before the restrictions on exit permits for Jews came into force. In particular she had become friendly with two young women, who left her in no doubt about what was happening in Europe. Vicki Ohrenstein had left Austria after the Anschluss. A secular Jew from an assimilated bourgeois family, Vicki had been standing with her gentile fiancé, watching incredulously as the Stormtroopers goose-stepped their way through the streets. All of a sudden, she became aware that the young man beside her had let go of her hand and had moved forward through the crowd as if in a trance, his arm outstretched in the Seig Heil salute. It was at that moment, she said, that it hit her with the force of a thunderbolt that there could be no future for her in her native country. She arrived in England in the mid-1930s, where she ultimately became the highly capable manageress of the main Sheffield book store, Wards, on Chapel Walk, and was my first employer when I took a holiday job there as a student.

The other young woman with whom Ena was to remain close until their deaths was Illa Wolfsfeld, who arrived in Britain in 1936 at the age of twenty-one. Illa was a slender, dark-haired beauty, who had trained as a classical ballerina. Her husband, Erich, thirty years her senior, had been Professor-Principal at the Berlin Royal Academy of Art and an eminent artist, whose work hangs in galleries across the world as well as on my own sitting room walls. When he asked Illa to come up and see his etchings, the invitation was no tired seduction technique. The etchings had won the Grand Prix de Rome in 1916 as well as numerous exhibition gold medals. Illa began modelling for him and their romance blossomed. In June 1936, the day after they were married, Erich was expelled from the Academy. Illa fled to Britain on a domestic servant visa. A guarantee of employment was the only sure-fire way the authorities would allow her to enter the country. With a portfolio of Erich's paintings taped into the lining of her suitcase, she found a job as a maid of all work in the house of a Sheffield University professor. It was a position for which she was singularly ill-suited and at which, as she readily admitted, she was quite incompetent. Coming from the Berlin intelligentsia, and a family who had retained both a maidservant and a cook, Illa had never even entered a kitchen until she came to England. On her first morning in Sheffield, her employer discovered her weeping, completely outfaced by the daunting task of making tea and toast. But when he saw Erich's work, he realised that here was something exceptional. The Director of the Sheffield museums was equally impressed and offered a one-man exhibition at the Graves Art Gallery in September 1939. It was Erich's ticket to safety. He secured a distinguished person's visa as part of the cultural quota that allowed a select few German Jews to come to Britain that year. He made it just a few weeks before war was declared, and in May 1940 was arrested by the British authorities and interned as an enemy alien on the Isle of Man, where he continued to paint using boot polish. Destitute on his release, he had to beg for a living. He eventually established a studio in London and continued his artistic career, although never to the level of acclaim he had once enjoyed.

With these stories fresh in her mind, Ena needed no persuading to join David in his efforts to help fugitive Jews, and she painstakingly translated letter after letter, often working through the night to cope with the deluge of appeals that flooded in. Their relationship came to a head only a few days before war was declared. My mother had a Swiss German-speaking pen-friend, Lucie, with whom she had kept up a regular correspondence since university days, and with whom she had spent holidays. Ena had been ill during the spring of 1939, possibly a result of the exhaustion brought on by her ceaseless refugee efforts, and Lucie suggested that she take an extended convalescence in Lausanne. An added attraction of this invitation was Lucie's handsome brother, Joggi, who knew and admired Ena from previous visits. The couple had gone skiing and skating together, sipped *glühwein* at little bars surrounded by massed, snow-capped mountains, and in the summer months had gone sailing on the lake and sunbathed on its shores. The pair had exchanged a series of increasingly affectionate letters, some of which have survived, and Ena was keen to renew their friendship. This is why, to my amazement given the benefit of hindsight, in August 1939, when England was preparing for war, she was to be found basking in the pleasures of the Swiss landscape, dividing her time between Lucie's townhouse and the family's mountain chalet.

Meanwhile the news from Germany was ever more troubling, stirring even my habitually slothful grandfather into action. In the middle of August, Isaac Glass wrote to his daughter suggesting she should cut her holiday short and come home as soon as she could.

But Switzerland was idyllic, Joggi a delightful companion, and Ena, cut off from both the English papers and the BBC, and in any case never one to follow her father's orders, blithely disregarded his advice. It was only when the very next post brought a letter from David Brown, imploring her to return before the European borders became impassable that she grasped the urgency of the situation. It was a wake-up call.

She packed her bags that night and managed to get a seat on one of the last trains to Southampton before the Swiss authorities closed the borders. It was a hair-raising journey, the carriages packed with those who were using Switzerland as a last-ditch escape route. The train made multiple halts through Belgium and France, was subject to heart-stopping delays when no one knew what was happening, and at each frontier, guards boarded the carriage, demanding passengers produce their papers for scrutiny. Ena arrived in Southampton, exhausted and shaken after a forty-hour trip. It was David's intervention that had saved her from being trapped abroad for the next six years, and who knows, perhaps forever. From this point on there was only one direction in which their relationship could go.

Ten

The Little Tumblers: Sheffield 1920–1970s

"The effect of her being on those around her was incalculably diffusive:
for the growing good of the world is partly dependent on unhistoric
acts; and that things are not so ill with you and me as they might have
been, is half owing to the number who faithfully lived a hidden life and
rest in unvisited tombs."

GEORGE ELIOT, *MIDDLEMARCH*

"I grew up in two worlds," wrote my mother at the age of ninety-
four. "The one typically English middle-class where I read *Alice in
Wonderland*, learned to recite Shakespeare at school" – she then went
into a rendition of 'Friends, Romans, countrymen...' – "collected a
penny for the guy in winter and in summer ran three-legged races.
And then there was the other. Side by side my two worlds existed so
that I was always different from the others. They gave me the feeling
of being on the outside looking in." This sense of being a spectator
never left her. She projected her own fantasy into a story about a rabbi,
who, while delivering his sermon, found that he could peer into the
hearts of his congregants. Yet while she cherished her status as covert

observer, she was rarely prepared to let people into her own life. She described her vision of hell as "having to live one's life over again with one's thoughts revealed to the person to whom one is speaking." Her worst fear was to appear naked either physically or philosophically – she refused point blank ever to try on clothes in a public changing room. Privacy was her safeguard.

I have a photograph of my cute, one-year-old mother with her brother, Harry, and older sister, Rae, the girls in lacy white frocks, with ankle socks and button boots. Harry stands behind them, one arm protectively round Ena to stop her toppling over. And another of her with Rae and a heavily ringleted Rita, evidently before Nancy arrived on the scene. Harry and Rae above her, Rita and Nancy, the little ones, below. My mother never had a natural ally. It seemed obvious to keep her distinctiveness intact, and to sleep in arctic splendour in the attic, a blessed retreat from her squabbling sisters. Life at 49 Montgomery Road was loud with activity, chatter and games, with the comings and goings of friends and neighbours as well as five boisterous children, and my grandparents' approach to childcare was casual in the extreme. The girls took for granted the dancing classes and piano lessons, the tennis tournaments and the swimming galas, the outings to the races and the frequent holidays. Blackpool in particular featured prominently in their early lives, not just in the summer but at Easter and Christmas as well. One freezing December, as they drove across the Pennines on the way to Blackpool, snow falling and the road surface slippery, the car with its seven passengers slowly slid sideways into a ditch. "I can still see my father in his heavy overcoat," reported my mother nine decades later, "standing in the middle of the road, banging his arms across his body to keep warm, and flagging down passing motorists to take his small children in ones or twos to Manchester station from which they could catch the train to Blackpool." It never crossed my grandparents' minds that there might be other perils for little girls entrusted to the care of a total stranger. And, in truth, they all arrived safely.

From early on Ena was acknowledged as the clever girl of the family. The first *bon mot* she ever remembered making was when she was five years old, racing up and down the kitchen, a headscarf tied around her head, shouting "I'm a Rushin' peasant". My grandmother, standing at the stove cooking, was oblivious to puns though indulgent to high spirits. Ena's delight in language lasted a lifetime. She wrote her first poem when she was nine and always loved word games, literary quizzes and inventing children's puzzles that featured jumbled words or a test to turn 'Lot' into 'Jew' one letter at a time. She would produce verses at the drop of a hat, not just for birthdays but in thank-you notes to friends and replies to invitations. "Let the tumbril rumble", went her acceptance for a party given on 14th July, "And as we sit – mustn't grumble / We'll chat and knit. / For the tri-coloured invite, thanks a lot / But don't expect us sans culottes".

After she was married and burdened with me and Julian, she started to write light articles for magazines and also became the Sheffield correspondent of *The Jewish Chronicle*, a job she held for forty years. Journalism could be easily interspersed with household chores. Her subjects were typically women's issues, Jewish life and her other great passion, gardening. "O Sweet and Lovely Wall", she wrote with apologies to Shakespeare in an article on climbing plants for *Popular Gardening*. "The Synagogue and the Kitchen Sink" appeared in *The Jewish Chronicle* and "When Knitted Sports Knickers Were All the Rage" in *The Lady*. They give an accurate indication of her range. When I went through her papers after her death, I found that she had kept a systematic record of every piece she ever sent for publication, including a list of all her rejections, plus the rejection slips. Most writers bin them immediately. She liked to be reminded of her limits. At the age of eleven, she had won a scholarship to Sheffield Girls' High School, and when I visited the school a few weeks ago, I saw her name in gold lettering on the Honours board as one of six who went to university in 1933. She was hugely competitive, small, wiry and a good tennis player but she was always the last to be picked for the netball team when the captains were choosing sides. At first she worried that this was a personal snub, only marginally reassured by the fact that the first person to be selected was always Dorothy "the lamp-post" Wharton, who could pop the ball in the net just by stretching out her right arm.

Her first taste of being different was when she was five and came face to face with Christmas at the infants' school party. As the children dived into the magic mountain of cakes piled on platters on a long table, she sat apart to eat the solitary bun provided by her mother, baked according to strict Jewish dietary laws. "I found myself separate if equal," she remarked. "The pattern was set." That pattern dominated my mother's version of who she was. "All right," she insisted, "so I didn't have a chocolate Easter egg but the Passover celebration lasted a week. All right, so I didn't have an angel-topped Xmas tree dripping with gold and silver baubles but I had the coloured candles of Chanucah, also lasting a week." There's more than a touch of defensiveness in her tone. She never let on how mortified she was by the frequent notes in my grandfather's elegant script, "Dear Miss Neal, will you please excuse my daughter from school next Monday and Tuesday as these are Jewish Holy Days". "And," said my mother, "if anyone wants to know why I never mastered logarithms or the principal rivers of South America, the reason is that they were on Mondays and Tuesdays."

Worst of all though were parties at the homes of school friends, not because she didn't know how to "bite an inch off a red-hot poker" but, oh terror, how to refuse politely the potted meat sandwiches. Incidentally the solution to the red-hot poker conundrum is to gnash at the empty air while standing one inch away from the fiery object. It was a challenge that defies all today's regulations, and was still around in the 1950s, when I too had to endure the nightmare of party games with their forfeits and "dares". Reading my mother's jottings about her childhood makes me wonder why she condemned me to repeat the embarrassments she suffered when she had to stand in the corridor during school prayers, was made to sit outside the classroom in scripture lessons and was excluded from the annual carol service. I longed to blend in unnoticed – some hopes. My mother, who was reprimanded at school for croaking like a frog, was put off singing for life and forever after silently mouthed the words to any choral performance, even to "God Save the King", which was ubiquitous at public events, including school speech days and at the end of the feature film in cinemas. Carols were completely off the agenda for her, and by extension for me.

In contrast to her sisters, Ena had little interest in being fashionable or flirty. While they thrived on gossip and dates, she found comfort in solitude, where there was no one to impress or make an effort for. As Edith Wharton, the American writer, whose works my mother greatly admired, once said, "When I'm on my own, the conversation's so much better." She renounced cosmetics on the grounds that they were artificial, her one compromise being a deep red lipstick for formal occasions. The same one in its metallic casing was dragooned into use for about two decades until it was completely ground down to its base. I can't ever remember her buying a new one, and she certainly never visited a make-up counter or read a newspaper beauty column. Gifts of perfume were stored in a drawer and forgotten about. She remained oblivious to changing styles. For years she kept hanging in her wardrobe a "costume" of sober grey jacket and skirt that had been hers in the 1930s, and that still had "lots of wear in it", with the intention of passing it on to me as soon as I was the right size to fit into it. As my teenage years coincided first with rock 'n' roll and then with the era of the mini-skirt, I naturally refused to have anything to do with it (it smelt of mothballs anyway), and eventually to her deep regret, she had to consign the outfit to the jumble sale. "Such waste, Judy!" she scolded, as teen culture passed her by undetected.

The sibling with whom she felt most affinity was Harry, clever, polite and well-behaved, qualities he carried into adulthood, and without the spikiness with which my mother cloaked her shyness and which used to alarm my friends. His only misdemeanour as far as I can tell was at the age of eight when he put Ena, then three, into the garden wheelbarrow and ran down the hill with it, letting go of the handles as soon as he felt the vehicle had gathered enough momentum to fly independently. My mother bore the scars to her dying day. Sedate in every other respect, Harry retained his love of speed, and bought fast cars as soon as he could afford them. He squired his sisters to dances, partnered them at tennis, and accompanied my mother, the only one who appreciated classical music, to the symphony concerts at the City Hall. They went on holiday together, memorably to St Moritz in 1938, where they were photographed in ski gear on the slopes, pictures that now elicit unchecked hilarity in my grandchildren, who knew my mother only as an arthritic old lady who couldn't get in and out of the car without help.

When Harry contracted scarlet fever as a teenager, he was considered too precious to be sent to hospital. My grandmother was convinced that if you went into hospital you never came out again except in a coffin. She passed this fear on to my mother, who avoided hospitals like the plague and only ever spent one night there in her nineties following a bungled cataract operation. Instead, Rae was given the important task of nursing Harry at home. For six weeks a sheet soaked in antiseptic hung across the door of his bedroom as protection, while Rae ran up and down stairs with glasses of barley water to keep his temperature down and bowls of chicken soup to restore his energy levels. Unsurprisingly she soon became infected, quickly followed by Nancy. The two girls were packed off to a nursing home at Lodge Moor, set in green fields on the city boundary. They were allowed visitors only on condition that they stayed outside, so Ena and Rita would loiter in the hospital grounds, throwing sweets into the ward and chatting to their sisters who leant out of the windows. Rita, who was eleven, was then despatched to Aunty Millie in Manchester but a few days after her arrival the tell-tale rash appeared. Scarlet fever was notorious as a frequent cause of death in young children, and Millie, who had a new baby, panicked. Without a second's thought, she shoved Rita out of the front door, where she stood shivering in the porch – it was raining – until a taxi came to cart her off to Monsall isolation hospital. Quarantined for five weeks, Rita languished in solitary detention, her only consolation a huge, square basket of fruit, sent to her by a kindly friend of her father's, packed with hothouse luxuries, including grapes and apricots. The sight of it, unfortunately, was all there was for her to enjoy as – and Rita resented this until her dying day – the nurses' eyes lit up when they spotted it, and the tearful patient could only look on as they shared the goodies out between them. Ena was the only one to remain immune to the infection, possibly down to her robust constitution and the polar solitude in her attic, so glacial that it presumably killed off any lurking microbes.

The black and white photograph on my mother's dressing table showed a society wedding straight out of the pages of *Tatler* or *Country Life*. A happy bride in a flowing wedding dress and long, gauzy veil stands on a manicured lawn. At her feet pose three young women, her bridesmaids, in white full-skirted gowns with puffed sleeves, embroidered with sprays of lily-of-the-valley, and wearing veils held in place by coronets of flowers. Each is holding an enormous floral bouquet more suitable for a bride than for her attendants. This tableau is artfully framed by the spreading branches of elm trees and weeping willows and set off by a background of huge rhododendron bushes in full bloom. The photograph was a permanent fixture in Glass family households. It was displayed prominently on my grandmother's sideboard, and in my Aunt Rita's bedroom, and again on the cocktail cabinet in my Aunt Nancy's lounge. It showed the apotheosis of a romantic idyll, a blessed marriage of a charmed couple in the garden of their country estate. Who said that photographs can never lie?

The picture is of the eldest Glass sister, Rae, and her wedding to Manuel Goldstein in the summer of 1938. It was taken in a public park. None of the women in the photograph would ever have such magnificent dresses again. Nor would the bridesmaids have such fairy-tale weddings themselves. Quite the reverse in fact as they were all married during wartime. In the fairy-tale, Cinderella effects the transformation from skivvy to princess partly through the effortless magic of a perfect ball gown with fragile slippers to match, slippers that won't fit any foot other than hers. Her petite shoe size is a sure-fire sign of her sensitive spirit and innately noble character, a marked contrast to the great clodhoppers of those normal mortals, her stepsisters. As it happens, Rae's shoe size was two-and-a-half, the tiniest adult shoe size available, and throughout her life she had great difficulty finding shoes to fit. There was, however, no handsome prince to slide the slipper onto her toes, thereby rescuing her from a lifetime of drudgery. Rae's elaborate wedding dress, hand-stitched by Miss Ruby, the dressmaker in Manchester who made my grandmother's clothes for special occasions, was equal to anything in the Perrault classic or even the Disney film. But the silks and satins soon reverted to rags and even the delicate shoes couldn't save the girl who became a princess for one day only. It was the first and last grand wedding in the family, and it marked the final day of Rae's protected life.

Rae took after my grandmother in character. Chatty and sociable, she had an infectious giggle, and could spend endless amounts of time window-gazing, going to the movies and burbling on about trivia with her friends. Her story is one of decline into the sort of ordinary tragedy that goes unnoticed in so many lives, a mundane story of waste, deceit and abuse, suffered mostly in silence and ending in a death among strangers in an impersonal hospital ward. Without the self-determination that characterised her siblings, Rae had no thoughts of a career. For a couple of years she had attended Minerva College, a girls' boarding school in Leicester, and on leaving never trained for any profession other than household management, and she certainly wasn't a natural at that. With a maid at Montgomery Road to launder her immaculate tennis whites, why should Rae be an expert at scrubbing floors? The family paid a charwoman to come in daily to do that. The result of this was that when Rae had her own home, it was a total mess, with dirty dishes lying on every surface, old cartons under chairs, bits of clothing draped over furniture, and the entire place so squalid that my father, dropping by for a cup of coffee one day when he was in the area, could not bear to let his lips touch the cup.

Once she reached her twenties, with her sisters either at college or at work, Rae's life was empty. She devoured glossy magazines, and did embroidery, embellishing cushion covers and table linen with floral designs. Her stitching was beautifully neat, and I still have a tablecloth she gave me, decorated with pink daisies in shaded silks on a background of meticulous cross-stitch. She spent her summer afternoons playing tennis and winter ones at the cinema. She took in a handful of private pupils for elocution, reprocessing the lessons she had learned at Minerva, but this could never be described as a serious career move. In any case she had her hopes pinned on Harry Cohen, a young librarian from a respected Sheffield family. With a group of like-minded companions, they would set off at weekends on rambles around Grindleford or Bakewell in the Peak District, or motored to the seaside at Filey, Bridlington or Scarborough. I've got all the photos. They enjoyed ballroom dancing and concerts, and they played tennis at Greenwood, which had become a centre for the Sheffield *jeunesse dorée* of the period. Rae Glass and Harry Cohen were part of the in crowd and an acknowledged couple.

Harry was bespectacled, slim and good looking with an Errol Flynn moustache and a twinkling smile. His charm and convivial nature, however, were to be his downfall. For at the same time he was conducting his chaste and totally above-board romance with Rae, he was also engaged in dalliance with a pretty cinema usherette, Elsie Suckley, a rather more lax arrangement which permitted greater freedoms. Shortly before Christmas 1936, Elsie revealed the unwelcome news that Harry was soon to be a father. It was not an announcement greeted with unmitigated joy on either side. To his credit, Harry duly stood by the mother-to-be, and the couple were married quietly in a civil ceremony in Sheffield Registry Office early in 1937, smashing Rae's dreams in the process. Their son, Tony, was born a few months later. In September 1939 at the outbreak of war, Harry joined the armed forces, and rose to the rank of Sergeant in the Royal Army Ordnance Corps. He died of an insect bite on 3 April 1942 in Persia-Iraq, leaving his wife and two children – their daughter Angela had been born before he left – to survive on a war widow's pension.

I learned all about Elsie's sorrows because my father had been a friend of Harry's, and after his death did what he could to help the young widow. As well as the occasional cash hand-outs, this consisted of offering her child-minding duties, including sending me to stay at her house when my parents enjoyed a night out. These visits were always solitary ones. Julian could be farmed out to one of my mother's sisters, who had children roughly the same age. I was less malleable. In retrospect I realise that of course this was a financial arrangement, though at the time I just thought Elsie enjoyed having me around. Her house was quite unlike ours and I had to squeeze past push-bikes in the alley between the houses to enter a side door that opened straight into the kitchen, which also served as the main living room. The downside was that the house had no indoor sanitation, which meant that the lavatory was in an outhouse across a yard. I quite liked the fact that the wooden seat was much warmer to sit on than our chilly porcelain one at home but I was unnerved by the spiders which crouched in thick webs that festooned the corners of the dank little shed, and I got scared crossing the yard after dark as it was pitch black out there. I was also permanently nervous in case someone walked in on me, as the ill-fitting half-stable door, which closed with a big black latch, was rickety to say the least. And at night I was deeply embarrassed by the chamber pot, which sat underneath my bed, and was impossible to use quietly. Oh, the shame!

The introduction to Manuel Goldstein was made while Rae was still on the rebound from Harry. It was a match that she at first resisted. Tall, confident and with a smooth manner, Manny ultimately sweet-talked his way into Rae's affections. Even though my grandfather was keen to see Rae married, he was nonetheless suspicious of this virtual stranger, and made enquiries in Liverpool, Manny's hometown, about his prospective son-in-law's credentials. He can't have looked very hard. Manny represented himself as the owner of three shops in Liverpool and Southport, all apparently flourishing. With his doubts satisfied, my grandfather went ahead and gave Rae the lavish wedding of the photographs, handing over a substantial dowry to Manny to future-proof the match. Adorned in her bridal extravaganza, Rae beamed her way down the aisle of Sheffield's new Wilson Road synagogue in June 1938, followed demurely by her three maids of honour. The white-tie, seven-course marriage feast at Sheffield City Hall for a hundred guests – the menu still survives – began with *hors d'oeuvres* and *consommé de nouilles*, continued with *pâté de pigeon* and a sorbet before the main course of *poussin*, and ended up with *poire melba, savarin de fruits*, coffee and dessert. It doesn't take Miss Marple to detect that this bill of fare is merely my grandmother's Sabbath lunch of chicken noodle soup, chopped liver and roast chicken translated to swanky surroundings.

The day marked what was one of the last happy days of Rae's life. The pair moved to Southport, where it rapidly became apparent that his talk of being a successful businessman was just talk. It was true that an uncle of his did own shops but Manny himself was essentially unemployable. He was an arrogant bully, a fantasist who had ideas that were above both his station and his capabilities. Starting out as a salesman in his uncle's furniture store, he refused to take orders from his superiors, and had an inconvenient habit of telling the manager how he really ought to run the place. Predictably, he habitually got the sack.

At home he made Rae's life a misery. She cooked, washed, cleaned, mended and made do on their sparse and uncertain income while he ordered her around, shouted and resorted to violence if matters weren't to his liking. Rae, who had been used to a household which ran apparently under its own steam, where there was rarely a cross word and never a blow, was cowed. Her joy at being in charge of her own little love nest rapidly evaporated. An incompetent housekeeper and unsure how to stand up for herself, she became a virtual prisoner, allowed out only on rare occasions to shop for food. Manny refused to allow visitors, and the young wives from the local community, who might have been a source of comfort to Rae, found their gestures of friendship rebuffed. As their finances, a product of my grandfather's initial generosity, dwindled and Rae became increasingly isolated, she turned to her sisters for help. This was an act of great subterfuge, which had to be carried out behind Manny's back as he strictly forbade her to breathe a word to her family about their penury. Both my mother and Rita regularly sent Rae cash from their own meagre savings, shocked at the conditions in which she lived and worried that she was sometimes dangerously malnourished. The sunny bride in the portrait on the mantelpiece became thinner and more pinched in appearance.

Their daughter, Eta, was born in December 1944, six years after the wedding. Her unusual name came from a story in a sentimental magazine that Rae had picked up – she was a regular at Southport's public library. Eta resembled her father both in looks and behaviour. Strong-willed and taught to answer to no one, she grew up colluding in her mother's servitude, ordering her around and ignoring any timid requests Rae made for help about the house. I dreaded our intermittent visits to Southport, where I was expected to befriend her, and I could never think of her fondly even though it was constantly pointed out to me that she didn't have my advantages in life. Advantages? She was taller, stronger, bolder and could get her mother to do whatever she wanted. As far as I could see, I was the one who deserved sympathy.

Rae's appetite for popular literature did not do her any favours. She was a great believer in the supernatural and was positive that lifts in derelict buildings ran up and down without the benefit of electricity, powered by the ghosts of previous inhabitants. When she became ill with the cancer that would kill her, she turned for succour to a faith-healer, whose card she had seen in the local post office window. Audrey claimed to have spiritual powers that could cure virtually every known illness, and credulous Rae, desperate for a crumb of comfort, placed all her trust in this middle-aged fraud with the low voice and no qualifications. Twice a week for four years, Audrey came to hold Rae's hands and mutter prayers over her closed eyes, assuring her patient that she had a direct line to the Almighty. She persuaded her that her normal diet was poison, exacerbating her corrosive illness. The result was that Rae, unable to afford the special foods recommended by Audrey, became progressively weaker, her decline undoubtedly hastened by such spurious advice. When her sisters found out that she was paying this charlatan eight pounds a month, they made her promise to stop but to no effect. All through the months when Rae was crying to them over the phone that she had no money for food, she continued to have two sessions a week with Audrey at a pound a time.

Rae had been diagnosed with advanced leukaemia. Manny refused to accept that she was ill, despite her increasingly skeletal appearance. As she grew frailer and in urgent need of treatment, she made twice-weekly visits to Liverpool Royal Infirmary to receive the blood transfusions that were keeping her alive. The bus journey, which she took unaccompanied throughout the long, harsh winters of 1971 and 1972, took almost two hours in each direction. By the time she arrived back in Southport, she could barely trudge up the hill from the bus stop. Manny continued to demand meals on the table on time, expected her to drag up buckets of coal from the cellar and to keep the front steps of the terrace house whitened. A few weeks before she died, Rae somehow managed to scrounge enough cash to buy a steak for Christmas dinner. When she served it up, Manny took one look and hurled the plate and its contents across the room.

After her death, my father, who had been intending to offer Manny some cash to tide him over, was so appalled by his behaviour that he withheld the gift. "He is beyond pity", he wrote in his diary that day. He had reckoned without Rae's siblings who clubbed together to give the bereaved husband a hundred pounds. Back at the house after the funeral, Rita, who was the only other person in the family with those dainty feet, asked Eta for a pair of Rae's shoes as a keepsake. Eta, who had been about to throw them out – there was not a huge second-hand market for ladies' shoes size two-and-a-half – agreed to sell them to her for five pounds, a pretty steep market price. Rita, uncharacteristically dumbstruck, handed over the sum, but never forgave her. When Manny died three years later in the hottest recorded August for a century, the house, which had been stripped bare, needed to be fumigated before it was put up for sale. He had sold off its contents and amassed a huge overdraft at the bank. He died alone of heart failure, most likely, the coroner concluded, brought on by malnutrition. His body lay in the empty house for several days before it was discovered and was so decomposed that the police refused to let Eta see it for purposes of identification.

Rae's wretchedness tormented her sisters, who always felt guilty that they could not do more to save her. They had remained in Sheffield, apart from Rita's brief foray to Middlesborough with her husband, Harold Simons, shortly after the war, and Sheffield was where they brought up their families. I can still remember the joy at Grandma's house when Rita returned to the nest in 1952. I was especially fond of Rita and would often drop in uninvited for tea on my way home from school. Her house was light and cheerful and seemed much more welcoming than my own home. The food was a lot better too, and Rita, with her hugs and cries of delight, always gave me the impression that a scruffy, ravenous seven-year-old girl was exactly the person she most wanted to see. In spite of her neat appearance, as a child she had somehow earned the family nickname of Big Fat Lump. Letters from Harry and Ena in envelopes addressed to "Miss B.F.L. Glass" would drop through the letterbox with unerring regularity whenever they were away from home. "My Dear Big Fat Lump" opens one letter from Harry in 1933, during his period as an articled solicitor. "The train that carried your skinny brother back to London covered the 165 miles at an average speed of 35.75 m.p.h… I have just been listening to Henry Hall [host of a radio show]. 'How are you Mrs Glass? How's your husband, Mr Glass? And are all your little tumblers keeping well, well, well?'"

Rita had wanted to be a hairdresser but her father felt that this was no job for a Jewish girl and sent her to secretarial college after she left school. When she found work in the offices of a large steel firm, it didn't take long for her employers to spot her gift for organisation and she was quickly promoted to manager, only to discover that she was getting paid half the salary of her male colleagues. She felt the injustice keenly but knew that women didn't complain about unequal pay for fear of losing their position. Take it or leave it was the bosses' mentality. Rita took it. She greeted life with a stoicism that embraced all eventualities. "What can you do?" she would ask rhetorically whenever faced with any misfortune, whether this was spilling a drop of Palwin's No 5 on the tablecloth or the unwelcome news that Labour had won the 1964 general election.

After her death, I came across a much folded and re-read piece of paper in a secret drawer of a box of Rita's treasured mementoes. It was her horoscope, a free gift with tickets to *The Clairvoyant* with Claude Rains at the Gaumont cinema when Rita was seventeen. "You will become a really affectionate and religious nature, which likes more to give than to receive and then you will have few enemies but many good friends," predicted the "famous Psychologist", Dr Leopold Thoma, with uncanny if ungrammatical accuracy. "Women born under the sign of Aquarius will make very good and sincere housewives... Their loyal sense and serious conscientiousness enables them to be very faithful and to become happy while married." And so it proved. In December 1942, Rita unpacked Rae's still pristine dress from its tissue paper and wore it to her own wedding. She and Harold honeymooned at the Cumberland Hotel in London, where the bill for five nights, including early morning tea, amounted to the princely sum of £5.13.6. The following year, Harold, who had volunteered for the RAF the day war was declared, was awarded the DFC for being "an outstanding member of air crew", displaying "skill and courage of a high order". To the end of her life, Rita kept his photograph in uniform next to their wedding picture, where she could see them from her bed. In the 1980s, when to Ena and Nancy's dismay Rita moved to London, she immersed herself in charity work with the Cockfosters & Southgate synagogue. For twelve years she was Vice President of the Ladies' Guild there and in 1994 was named their Lady of the Year. Even into her nineties, she kept busy delivering meals on wheels to the "old people". That term of course never applied to her. She remained youthful, her hair, a stranger to artificial colouring, the same dark brown it had been when she was young, with just a distinctive single white streak at the front, and a few lone grey strands.

Rita's resilience to life's adversities was unfortunately not inherited by Nancy, the youngest but in a family of vertically challenged individuals, by far and away the tallest of the little tumblers. Although Nancy was present throughout my childhood and much of my adult life, she still remains a somewhat blurred figure. She had been a petted child, and grew up constantly seeking protection, usually finding it. Despite this inherent neediness, she was the only one of the sisters to have a full-time career. She had trained as a teacher on Sheffield's Collegiate Crescent, and, although seemingly of a nervous disposition, was quite capable of handling a class of over forty wayward children at Carterknowle Junior School. She was a great proponent of the cane on recalcitrant pupils, which probably explains it, and, in line with standard pedagogic practice at the time, could not conceive how a teacher could maintain discipline without it. Her own vivid memory of being beaten at the age of five didn't put her off. "We were learning to read," she told me. "The teacher had written the word 'and' on the blackboard and I didn't know what it meant." Latterly she spent several years in the home tuition service of the local education authority, her gentle nature perfectly attuned to dealing with sick or disturbed youngsters who were unable to attend school. For many years, she was also a star of the local tennis circuit as well as a formidable table-tennis player – her lanky frame and elongated reach were a great advantage. She shared this love of sport with her husband, Neville, an inoffensive and kindly individual, and a leading light in the Sheffield Jewish sports club, Maccabi.

Yet every encounter for Nancy in later life was something of a trial, and she greeted every new opportunity or invitation as a threat. As she grew older, she became visibly more neurotic. Visits to the dentist were fraught with more than the usual foreboding because she insisted that anything other than food that went in her mouth made her gag. Consequently she would sit in the dental chair and refuse to "open wide" for even the most routine examination, posing a particular challenge for the long-suffering practitioner. In fact all medical procedures turned into an ordeal as, having manfully conquered her fear of needles, she was also terrified that she might be allergic to anaesthetic. She grew pathological about germs in the atmosphere and wouldn't enter a building if illness were anywhere in the vicinity. My daughter has never forgotten how, in pre-pandemic times, Nancy refused to set foot in the house on hearing that Victoria was recovering from a cold, and turned tail to seek the safety of her own trustworthy lounge with its twenty-six inch TV screen and walnut cocktail cabinet. Any journey for Nancy was a nerve-wracking prospect in case of rain, fog, poor road conditions, traffic accidents or falling ill away from home. Her worst fears about air travel were confirmed when four of her best friends were killed on a holiday flight when their plane crashed into the side of a mountain as they landed in Tenerife, a tragedy of epic proportions that caused shockwaves throughout the local community and might well have unsettled even the hardiest temperament. More and more Nancy came to rely on her older sisters for support, who would answer the incessantly ringing phone with trepidation but who always sprang into action, if "sprang" is an appropriate verb for women who were by that time nearing eighty. Oh, the tyranny of the weak! My habitually reticent mother, not given to complaining as a rule, took to referring to her as "your aunt" in my presence or "your sister" in conversation with Rita, a danger sign if ever there was one.

Eleven

Amazing Aunts: Sheffield 1954

*"Speak in French when you can't remember the English for a thing –
turn your toes out when you walk – And remember who you are!"*
LEWIS CARROLL, *THROUGH THE LOOKING GLASS AND WHAT ALICE FOUND THERE*

In my study at home, a tapestry fire-screen guards the stone hearth,
where once it shielded a grate (which I never saw lit) in Rose and
Maude's little drawing room. The screen is delicately worked in
shades of pink, gold and green, and the picture shows two figures
in stiff seventeenth-century court dress on either side of a tree, their
arms outstretched towards one another. The male figure, holding a
crown, looks like Charles II. Judging from the expression on her face,
his sulky lady friend could well be his wife, Catherine of Braganza,
silently expressing her disquiet with his philandering. The hybrid
landscape on which the two figures hover shows a squirrel, hunting
dogs, fish swimming in a little brook, and, inexplicably, a camel with
a cheery driver, wearing a fez, urging it along. I would never dream
of buying such a thing today but I was captivated by it as a child, and
I have to admit that it comes in very useful now, as it also tips up to

become an occasional table. Embroidered by one of the seamstresses in Rose's workshop, it is a constant reminder of all the Sunday mornings when I was taken to visit my great-aunts. Preserved under glass, the colours in this picture, like my memories, have remained vivid and unchanging.

Colours, objects and smells – they float through the backdrop of my brain and provoke instant recall. The smell of freshly-baked biscuits for instance means that is Sunday morning in 1954, when my father would collect my brother and me from *cheder*, and take us on our weekly visit to Rose and Maude, who by this time lived together in a bijou, semi-detached residence in Ecclesall. It might only have been a couple of miles up the road but with its neat, spick and span frontage and pretty garden, 225 Tullibardine Road was a world away from Broomhall Street. As we went in through the front door, the smell of those biscuits wafted towards us. Sundays were Maude's baking mornings, and the biscuits stood cooling on a wire rack. Just as she had done in those impoverished days of the 1920s, it was Maude who kept the house gleaming, who shopped for groceries, and who did the cooking. But mingling with the baking smells there was another, flowery aroma that was more powerful than the rest. That one is a direct path to the majestic figure of Aunty Rose, or Queen Rose as my father would call her out of earshot, the unacknowledged head of the Woolman tribe.

Elizabeth Arden's Blue Grass perfume, spicy, floral and sophisticated, was created by Fragonard in 1934, and is still on sale at select beauty counters today. Just a whiff of it and the years fall away for me, and Rose is in the room. The fragrance permeated her clothes and her lacy pocket handkerchiefs and followed her wherever she went. Rose was easily the most *soignée* member of the family. Tall and stately, she remained impeccably groomed even in her late seventies, and was held up to me as a model of perfect deportment. My father used to make me practise walking the length of our lounge while balancing a book on my head so that my posture would develop into something approaching Rose's ramrod stature. As I was about half her height and had only a fraction of her poise (on a good day), this was an improbable goal, but I did eventually learn not to wobble. When I finally managed to keep the book steady for a couple of circuits, the bar was raised to two books or even three. I could never win.

Rose had high standards regarding fashion and indeed just about everything else, and she and Maude, who somewhere along the way had added an 'e' to her name to make it appear more refined, constantly impressed upon me the importance of attention to detail. This included making sure my handwriting was all sloping at exactly the same angle, sautéing onions in *schmaltz* until they were "just golden" for the perfect chopped liver, or checking that the seams of my stockings were straight before leaving the house. My children now mock my fastidiousness and shriek with laughter when I straighten pictures by a millimetre when I enter a room, but it's just a vestigial throwback to my Woolman training.

At the age of fourteen, following in the family tradition, Rose had been apprenticed to a draper, and gradually progressed from assistant to *vendeuse* and eventually manageress at a local couturier, Maison Sonia, now defunct, where she was in her element bossing everyone about with her blend of firmness and charm. Her lover had been killed in the First World War, and a photograph of this handsome young man in his RAF uniform stood on her dressing table. By the 1950s she was the proprietress of a smart boutique in Sheffield city centre, which had her name, promoted to Rosa Woolman, inscribed in elegant curling script on the shop front. The real owner of the shop was tall, portly, good-looking and married Mr Wiseberg, with whom, rumour had it, Rose was conducting a steamy love affair. The shop interior was very grand, and the window displays were furnished with white-painted, wrought-iron frames against which stood headless dummies with frocks draped around their curvaceous forms. There were spindly gilt chairs and a chaise longue with satin upholstery for customers to sit on while Rose and her assistants brought out modish little costumes with matching jackets and skirts, afternoon tea-gowns or evening dresses for display. Sometimes these were modelled by the salesgirls, who were selected for their height and graceful carriage – obviously they had all passed the book-on-head test with flying colours. It was out of the question for customers to go rifling through racks of clothes with their dirty fingers. Zara it was not.

While Julian and my father munched warm biscuits with Maude in the pristine dining room with its figurines of Chinese horses brought back by Aunt Lillie from Hong Kong, I would go upstairs to visit Rose, for whom Sundays were her only chance of a lie-in. As it was invariably approaching one o'clock when we arrived, it was a very late lie-in indeed, and I thought this indolence the height of luxury. In her bedroom, the heady fumes of Blue Grass took over big time from the baking. Rose, then in her sixties, welcomed me from the piles of pillows in her elaborately carved double bed, her blue-rinsed hair kept in place by a lacy hair net. I was allowed to sit on the cushioned stool in front of the triple-sided mirrors at her cream, kidney-shaped dressing table and try on her jewellery. Huge pearl earrings, glittering diamond rings, strings of shiny pink and oyster-coloured beads were mostly paste but who cared? There were bowls full of long hatpins with sparkly rhinestones on the ends, and translucent alabaster dishes for lipsticks, and a massive pale-pink swansdown powder puff in its own special circular cardboard box. It was a million miles from my mother's austere bedroom at home with its gloomy mahogany furniture. Everything was soft in Rose's boudoir and most of it was like her, delicately coloured and gracious. She lay back against the heaped pillows and talked me through her wardrobe as if I were a grown-up. To a little girl in those drab post-war years it was heaven.

Despite the surface fluffiness, Rose was a formidable businesswoman with a tough commercial brain and firm ideas about what was proper, somewhat ironic given what I later discovered about her own love life. After their deaths, I went with my cousin Zelda, Cissie's daughter, to clear out the apartment in Hove, where Rose and Maude lived post-retirement. Rose's boudoir was just as it had ever been. Decked out in all its pink and cream décor, with its acres of wardrobes and adorned with swags, ribbons and bows, the room had merely relocated itself a couple of hundred miles down the motorway. As Zelda and I went through the tailored jackets, crepe-de-chine blouses and more intimate garments to sort them into bags for the charity shop or the tip, there, buried among the silky nightdresses was a champagne cork and the dried-out remnants of a long-stemmed red rose, tied together with a faded satin ribbon. We could only guess at the night of passion they commemorated. Given what I now know, perhaps I shouldn't have been surprised by the fact that Rose was one of the first paid-up members of Hugh Hefner's Playboy Club, when it opened on London's Park Lane at the height of the Swinging Sixties. Even though everyone swore that she only went there for the restaurant's fine dining, I had visions of my dignified aunt, then in her seventies, sharing racy jokes or rolling dice over bottles of bubbly with Michael Caine and Sean Connery.

After my great-grandmother Fanny's death in 1933, and in truth even before, Rose ruled the roost for the Woolman family, and my father was always slightly in awe of her. She was afraid of nothing, apart from a preternatural terror of birds, so powerful that she refused to stay anywhere if there were stuffed game birds in glass cases, pictures on the walls featuring birds, and couldn't even bear to sit in a chair if the upholstery featured feathered embroidery. Much to the family's admiration, after the war Rose had bought a car and learned to drive it, and when I knew her, she careered around Sheffield in a smart little Morris Minor. She seemed to be able to get anywhere she needed despite the fact that she had never mastered the technique of putting the car into reverse. Apparently during her driving test she had flatly refused to do a three-point turn, and so potent was the force of her personality that she somehow induced the examiner to reverse the car for her, and still award her a pass. Everyone was far more impressed by this evidence of her authority than by her driving licence. Subsequently on one occasion, she drove the wrong way down a one-way street and was stopped by a vigilant police constable who happened to be on his beat at the time. She rolled the Morris towards him and described her predicament – she couldn't go forward because of the one-way system and couldn't go back because she didn't know how. In the end the officer agreed to walk alongside her and talk her through the process as she slowly backed the car down the admittedly narrow lane. Having negotiated this arrangement through the car window, she then wondered why he stayed rooted to the spot. "Madam," he patiently explained, "Your car is on my foot."

Rose and Maude took a special interest in me and my brother. As neither of them ever married, we, and Zelda, were the closest they had to grandchildren. In the school holidays and at half-term, they would take me out into town for "a treat". Either Julian was considered too young to accompany me – I was expected to manage the bus unaided – or he refused, very sensibly, as these were strictly feminine occasions. Mostly the treats took the form of elevenses at one of the ritzy cafes in Sheffield city centre. Although my mother dressed me with special care for these events, I never quite measured up to expectations.

Rose and Maude would look me over critically, inspecting my hem, my buttons, my cuffs, and ask challenging questions, such as, "Judy, where are your gloves? A lady is never seen without gloves." I would have been about eight at the time. They were immaculately turned out of course, with perfectly fitting leather gloves, handbags that matched their high-heeled shoes, and hats perched on their perfect coiffures. Davy's teashop, their favourite rendezvous, was a lovely place, smelling strongly of freshly ground coffee and serving delicious, hot, toasted teacakes dripping with melted butter. Sometimes for a change we went to Walsh's, the classiest department store in Sheffield, later to become a branch of House of Fraser, where there was a restaurant on the top floor, or to Marshall and Snelgrove, which specialised in exclusive couture. As we daintily sipped our drinks, cocoa or Tizer for me, we watched the mannequin parades, where young women would sashay around the tables showing off the latest fashions on sale, holding up cards in front of their chests with price tags – for the clothes, not the models – prominently displayed.

Maude and Rose were warm and affectionate. They hugged and kissed and always wanted a cuddle, which I found rather a bore. Their favourite term of greeting, used for babies and small children was "chuckely sponge cake", as in "Come and give me a kiss, chuckely sponge cake", accompanied by a pinch on the cheek. Pinching on the cheek was a speciality of my great-aunts. Occasionally, the endearment was amended to "chuckely *bubbele*" but the pinching part never changed. They felt sad that our visits to them were rationed, and it was only later that I became aware of the tension that existed between them and my mother, who cared nothing for what happened to be in vogue that month, and who begrudged their proprietorial attitude to my father, who for them was always the forlorn little boy they had rescued from a fate worse than death – i.e. Barrow-in-Furness. They were always trying to turn me into a lady and improve my own sartorial sense but as this was entirely in the hands of my mother, it did little good, as spending money on fancy clothes for children was frivolous in the extreme as far as she was concerned.

When I was twelve, to my great joy I was asked to be a bridesmaid at Zelda's wedding, which was to take place in London at the end of the year. I was ecstatic at the thought of the frilly bridesmaid's dress and staying overnight in a swish hotel, but my parents would not consider it. Despite pleading from Rose, Maude, the bride and the bride's mother, they were adamant. It would involve too much "fuss" – "fuss" was a taboo concept in our household – and would give me ideas above my station. Little did they realise that the ideas were already deeply embedded. Rose and Maude were experts in the psychology of little girls.

In old age Rose's hair turned silver, though her regular weekly visits to Marjorie Dalton's hair salon usually modified it to a tasteful blue or even pink. Maude's dark hair on the other hand gradually mutated into a startling shade of orange. Although like Rose, she was determined to be elegant, she somehow just missed her goal, most likely because her schoolteacher's salary never amounted to much more than a pittance. We talk today about the iniquity of the gender pay gap but then, women schoolteachers were paid a scandalous forty per cent less than their male counterparts. Maude also of course did not have the same access as Rose to high fashion at wholesale prices. The aunts were eternally youthful, their faces virtually unlined in the pre-Botox era even as they approached their eighties. They were invariably heavily made up in the cosmetic style of the 1920s, the period when they were in their prime, with powdered complexions, bright red, lipsticked mouths and the pencilled-in arched eyebrows that had been all the rage thirty years earlier.

As far as anyone knows, Maude had never had a male admirer. She admitted that once, when Zelda was a baby, she had taken her out for a walk and fell into conversation with a rather dapper young man on a bench in the park. Unfortunately, just as they were getting on really well and she had hopes of being asked out on a date, the baby woke up, and she had to disclose ownership. Before she had time to explain the baby wasn't actually hers, he had fled. Both she and Rose remained fascinated by stories of romantic intrigues and marital problems, and became confidantes for most of the Jewish community, many of whom were Rose's customers and found the intimacy of the changing room a perfect place for whispered secrets.

Maude was a natural with children and taught second grade at Hunters Bar Elementary School for over forty years, where generations of children learned to read and write under her care. The school had a mixed intake of children from a range of backgrounds, not all of whom were grateful for the benefits of modern education. She loved telling the story of a boy in her class who brought in a sick note from his mother after several days' absence. "What's been the matter with you?" enquired Maude. "I don't know Miss," replied the child, "I haven't read the letter." This note predictably did not form part of the bundle of letters that Zelda and I discovered in a cardboard box at the Hove flat. Grateful pupils and their parents all recalled her seemingly endless patience and her considerateness, as she went out of her way to help struggling scholars, often staying behind after school to go through their spellings with them.

She herself was a great letter writer in the days before email and texting began to dominate communication. I can now see that her epistles were brilliantly insightful precursors of text-speak and way ahead of their time, peppered as they were with abbreviations, so that they resembled an obscure cryptogram that had to be deciphered before the full meaning revealed itself. They frequently collapsed words to save space – just as in txt spk – and always used initials instead of names, for instance, for relatives, friends or for places they had visited. Thus ZA would be Zelda Arden, M&S would not be Marks and Spencer's (this was always referred to as Marks) but Marshall and Snelgrove, and B&H stood for Brighton and Hove. In addition, at least every other sentence would include the acronyms TG, PG or ABW. These corresponded to the phrases that coloured Maude and Rose's lively conversation, and respectively stood for "Thank God", "Please God" or "All Being Well". Occasionally their use was strangely inapt as in a memorable line from one of Maude's letters after her retirement to B&H, which expressed the hope that "when I die PG, I'll be buried in Sheffield ABW". Given this penchant for coded messages, it's no surprise that Maude was adept at the *Daily Telegraph* crossword, which she completed every day, and helpfully passed on to me her hints on crossword technique, such as to "always look for the embedded word" – the word hidden between two others – as the easiest starting point.

I adored going to their house, and my biggest treat was being allowed to stay there overnight, where I had my own very clean and tidy room, and in the morning made my bed as my mother had instructed me, only to get told off by Maude for doing it before it had been given a chance to air. Rose died of heart failure in 1968, having suffered from angina for the last decade of her life. Maude, more robust, stayed wonderfully energetic throughout her retirement years. She was killed at the age of eighty-two by a speeding motorist, who raced through a STOP sign, crashed into an approaching vehicle, spun round at a ninety-degree angle, and landed on the pavement, ramming into Maude who was standing on the corner, waiting for a lull in the traffic. Hit just before 4.30 in the afternoon, she was fatally injured and died in hospital just over an hour later. There was an oddly tragic irony about her mode of death, as at the time of the collision she was on her way to her part-time volunteer job, shepherding old people safely across busy roads. The coroner recorded a verdict of accidental death, a judgement I still can't quite come to terms with.

From time to time our Sunday excursions would feature my father's uncle, Joe. Mild-mannered, twinkly and amiable, Joe was by this time retired from his job as head of research at Firth Brown. He devoted most of his time to his twin passions of billiards and bridge, and seeing him relaxing in his cardigan and slippers, I never fully appreciated how distinguished he had been in his professional life. In any case he was always somewhat overpowered by the controlling presence of his sharp-tongued wife, Fanny, for whom no one in the family seemed to have a good word. The couple had become engaged in 1926 when Joe was a modest young scientist, set for a high-flying career. He was ultimately to become a Fellow of the Royal Institute of Chemists and could put the initials F.R.I.C. after his name – I'm surprised Maude didn't pick up on it for her letters. His fiancée was Fanny Millet, a young woman from an affluent Southampton family, who owned outfitters' shops in the South of England, which in the 1940s and 1950s were to become a well-known national chain, Millets Stores. Fanny, who always insisted that her name was really Fanette, an illusion in no way verified by her birth certificate, was tall and elegant, her hair cut into a modish Eton crop. In a studio portrait taken before she was married, her aquiline profile and swan-like neck are shown to advantage, set off by the dark grey turtle-neck sweater she is wearing and her fitted velvet jacket. Very Noel Coward and very unisex. She looks stunningly modern, a creature from a more urbane society in comparison to my great-aunts, who despite their efforts, at this stage in their lives come over as deeply provincial.

Fanny made only one catastrophic, pre-nuptial visit to Sheffield, when she came to be introduced to her prospective in-laws. Joe had invited her to stay for a weekend at 14 Broomhall Street, a very different abode from Botleigh Grange, the porticoed mansion her family occupied in Hampshire, which is now a country-house hotel. Naturally his mother and sisters were eager to make a good impression, and Maude spent her savings on decorating the front parlour, ready to welcome the future bride. She claimed that this was the first all-white parlour in Sheffield and the height of interior decor chic but Fanny was immune to its charms. The weekend was an out and out disaster. Fanny made no secret of the fact that she was vastly superior to the Woolmans, who were several rungs lower on the social ladder. It would become her mission to rescue Joe from his primitive background. As the family sat down to Friday night dinner, always a significant meal at Broomhall Street, when everyone gathered together, Fanny looked around her with the haughty expression of a well-bred racehorse. Maude, who was invariably in charge of these occasions, had magicked up a spotless white cloth to adorn the table, which was laid for once with matching plates and cutlery. As they sat down to eat, Fanny ostentatiously picked up her knife and fork and scrupulously examined them for possible stains. She then proceeded to wipe them on her table napkin to remove imagined specks of grease. Rose, infuriated by the implied insult, and by this time utterly exasperated with Fanette's airs and graces, which included her high-falutin' name, went upstairs after supper, extracted Fanny's delicate lawn nightdress from under the pillow where she had stowed it, brought it downstairs and stuffed it up the kitchen chimney. Fanny, oblivious to the fury she had provoked, was meanwhile enjoying a quiet, romantic walk around Sheffield's scenic high spots in the company of her intended. Relations between the sisters-in-law never really improved much after that.

That summer, Joe and Fanny had a sumptuous wedding in Southampton on a glorious June afternoon in one of the oldest synagogues in England. Wearing a wedding gown made out of faille, a heavy corded silk fashionable at the time, Fanny for once belied her surface composure and found herself trembling like a leaf under the wedding canopy, beset by sudden doubts. Thoughts of cancelling the whole thing went through her mind. "What am I doing? I am marrying a stranger," she confessed to me many years later, unnerved by the finality of the prospect before her, though probably not unlike other virgin brides of the time. But it was too late to turn back. She was also more than somewhat miffed by the fact that the groom's elder brother, Wilfred, by now a lieutenant in the Royal Navy, had arrived at the ceremony, splendid in full naval dress uniform with a cocked hat and a sword, outdoing the bride in his finery and getting all the attention, a point that Fanny forever held against him. The lavish wedding reception was held in the large, rose-scented garden of Botleigh Grange, where the guests were treated to home-grown strawberries, gallons of cream, and champagne brought up from the cellars. The champagne was placed in ice-buckets on the grand piano in the magnificent drawing room, where a tail-coated butler stood waiting to pour it into crystal champagne coupes. Because of the blazing weather, the guests congregated on the lawns, under the shade of the trees and hardly ventured into the house at all. As the butler seemed to think it below his dignity to move from his allocated position, the only people who drank the champagne, according to Fanny, were the chauffeurs, who were lounging around outside the windows alongside the cars, waiting for their owners. It was quite a come-down for Fanny to relocate to the grim steel city, and I don't think she ever quite got over it.

Joe and Fanny had one son, John, who was more punctilious than even Maude and Rose could have wished. He compiled a scrapbook of cuttings of mistakes he had spotted in the daily papers and kept an egg-timer on the wash-stand shelf to regulate the prescribed 180 seconds he needed to brush his teeth. If he didn't perform this within five minutes of eating, he felt defiled. As a result, he rarely ate anywhere except in his own home, where he knew he had immediate access to a toothbrush. He was a clean, handsome but withdrawn boy, who by the time he was in his forties, had developed delusions that he was a victim of persecution, an unwelcome effect of his OCD syndrome. He grew to resent his parents and everything they stood for, including their Jewish background. His antipathy intensified to such an extent that in the 1970s he left England to make his permanent home in Nuremberg, Germany. The symbolic significance of the location of Hitler's notorious rallies could not have been more pointed.

Our final Sunday port of call, though much less frequent, was to the youngest of my father's aunts, Cissie. There had been no love lost between them ever since his sudden arrival in Broomhall Street in the winter of 1915, when he appeared like a fledgling cuckoo to take over her place as the baby in the Woolman nest. It was also a bone of contention for my father that the savings from his university scholarship money, £50 of which had been put aside each year for his future, were commandeered to foot the bill for Cissie's marriage to Myer Auerbach in September 1932. In the late 1940s when I first remember visiting them, Cissie and her husband were living in a flat above their shop in Walkley, an unprepossessing area of Sheffield. When they were trying to establish themselves financially, Mick, a warm, genial man, had found that customers were suspicious of conducting business with the foreign sounding Myer Auerbach, and the attempt to establish a growing concern frequently verged on bankruptcy. In a stroke of genius, he changed his name, and overnight metamorphosed into Colonel Michael Arden. No one ever enquired into the legitimacy of his title, and customers flocked in. Forever after, his clients and colleagues referred to him as "The Colonel". He and Cissie had originally met during her extended visits to her sister Julia in Barrow-in-Furness, where the Auerbachs had settled. Having been forced to leave school at fourteen, in spite of the fact that she regularly came top of her class, Cissie spent most of her teenage years in Barrow as an extra pair of hands, coping with Julia's unruly family, or working as a salesgirl for Browns the Busy Bee, still at that time operating out of Crellin Street. The marriage had its ups and downs that were more protracted than most, and my father was regularly assigned to go and retrieve the errant Mick, who had left home yet again, and who, more often than not, was to be found hiding out in Scarborough, Liverpool or Blackpool.

The main attraction for me on these Sunday excursions was the thought of Cissies's mouth-watering, home-made ice cream (she later told me it was just frozen custard) and the hope that I might see Zelda, who was eleven years older than me, and whom I hero-worshipped. The ice cream didn't really compensate for the fact that Zelda was hardly ever there. She had been packed off to boarding school in Wales so that Cissie could devote herself to building up the business with Mick, and the nearest I got to her was her teddy bear, who lay on her pillow looking lonely, waiting for her to come home. I used to hug him for comfort – it worked both ways. Around 1953 the Ardens moved to a much more splendid house in Ecclesall before being the first of the Woolmans to up sticks to B&H when they retired to an elegant, bow-windowed apartment in one of Hove's gorgeous Regency terraces.

Zelda was a lovely girl, a mixture of fun and practical common sense, who lived life at a pitch of high drama, where everything was either a catastrophe or a triumph, both usually accompanied by gales of laughter. She subsequently worked as a secretary on Fleet Street for Hulton Press, part of the IPC group, which produced the comics that my brother and I used to have delivered weekly. Julian's publication of choice was the *Eagle*, an action-packed adventure comic, which featured the science fiction hero, Dan Dare, Pilot of the Future, on its front page throughout the 1950s. Dan Dare's enemy was the lurid green Mekon, whose distinctive evil energy made him secretly my preferred character. My own comic was *Girl*, the much tamer sister companion to *Eagle* but which I eagerly looked forward to as it plopped through the letterbox every Tuesday. The stories in both were all in comic strip form, and I was an avid follower of the adventures of "Lettice Leefe, the Greenest Girl in the School", and "Belle of the Ballet", which I humiliatingly and mistakenly pronounced as "Belly" to the outrage of the aunts, who didn't hesitate to put me right. "Belly" was a rude word in those unworldly days. When Zelda showed us round her office on one of our rare trips to London, it seemed tremendously exciting and definitely one up on my school-friends that I had seen the actual drawing boards, which disclosed what was going to happen in the serial three weeks ahead. I was sworn to secrecy, and despite temptation, never once let the cat out of the bag.

Twelve

The Gatekeeper: Auschwitz 1944

*"You have given the world a personal connection to history...
far into the future, people will always remember."*

STEVEN SPIELBERG LETTER TO HARRY LOWIT

I can't remember a time when I didn't know about the Holocaust. My parents' house always seemed to be filled with people with foreign accents who had escaped the horrors of the Nazi regime, many of whom owed their lives to my father. I met young students, scientists and teachers, who had been children when they said goodbye to their parents on the platform of a distant German railway station, never thinking that the urgent, clinging embrace would be the last time they would ever feel their mother's touch. I met elegant women with immaculate coiffures, who made melt-in-the-mouth *sachertorte*, and whose sitting rooms featured tapestried chairs and grand pianos. I met men with beards and sad eyes and guttural voices who had emerged from the hell of the concentration camps. Rarely during my childhood years did any of these people indicate that they had lived previous lives, nor did they betray by any slight unguarded gesture a shred of bitterness about the terrors they had endured.

Individually, they all had unique stories to tell, even if I was only dimly aware of the details. The one who made the most striking impression on me was Rev. Abraham Brysh, minister to the Sheffield congregation and a close friend of my parents. Gentle, calm and overwhelmingly tolerant of human failings, he appeared to bear no enmity to a single soul. One day, alone with my father in a moment of rare intimacy, he spoke impassively and fleetingly about his history. Born in Poland in 1920, he was sent as part of a transport to Auschwitz, where the rest of his family were murdered. Aged twenty, he was put in a work unit of young men and teenage boys who were marched each day to a quarry, where they were required to dig stone and smash rocks with only the most primitive of tools. It was back-breaking work. In the depths of winter, their hands torn and feet numb and frostbitten, they managed to find some slight protection against the sub-zero temperatures by stuffing their shoes with felt, a makeshift lining, filched from the nearby railway depot. When their ruse was discovered, two of the group were singled out to be hanged as an example to the rest. Abraham Brysh was one of the two.

As the young man was led to the gallows in front of his comrades, the overseer who had supervised the work detail stepped forward to petition the SS officer in charge to lighten the sentence. This Jew, he declared, pointing to Brysh, still strong and able-bodied, happened to be a particularly industrious labourer, who could continue to be of use to the Reich. The sentence was commuted to twenty lashes and a beating with an iron bar. Afterwards, lying on the ground, bleeding and barely conscious, Abraham somehow managed to crawl towards the guard who had inflicted the punishment. Stumbling to his knees, he thanked the man for not killing him. A few years after the war, his home community in Poland published a memorial volume in tribute to all those from the village who had perished in the Holocaust. It was in this book, scanning the list of his relatives and neighbours, with their accompanying photographs, seeking for evidence of what had happened to his school-friends, that Abraham discovered his own name.

My childhood was peopled with heroes such as Abraham Brysh, men and women who had been victims of unutterable physical and psychological torment: displaced from their homes, wrenched from their loved ones, starved and beaten, and witnesses to death on a daily basis. Their backstories were woven imperceptibly into the fabric of my upbringing. Yet their earliest years were not dissimilar to my own. Cocooned in innocence, they had sat at school desks, greeted their fathers after work, went to the park for ice creams, obediently did their music practice and were taken on trips to the seaside. I devoured the diary of Anne Frank, who grew up like me in a settled middle-class home. As she trotted off to school each day, she had no premonition that she would spend her teenage years in hiding, concealed behind a bookcase in an office, where days and nights were turned topsy-turvy and she emerged from whispered silence only when the building was empty. She dreamed of a brilliant future, yet her life ended before her sixteenth birthday. In February 1945, bald, emaciated, covered with scabies and racked with typhus, this once lively, imaginative girl died in Bergen-Belsen together with her beloved sister, Margot, and a few short weeks before my own birth. I knew that it was only by a trick of timing and a mere decade that I was spared her fate.

Like all Jews of my generation, my sense of identity was shaped in the shadow of the Holocaust but it was only when I was twelve that its presence made its dramatic entrance into my own family. In 1957, after a whirlwind three-week romance, my cousin Zelda became engaged, triggering unalloyed outpourings of delight from the great-aunts. Her fiancé, Harry, a young engineer, was charming and debonair with a grin that lit up the room. We all fell in love with him. Then we learned about his background. Among the many accounts of supreme courage and audacity that have come to light from the war years, Harry's story remains one of the most powerful. It now forms part of the Shoah archive of the Steven Spielberg Foundation, and can be accessed in museums around the world, including the Imperial

War Museum and the Holocaust Memorial Museum in Washington. Rescued from Dr Josef Mengele's murderous selection process by the daring of another young boy, Harry survived six concentration camps to emerge in 1945 as a fifteen-year-old savage, brutalised by camp culture and, as he later acknowledged, "with no understanding of right or wrong". Stealing, violence and callousness had been the tools of his existence in a world where atrocity was routine. Each morning as he stepped out of his hut at Auschwitz-Birkenau, he kicked aside the bodies of those who had died during the night in order to clear his path. Zelda, with her blend of warmth and inner strength, became his redeemer, rebuilding his confidence, taking the place of the mother he had seen snatched from him, and restoring him to a full sense of self and family. He became a cherished figure in all our lives, the scars of his childhood securely camouflaged. Until he was asked to record his experiences for the Shoah archive, he had never spoken about the details of his past.

Born in Prague into a wealthy orthodox Jewish household, Harry had a cosseted childhood, surrounded by comfort and attention. His father, Karel Lowit, owned a waterproofing factory, and the family lived in luxury in a modern villa on the outskirts of the city. As a toddler, Harry's sunny personality was so appealing that he became a child model, his photo featured on advertisements for tinned foods. He was nine when the Nazis invaded Prague. When the laws forbidding Jews to own property came into force, the family were forced to sell the factory for a nominal sum, give away their home and move, first to a rented apartment and then to his grandmother's country house, where they had spent carefree summers and where, like many other misguided Jews, they hoped that the combination of rural seclusion and their deep coffers would protect them from SS scrutiny. How trusting they were. Karel's brother, Rudi, had recognised the warning signs and fled to England but Karel misjudged the gravity of the situation and determined to stay put. In December 1939 he was duly arrested and sent to the Gestapo headquarters at the Petschek Palace, where in the basement torture chambers he was interrogated as a suspected resistance fighter. Harry and his mother heard nothing from him until they were called to attend his funeral. He had been executed for "unspecified crimes".

In June 1942 mother and son were sent to the Terezin ghetto, sixty kilometres northwest of Prague, and effectively a transit station for deportations to the extermination camps in the East. Largely self-governed by Jewish leaders, Terezin later acquired notoriety as a showcase, used by the Nazi propaganda machine to deceive a Red Cross inspection team as to the supposedly humane treatment of its inmates. The reality was very different. Harry and his mother were directed to a cell bare of furniture, which for the next year and a half they shared with fifteen others. Bewildered and terrified, the eleven-year-old slept on the floor curled against his mother for comfort in a world from which normality had been stripped. In September 1943 they were on one of two transports sent from Terezin to the family camp at Birkenau, a three-day journey by cattle truck without food or drink and packed together so tightly that even the slightest movement was impossible.

I listened to Harry's testimony in the reading room of the Imperial War Museum. Recorded over several days, his voice remains calm and dispassionate as he takes his listeners through his journey from civilisation to barbarism. His voice breaks only once, at the point where he describes how on 8th March 1944 when the family camp was liquidated, he watched his mother taken away to the gas chambers. He pauses, choking back tears, and cannot continue. Beneath Harry's unfailing good humour and impeccable control were wounds too deep for healing. At the age of thirteen, Harry, prisoner number 170519, was on his own.

He was moved to Auschwitz D, Dresdner Barracks, where his good looks and mop of curly hair (prisoners in the family camp had not had their heads shaved on admission) caught the eye of the SS guard Irma Grese, whose sadistic excesses later earned her the nickname the "Beautiful Beast" when they were reported at the war crimes trials. Under her protection, Harry became a *"Laufer"*, a messenger boy, who moved unimpeded through the vast acreage of the camp. As his duties included visiting the kitchens, he was able to scrounge the scraps that saved him from starvation, and which he could secrete to share with others in his hut. Irma later passed him on to her lover, Josef Kramer, commandant of Auschwitz and subsequently Belsen. Harry was exposed to scenes that no child (or adult) should ever have to witness. His errands took him into the gas chambers where he was besieged by the shrieks of the dying and the sights of the mounds of bodies who a few moments earlier had clawed helplessly for life, now waiting to be slung into crematoria. In the summer, equipped with a blue uniform and boots, he was put to work on the main gate at Auschwitz with its heinous motto *"Arbeit Macht Frei"*, where he lifted the bar to admit the incoming transports of traumatised Jews to stumble through to their deaths.

Yet he was not exempt from the random selection processes, the threat that hung over all camp inmates. In July 1944, he was part of a line-up of naked prisoners filing in front of Dr Josef Mengele for inspection. Those sent to the left were assigned fit for work and a temporary reprieve while those sent to the right were condemned to death. Harry stood in line next to his friend, Hellmuth Szprycer from Berlin, who had adopted him as a surrogate brother after they had arrived in Birkenau almost two years before. The boys had been inseparable ever since. Both were directed to the right. With the chutzpah of someone who has nothing to lose, fourteen-year-old Hellmuth broke ranks and approached Josef Mengele. Unafraid, he looked him straight in the eyes, clicked his heels in a parody of an SS officer and pleaded in German for his life. "I want to work for you. I will do anything – clean your shoes, your motorcycle. Don't put me in the gas chamber." On hearing that Hellmuth was *ein Berliner*, Mengele relented. But as Hellmuth turned back to join the queue for the living, Harry called out to him to save him too. It was a strategy fraught with peril. Surrounded by a posse of guards with whips and loaded guns, Hellmuth could have thrown away both his own and Harry's chances in that place where Jews' lives were worth less than those of the dogs trained to tear them apart. In an act of unbelievable bravado, he approached Mengele once more and implored him to spare his friend. This time, Mengele held out two matches. "The one who takes the longest match will live," he declared. "The short match will go to the gas chamber." When Harry picked the short match, he cried again to Hellmuth, "I don't want to die." A third time, the lad approached the Angel of Death. "What is one more life to spare?" he asked. Miraculously Harry was saved.

Over fifty years later, when Harry was recording his testimony for the Shoah Foundation, one of the researchers thought that this tale sounded familiar. Checking back, she discovered that a previous witness, a retired antiques dealer from Ghent, had provided a remarkably similar statement. It was Hellmuth Szprycer. On a murky February evening in 1997, the two were reunited. "My dear boy," said Hellmuth as they embraced in the lobby of the Hilton hotel on London's Park Lane. "This is history."

But in 1944 survival was by no means a foregone conclusion. During the evacuation of Auschwitz in January 1945, nine days before the arrival of the Soviet Red Army, Harry was forced onto the infamous death march, walking thirty-five miles through snow without food or shelter before being loaded onto an unheated freight train in sub-zero temperatures. His destination was Mauthausen in upper Austria. In March he was transferred to the sub-camp of Melk and finally in April, Ebensee, near Salzburg. Ebensee was designed to provide slave labour for the Nazi regime, including the construction of a maze of underground tunnels to be used as armaments stores. Although not primarily an extermination camp, the death rate at Ebensee was abnormally high due to the exceptionally harsh conditions and the casual brutality of its staff and ruthless commandant. Almost half the prisoners died of exposure, malnutrition and disease, and desperate men, pushed to the limits, resorted to cannibalism. Shortly after their arrival, Harry and a fellow prisoner, Leo, from Belgium, were put to work hauling coal from town in a truck when they overheard SS soldiers discussing the imminent end to the war and the coming of

US forces. The Nazi plan was to obliterate all evidence of the camp's cruelty by marshalling the prisoners into the tunnels, which were mined and were then to be blown up. While the guards were enjoying a beer break, Harry and Leo brazenly made their escape, driving the truck away into the mountains virtually under the eyes of their captors. For three weeks, they laid low, hiding in forests, in farms and outbuildings, waiting for the Americans to appear.

The fearless breakout from Ebensee was the start of Harry's re-introduction to a world that itself was just beginning to come to terms with the aftermath of war. Haunted by memories of his lost family, and unable to bear the thought of going back to Prague, Harry made his way with Leo to Belgium, partly on foot, across treacherous terrain, mountain passes, bombed bridges and a devastated landscape, finding shelter where they could. Leo's family gave him temporary refuge but he remained essentially a drifter, homeless, uneducated and without sanctuary. After months of this hand to mouth existence, he was advised to contact the Czech embassy in Brussels. Once again he was to encounter an extraordinary stroke of fortune that would be his salvation. As he gave his particulars to the officials, his surname struck a chord with one of the embassy staff, who recalled having met a Rudolf Lowit at a party in London some months earlier. On the off chance that there might be a connection, she located Rudi's contact details to ask if he might have a fifteen-year-old nephew. This is how Harry, the sole survivor, came to England to be reunited with the uncle who had the foresight to leave Prague while he still had the chance.

Eventually Harry did summon up the courage to revisit Czechoslovakia. At his grandparents' former home, he discovered a cache of family photographs that had been hidden in the rafters and kept safe by neighbours throughout the war. He also recovered a large oil painting, a portrait of himself at the age of two, nestled in his mother's arms. This picture hung in Zelda and Harry's home all their married life and is now prominently displayed on their daughter Julie's sitting room wall. It is the constant reminder of Harry's old life of untroubled innocence and remains a silent witness to everything that he lost. He went on to become a successful businessman, hugely proud of his own beautiful home and family. It was easy to forgive him his inordinate and almost childlike pleasure in possessions. The Rolex watch and top of the range Jaguar remained symbols of how triumphantly he had rebuilt his cover. Only occasionally would tiny details betray him, as Zelda watched over him and continued to cut up his food at mealtimes just as his mother had done when he was a small boy.

Thirteen

Rootless: Sheffield 1960s

"As they say, history does not repeat itself, but it rhymes."
MARGARET ATWOOD, *THE TESTAMENTS*

It would be amazing if, in a family as large as mine and with such a tangled history, there were not more than a few casualties. The Woolman/Brown family certainly had its quota of damaged individuals, for the most part kept under the radar until they could no longer be ignored. My father himself was remarkable for the way in which he overcame the ordeals of his childhood and established himself as a mover and shaker in his local community, a rock to whom others turned, and generous to a fault. But he was always gripped by the fear that what he thought of as the toxic legacy of the past would at some point catch up with him. "Causes of schizophrenia can be 80% environment and 20% genetic," he noted in his diary after a discussion with a psychiatrist friend, "possibly due to uncertainty of identity in very early age or stemming from a Mother who only pretended love. I thought this might well apply to my sister Sadie, adopted when her mother died. Or Ray with a stepmother at the age of two. Perhaps I was lucky to have brothers to normalise me."

The intimacy with his brothers, especially Alex, was pivotal to his wellbeing. Whenever he felt particularly low and in need of a soul mate, he would nip off to Barrow, sometimes at just an hour or so's notice, returning with his batteries recharged, and restored to his usual buoyant self. In Barrow, life was simple and uncomplicated. Windowsills flaunted plastic flowers, china puppies and souvenirs from Blackpool or Benidorm. There was no need for airs and graces. Everyone knew everyone else, and Alex couldn't walk down a street without being hailed by a friend or customer. Similarly, Alex, who never lived anywhere other than his hometown, would turn up on our doorstep, or ring without warning from a pub when he was already halfway across the Pennines. A fanatical bridge-player, he would regularly phone at midnight or even later after a match at Barrow bridge club, and without any preliminaries, his disembodied voice would emanate from the mouthpiece, "You hold ace, king five times spades, queen and three little hearts…" Even though my father would often be woken up just as he had managed to nod off, these shared problems over bidding strategy helped to take his mind off the family crises with which he was surrounded. He had more than his fair share.

My father's other brothers, demobbed after the war, were relaxed, lovable layabouts, never able to make much of themselves. Joe, a strong candidate for the award of worst conversationalist in the world, worked in a bookie's in Cornwall. I always knew it was him when I picked up the receiver and there was total silence at the other end of the line. There was no mistaking that distinctive heavy breathing for anything more sinister. He had distinguished himself in the RAF air bomber command during the war, and I learned more about him from going through the photograph album of his war years than from any exchange we ever had over the sixty years I knew him. The snapshots from India, Burma and Singapore show a vigorous young man in khaki, wearing a huge grin, and hardly able to believe his luck at having traded the grimy streets of Barrow for wall-to-wall sunshine. After being assigned to overseas service in Canada in 1943, he cadged a lift to New York one leave, and Central Park looks leafy and civilised, the oasis in the heart of the sky-scraper city. He wasn't demobbed until 1946, went to London to seek his fortune, which never materialised, and emerged with an alarming wife, fifteen years older than he was, who had been his landlady and had inveigled him into marriage. Joe eventually managed to extricate himself from this liaison, and fled to Cornwall, presumably the place he could think of that was furthest away from her.

My father's youngest brother, Harry, was another happy-go-lucky character with the easy charm of all the Brown boys plus a fatal penchant for women. Before the war he had been a car salesman at a Premier service station in Barrow, but once demobbed couldn't find any gainful employment. With typical liberality, Alex made him a partner in Browns the Busy Bee, which by the 1950s he had built into a flourishing concern. The partnership was designed as a helping hand to set Harry on his feet but Alex's kindness backfired. A few months after signing the papers, Harry's car skidded out of control on an icy surface one freezing December, straight into the path of a tanker on the A6 near Preston. He was killed almost instantly. His was the first death I remember. The previous year, he had married a young woman on casual acquaintance, Doris Maitland, whom the family never met. She emerged from the shadows, a grieving widow, to claim cash for half the value of the Busy Bee. Alex, hard-working and conscientious, was compelled to sell everything to meet her demands, and then had to start up again from scratch. The other consequence of the tragedy was that forever after, my father made us telephone him the minute we reached our destination on any winter journey, even if just driving from his house to ours, a couple of miles away.

But it was my father's sisters who were walking disaster zones. Two of them he barely knew until they exploded into his existence during the mid-1960s, with a shocking and disruptive impact. Unanchored, lost and directionless they had tottered through life, skirting catastrophe until the moment when their security blankets were pulled from beneath them. David's only full sibling, Ray, was a bewildered soul, constantly searching for someone or something to love. His half-sister, Sadie, a wounded and broken individual, also found little to sustain her. Neither married, and each suffered severe psychiatric breakdowns. Even Bessie, who had intermittently looked after him when he was a child, had deep-seated problems that were to materialise in her unfortunate offspring. These dark, gloomy pieces of my family history intruded from time to time during my uncomprehending childhood and teenage years. Only after reading my father's page-a-day diary, which he kept for from 1964 until his death twenty years later, did I start to understand how they held clues to the clouded years of the past.

My father's sister, Ray (not to be confused with my mother's sister, Rae), also lived in Southport. This unfortunate concurrence meant that the town, with its beautifully preserved Victorian arcades and promenades, for me never fulfilled its guarantee of seaside gaiety promised by the holiday posters. I have a vague recollection of being dragged down Lord Street and expected to admire a clock made out of flowers, but the town's undoubted charms took second place to the tension of family encounters, when one or other of my parents stood tight-lipped or sat uttering long-suffering sighs for an entire afternoon. Ray's little semi had been bought for her by Alex. It was 1954, and I was nine when my father took me and my brother to see her. The house had a cracked gate, from which most of the paint had peeled off, and what would have been a scrap of garden if it hadn't been so overgrown and littered with tin cans and paper.

As we walked down the path leading to the front door, I became conscious of a truly awful stench, which gradually got closer and stronger. I tried not to breathe. I got my hanky out of my pocket and held it over my nose. I looked at my father who didn't seem to register that anything was amiss. He rang the bell and we waited, Julian and I, on either side. Some summer holiday this was turning out to be. From behind the door I could hear a scary yowling noise as if a hundred starving cats were imprisoned there. The noise got louder as a crack appeared in the door to reveal a madwoman with wild grey hair. She peered out with staring eyes that seemed to look right past us. My father pushed me and my brother through the gap, following closely behind so that there was no possibility of escape. This madwoman was Ray. In a flash, I realised why my mother had stayed behind.

The sights, sounds and smells that filled that narrow hallway have remained with me only partially submerged over the years. It was a zoo behind that front door. It was a whirl of fur and litter and dead food. It was stale pee and old fish bones and saucers of rancid milk on every surface. There were piles of damp newspaper and cardboard boxes filled with rags and things that breathed. I had been wrong in my assessment. Perhaps not a hundred but at least thirty animals prowled across the floor and skulked in corners. Their tails stood high in the air or curled up behind them as they lay strewn across the carpet and on the stairs. The cats glared at us from over the bannister with their green and yellow eyes, and in what passed as a sitting room, they stretched themselves on the window sills, along the back of the settee, and lounged among the cushions in the armchair with its ripped upholstery. I hoped I wouldn't be expected to sit down. Even more, I hoped I wouldn't need the bathroom. Who knew what horrors might be lurking at the top of the stairs, assuming I managed to get past the monsters that guarded the steps? My old nursery rhyme book of the three little kittens, who lost their mittens, was illustrated with coloured pictures of dear, soft creatures, who lived in a basket and loved to be stroked, and who daintily lapped fresh milk from a china saucer with roses painted around its rim. They were a world away from these feral beasts, who roamed around the tangled forest of the house as if they were its rightful owners, and whose claws might scratch out our eyes at any moment. With a horrid fascination I recalled the Brothers Grimm's story of Rapunzel, where cats were perfectly capable of blinding girls, especially if they didn't behave themselves.

This was my first and last visit to Ray's house, which would now immediately be classified as a health hazard that would have brought the public health inspectors straight to her door instead of a young, timid nephew and niece. What on earth had happened to bring her to this pass? I can only speculate. Ray sits mumbling like a lost soul at the edge of the dynastic jigsaw with no obvious place in which to slot her, surfacing erratically and with an increasingly urgent sense of impending calamity. She is one of the sad, inscrutable figures who make my exercise in family history truly a puzzle. There are too many questions and not enough answers in her story, so that even my father, who detailed the progress of her final few years of decline at length in his diary, could only guess at how she ended up so damaged. He had been kept at a distance from her for too many years and found it impossible to unearth any scrap of natural affection between them. They had been separated in 1915 and from that moment on she had barely impinged on his consciousness, even during his visits to Barrow as a child. I can now see that like him, she was a victim of the displacements that dogged her early years. Unlike him, she never escaped or was able to build a life of her own. I ponder on the circumstances in which she grew up, an imaginative child searching for love. She had been two when her mother died, eight when she lost her father. "After that," wrote my father, "who could bother with her?" Within a few weeks of her father's death, her little brother had also gone, and she was left behind, an unwanted girl who could only make herself useful to her stepmother and the three younger boys in their infested two-roomed flat. All through her childhood she was on call, before and after school, to scrub the floors, clean the gas mantles, wash and mend, and run errands.

The group family portrait, taken just before my father was packed off to Sheffield, is one of the very few pictures in which she appears. She is the bashful child standing at the back, with her head tilted slightly to one side, wearing a smart pinafore, her long, straight hair held in place by an Alice band. There's an absence of almost thirty years before the next photos, taken at a cottage in Windermere during a rare hot spell in August 1942. In one, a sunburnt Ray, wearing sandals, sits awkwardly in a deckchair, her attention completely absorbed by the tabby cat on her lap, an unsettling foretaste of things to come. She holds the creature by its neck, turning it to face the camera – and say cheese? In another, she stands with her hands on the shoulders of two young girls, her nieces, Zelda and Nora, Cissie and Wilf's daughters respectively. This time, it is Zelda who is cuddling the cat, her beaming smile a marked contrast to Ray's glum features. And then there is a third photograph of her three laughing half-brothers, Alex, Joe and Harry, casual and happy in shirt sleeves with their arms around one another, a perfect vision of fraternal affection. Ray can be glimpsed in the background, framed in the doorway, wiping her hands on her apron. It's a telling snapshot of her place in their domestic arrangements.

In the intervening period between these images, she had by all accounts been an exemplary schoolgirl. During the First World War she had spent hours knitting socks and blankets, baking cakes and packing parcels for the forces from donations sent in by well-wishers, and on 19th July 1919, national Peace Day, she received a handsome certificate from the Mayor of Barrow. It formally thanked Miss Rachael Brown "for the many services so willingly rendered for our SAILORS and SOLDIERS during the GREAT WAR, 1914–1919". She was twelve. That summer, a few months after the Armistice, she left school. Her stepmother, Julia, even if she had wished, couldn't afford to keep Ray in full-time education when there was so much to be done at home and in the shop. Schooling wasn't for girls anyway, and Barrow generally didn't set much store by learning. When the shop was busy, she worked behind the counter, measuring ribbon and tape, finding wool and counting out buttons and packets of needles. Only in the evenings, when she'd washed the pots and scoured the pans, swept up the crumbs and darned the boys' socks, did she have time to herself. Then she would sit for hours by the fireside, gazing at copies of *Picturegoer* or *Girls' Cinema*, magazines aimed at the mass market of film fans, mingling news about forthcoming features with gossip about the private lives of stars. A dreamy, moody teenager, Ray had little else to occupy her imagination. Her demigods were the screen idols, John Barrymore, Leslie Howard, Errol Flynn and Clark Gable, sophisticated, glamorous and passionate, everything that her life was not.

Despite its status as the most working-class town in the UK, Barrow at the start of the twentieth century boasted three major theatres, all of which hosted live performances before eventually being converted into cinemas. Ray was crazy about both stage and screen, and wildly starstruck. She haunted the Tivoli and the Royalty theatres as well as the Palace movie house, a converted Salvation Army temple. These buildings were the construction blocks for her fantasy world, to which she would retreat to sit in the darkness and let the magic take over. I estimate that she was about seventeen when, perhaps predictably, she developed a crush on one of the artistes who regularly appeared at the Tivoli. Possibly he was a member of the Italian Signor Rino Pepi's company, which performed nightly in variety shows. Ray became fixated by this dashing figure, revealing even then the obsessive personality trait that was to have disastrous consequences. She wrote him adoring notes and hung around the stage door, hoping for a glimpse of her hero. When the tour moved on, without a word to anyone, she packed a few clothes and left home to follow him. The locations – Darlington, Middlesborough and Blackpool – could hardly have been less glittering, and there are no letters or family anecdotes that can reveal whether her love was reciprocated or even perhaps if she were seduced and abandoned, the fate of groupies everywhere. It hardly matters. After a few months, she returned to Barrow, desolate and unforthcoming as always.

"In all her lifetime, she had no one to love her," observed my father with a mixture of sadness and guilt. Together with Alex, he was to shoulder the burden of her care as her breakdown progressed in later years. The Southport house I remembered visiting as a child, inevitably became completely uninhabitable, its walls broken, its floor full of holes, and years of dirt and garbage piled up on every surface. Only the cats, well known as the most selfish of domestic pets, remained her contented companions, the children she never had. Ultimately, and not before time, they too had to be destroyed. Ray was distraught. Alex put the house on the market, and found her a modern flat in Ulverston, a few miles from Barrow, the town's sole claim to fame being that it was the birthplace of comedian Stan Laurel, whose statue dominates the main square outside the Coronation Hall. Ray, who had been kept conveniently apart from us all these years, went to pieces. "It's like having a split personality," she admitted one day with a rare glimmer of self-awareness. "One life with the cats, and one life with people." The problem was that with the cats gone, she had no idea how to interact with the people.

On New Year's Day 1967, Alex phoned. Ray had moved in with him while the new flat was being refitted but she was proving impossible. The following afternoon, out of the blue, he arrived on the doorstep with her in tow, haggard, dour and with only two teeth in her mouth, adding to her grisly appearance. For the next few weeks, she lived erratically, either in my parents' house or with Alex or occasionally in her own flat, where she spent days lying on the bed doing nothing, not even bothering to get undressed to go to sleep at night. She went out and forgot the key, so broke a window to climb back in – fortunately the flat was on the ground floor – and was scratched to ribbons, leaving awful scars on her arms and face. She could settle nowhere. Staying with my parents, she got on a bus to go shopping, and failed to return, found by the police after three days of wandering the Sheffield streets, safe but disoriented. Speechless and withdrawn during the day, at night she would emit a torrent of babbling words and pitiful gasps from her bedroom. My father knew she needed professional help. In early April he and Alex, after agonising deliberations, had her committed to Middlewood hospital, a huge Victorian edifice looming over north Sheffield that for a century had been notorious as the local "loony-bin". When I was at primary school, it had become intimidating shorthand – "Oo-er, you're a loony – ought to be in Middlewood, you ought".

After a few weeks on a strict drug regime, Ray grew calmer and less aggressive. Despite my father's misgivings that she would soon relapse, which proved to be all too accurate, she was discharged that summer. She returned to the Ulverston flat, although its antiseptic neatness dismayed her. My father advertised for seven volumes of vintage film magazines, which he hoped would revive memories of her younger, happier days. Alex bought her a kitten, a neutered tom just to be on the safe side, but she failed to house train it, and the smell soon became pervasive. She clung pathetically to the creature and refused to leave home without it. Out with my father for lunch in Southport, she insisted that the cat came too, stowed in a box on the back seat of the car. Ray gobbled her food, going outside after every few mouthfuls to check on its welfare. They called on my mother's sister, the other Rae, whose house almost rivalled Ray's previous home for untidiness, everything higgledy-piggledy, reported my father, unable to bear the sight of washing lying randomly around the room, and ancient, disused cartons under chairs. In the midst of all the mess, Ray suddenly blurted out, "Isn't it lovely here?"

Reading my father's diary for the next few years has been so painful that I can hardly bear to record it. The fantasy life that had sustained Ray for years ultimately became her reality, her inner "voices" took over, and she descended into darkness, losing her already tenuous grip on external existence, with only occasional flickers of understanding as to what was happening to her. I am still possessed by visions of her wandering, half-dressed, along the landing of my parents' house, a forlorn and ominous figure, whom it was impossible to reach. At night, she muttered incessantly, always in the third person. "Ray wasn't there, Ray was upstairs, Ray was upstairs. David's alright, David's good as gold, Ray was upstairs, under the covers – she wasn't there, David is like a father to me." And just once my father overheard the heart-breaking interpolation, "I'm sorry, David". In and out of hospital, first in psychiatric units and then geriatric wards, she was oblivious to the fact that the patients on either side of her, themselves highly disturbed, had to be moved out of earshot. She died in 1971 of chronic gastric ulcers. As she was dying, she called out to Alex, who was at her bedside, "Take me home".

When I was nine, I found Ray a frightening figure, and if I'm honest, was disconcerted by her dramatic reappearance in my father's house when I was in my twenties. My father's half-sister, Sadie, who surfaced in our lives at almost exactly the same time as Ray, was equally unsettling. Given the convoluted web of familial inter-relations, this is perhaps worth a recap. Sadie, the daughter of my grandfather Max's first marriage, was fostered as a baby by Ruben and Fanny Woolfe in Nottingham, and had never been part of the network of aunts and uncles which embraced me and my brother throughout our childhood. To all intents and purposes, she was the Woolfes' daughter, although she never took their name. I have a single picture of her, taken when she was about eleven at Gale's photographic studio in Nottingham, and sent to her real father in Barrow. It shows her looking wistful but composed and well cared for. One long ringlet is artfully arranged over each shoulder, she is wearing a bead necklace prominently positioned over her high collar, and, most impressively, is sporting a wrist watch, a real status symbol for a young girl at a time when wrist watches had just started to penetrate the market. Seated next to Sadie is a stolid lady of about forty, presumably Fanny Woolfe, dark hair parted down the centre, and wearing a patterned blouse and ankle-length, dark serge skirt. The portrait is my only clue to her having maintained any contact with my grandfather, who died at the end of 1915, shortly after the picture was taken. Sadie never went to Barrow and my father barely registered her existence. He never met her until they were both middle-aged.

In 1955, Fanny Woolfe, with whom Sadie had lived all her life, died, and it was at this point that Sadie resumed contact with her sister, Bessie. It was to become her most intense attachment. Then two events happened in close conjunction that completely overwhelmed her. Firstly, at the age of sixty, Bessie passed away, and shortly afterwards, Sadie retired from her clerical job in Nottingham. Rootless and without natural companionship for the first time, she saw her life disintegrating around her. She changed from being a self-reliant, sociable individual into a trembling, anxious little woman, who suffered what she labelled "nerve trouble". Unexpectedly, she turned for support to David, the half-brother, who though a stranger, nonetheless was family. As usual he rallied to the cause. At first she would turn up at Sheffield station to spend a few hours at my parents' home, having booked a cheap day-return rail ticket. As she became more reliant on my father's comforting presence, she would arrive with a suitcase and stay for days at a time, reciting her worries like a litany, and driving him to distraction. Her Nottingham neighbours, with whom she had co-existed perfectly amicably for the past thirty or more years, were now out to get her, she complained. They were anti-Semitic. Her proof? They turned lights on and off in the house next door for forty-five minutes at a time in order to annoy her with the noise of the switch. She agreed to seek medical help but when my father arranged a domiciliary visit, she asked to meet the doctor in a hotel. "My neighbour listens to every word," she fretted. "She is so clever – she is quick as a mouse if anyone comes." Even in her calmer moments, she was a tedious guest, having little in common with either of my parents, and without the shared familial history to draw on. Her frame of reference was narrow, limited to her own woes, and her talk was scattered with the sort of trite phrases that had gone out with nineteenth-century courtesy books. "I've had an elegant sufficiency, thanks," she would repeat without irony at each and every mealtime.

This state of affairs could not continue. Following a consultation with a specialist (not in a hotel), she spent a period in Mapperley hospital in Nottingham, where she received ECT, the electrical shock therapy that was not uncommon in the 1960s. Effective in about fifty per cent of patients with bi-polar or non bi-polar disorders, its use on catatonic patients was spectacularly and horrifyingly exposed in the 1975 film, *One Flew Over the Cuckoo's Nest*. In Sadie's case, the remedy only exacerbated her condition. She became increasingly timorous and confused. In 1968, on the anniversary of her sister Bessie's death, sitting alone in her front room in Skynner Street, in front of a lit gas fire, she committed suicide by swallowing anti-depressants, prescribed by her GP. At the inquest, it was reported that she had taken three times the lethal dose. The neighbour about whom she had grumbled so bitterly had been worried by her non-appearance, looked through the window, seen her lifeless form, and alerted the police. My father accompanied Bessie's son, Max, to identify the body, "thin, grinning, blotched and horrible – a nightmare" and then to the house that Sadie had shared with Fanny Woolfe for so many years, sickening in its filth. Not only had the interior remained almost completely unmodernised since before the First World War, but it was devoid of both food and cooking utensils. We all wondered how on earth Sadie had managed to survive for so long.

Although my grandfather, Max Brown, had sired eight children, Bessie was the only other one apart from David to marry and have a family of her own. Fat, jolly and uneducated, she could hardly have been more different from my father. She had married a market trader, Benny Roseby, and together they built a highly successful concern, selling curtaining materials from their stall in Sheffield's Castle Market. They eventually made enough money to facilitate their move into a grand house in one of the best areas of the city, but all their wealth could not help them with the greatest problem of all, their daughter. Bessie's children, Max and Doreen, named in memory of her parents, seemed to have inherited a cursed strain. Their son, Max, ground down by a combination of personal and professional problems, was to follow his Aunt Sadie's path, and in his fifties took his own life by swallowing a bottle of aspirin washed down with whisky. Their daughter, Doreen, born in 1936, was, in my father's words, a walking tragedy. She was saddled with a severe stammer, quite the worst I have ever encountered. People would cross the road to avoid meeting her, and as a callous and easily embarrassed child, I found being with her so discomfiting I did my best to get out of visits to Bessie's house if Doreen, then a teenager, was likely to be around.

Apparently she had been a normal, if fairly dim little girl, who went to school, made friends and gabbled away quite effortlessly. Suddenly, when she was twelve, everything changed. The room would go quiet as she struggled to speak. Her face went into a series of dreadful grimaces, her body contorted, and she sometimes managed to blurt out a few syllables, even words, before her tongue stuck and she had to give up in frustration, while kindly relatives tried to complete her sentences for her. It is now accepted that acquired stammering can occur in older children as the result of a head injury or neurological disease. More commonly, it is attributed to psychological or emotional trauma. Having established that there was no physical malfunction, Bessie spent a fortune dragging Doreen around the country to trauma specialists and alternative practitioners. But despite all the sessions on the psychiatrist's couch, the massage and the hypnosis, no one ever identified the source of her disorder, and certainly no effectual therapy was ever found. Aunt Rose pronounced authoritatively that Doreen's condition was a result of the shock she had received when she saw her pet dog run over by a car. Nobody was prepared to back her up on this, and family debate on the cause of her debility didn't seem to make much difference to Doreen. No one ever commented on the curious fact that the onset of her disorder coincided with puberty. Nowadays, in a climate more highly sensitised to safeguarding children, schoolteachers and social workers might investigate Doreen's family circumstances along with more intimate examination of her person but in the immediate post-war period, this was never a priority.

The extent of the handicap meant that it was impossible for Doreen to continue attending normal school. She spent most of her time mooching around at home, occasionally going out with other girls of her own age to the cinema or to dances at the Jewish youth club, where loyal friends tolerated her infirmity. It was at one of these club events in 1965 that she met Sydney, an unprepossessing but seemingly gentle young man, who proposed marriage. They bonded through the fact that Sydney also had a stammer, though nowhere near as disabling as Doreen's. The family were as staggered as they were relieved that anyone would be prepared to take their daughter off their hands. Here was their redeemer.

The euphoria was temporary. Sydney was an inveterate gambler, who stole Doreen's housekeeping money to bet on the dogs and the horses. His financial career was one of utter disorder to which he seemed oblivious, even when he was declared a serial bankrupt. Throughout the 1960s, after her parents' deaths, Doreen would arrive on my father's doorstep even more incoherent than usual because the bailiffs were at that moment stripping the house. Sidney was having an affair with a fancy woman (my great-aunts' phrase) who worked in his factory, manufacturing *schmatters*, the Yiddish for cheap, shoddy clothing. When he absconded with cash from the till and a girl who worked in his factory, my father, then in his sixties and in a farcical repeat of the Cissie and Mick scenario of the 1930s, was despatched by the aunts to bring him back to face the music.

All of this explains why, in contrast to the expected pattern, my family tree, especially on my father's side, resembles an inverted pyramid. My grandmother, Annie Woolman, was one of twelve children. My grandfather, Max Brown, with his three wives, produced eight. By rights, and in the normal course of events, there should be about a hundred cousins and second cousins in my own generation. Yet I can count them on my fingers. Rootless, unloved, abused and broken, my aunts never had a chance.

Fourteen

Beginnings

"Life can only be understood backwards.
But… it must be lived forwards."
SØREN KIERKEGAARD, *JOURNALS*

I began writing this as a personal memoir to give my grandchildren an insight into my childhood and the world of the 1950s in which I grew up, light years away from their own. Along the way, it turned into something quite other than the sketch I originally planned. As I started to reflect on my parents' lives and those of the preceding generation, I was swept away on the tide of the backstory that emerged from the crumpled bits of paper tucked away for years at the back of my mother's cupboards. The records of former lives in these carefully preserved documents drew me in, and I was beguiled as well as troubled by the discoveries that leapt out from the archives, not just in those boxes and the black and white photographs of relatives, some of whom I only vaguely recognised, but, as I searched further, in library catalogues, census records, museum repositories and online. Their presence, and the promises they hinted at, became increasingly seductive.

Other people's stories are always easier to write than one's own. My personal past is still too close for comfort, too complicated by strong emotions, jealousies, disappointments, and overcast by a brooding sense of failure that is a hangover from my school reports, which all insisted that I could do better if I only I made more effort. More importantly, I found that my own history paled into insignificance when measured against the dramatic scenarios of my grandparents' generation. As those official files blended with the private records, the diaries and the letters and the albums, to yield up their secrets, I realised more powerfully than ever before that I did not want the extraordinary stories they contained to be lost. They are stories that expose the hardships my predecessors faced, but which also prove their talent for making the most of opportunities, a talent in fact for life itself. This ordinary family accepted their privations stoically, were hardily self-reliant and took nothing for granted. They may not have been so different from others of that time, but to me, and hopefully to my children, they are exceptional.

My four grandchildren, Jamie, Madeleine, Max and Millie, live in centrally heated homes, where bathrooms are plentifully supplied with towels and where there's no limit on the use of hot water. No one hits these children if they question what they are told. If they are hungry, they go the fridge. If they are ill, which doesn't happen very often because they have all been inoculated against the whooping cough and measles that I suffered as a child, they can see a doctor without anyone worrying about the expense. They take these things for granted – and so they should. They own iPads, they Facetime their friends, they are taken to play-dates by car, they stream music and buy trainers at the touch of a mouse, and they are hardened flyers who have travelled the globe from New York to New Zealand. My one and only experience of air travel as a child was to Brittany in 1953 in a reconditioned military aircraft, in which the cabin was not pressurised for passenger comfort. The memory of the resulting, piercing agony has never left me – I thought my eardrums would burst – and I didn't go abroad again for another ten years. In any case, I was never keen on travelling anywhere very far, as sitting in the back of a car that didn't have proper suspension made me feel sick. I was six when my father became the proud owner of a black Standard Vanguard, his very first car and one of the first family saloons to be manufactured after the war. Every time we went on a journey for a distance of more than about ten miles, he had to keep stopping by the side of the road for me to get out and throw up. I must have been a complete pain to take on holiday.

Yet, despite the difference in our worlds, my grandchildren's very names are throwbacks to the ancestors they never knew. Jamie's middle name is David, in a conscious tribute to my father. Madeleine and Millie both have Rose as a middle name, after my father's redoubtable aunt who was like a grandmother to me, and Max pays homage both to my grandfather who died in Barrow over a century ago and to the great-grandfather who tried his very best to establish a Sheffield dynasty. It was not his fault that he failed. This enduring Jewish custom ensures that the dead are not forgotten and will live on through the names of our children. It is one reason why the same names keep cropping up in my history. It shows me too that their mothers, my daughters, also feel the pull of the past, and want to sustain a token thread of continuity between the former and the present generations. As I grow older, it is becoming a more urgent task to instil that fragile continuum with substance before its foundations are completely overlooked. The original David, Rose and Max of course all have starring roles in my family history.

The entitlement of my grandchildren's childhood did not materialise out of nowhere. It is a direct consequence of the circumstances that brought my grandparents to England rather than consigning them to the Nazi extermination machine that followed their departure. Its roots lie in desperation and poverty. The impulse to believe in and to strive for better was strong enough for them to have the courage to abandon the familiar for the unknown. My forebears on both sides were humble, unschooled and deprived of any advantage. They were also industrious, law-abiding and observant Jews, who only really felt comfortable socially with friends who shared their faith. In contrast, my adored grandchildren, with gentile fathers, are barely aware of what their Jewish heritage signifies other than occasionally sharing in the ritual of lighting candles, eating matzo and hunting for the *afikomen* at the Passover service, as well as knowing that they must not ask for ham sandwiches in my house if they wish to go home intact. They attend the occasional family bar mitzvah, observe the rituals of Jewish funerals, and sit shyly while the congregation mumbles prayers from books that open backwards. I have accepted the fact that there will be no one to say Kaddish, the prayer over the dead soul, at my own passing.

But that heritage infused my upbringing, and whilst it fed my thirst for arcane knowledge (the Bible was an endless treasure trove of weird facts – I especially relished the blessing to say when you see a dwarf), it also frustrated my inclinations. It effectively prevented me from joining my schoolfriends at Brownies ("they meet on Friday evenings"), taking drama lessons, which as a youngster I lusted after ("they clash with *cheder*") or going on school trips to Paris ("the French cook everything with bacon, even salad"). Perhaps this is the reason why I now feel the compulsion to make sure my grandchildren know about their antique relatives, even though, unlike my genuinely English friends, one of whom can trace her roots to the Domesday Book, I can only go back just over a hundred years. It's enough, however, to remind Millie and Max, Madeleine and Jamie about the cultural DNA that they carry with them in the twenty-first century. Their world is so far removed from my early years.

I started school in the spring term of 1950, a few weeks before I turned five. Abbey Lane Primary wasn't the nearest state elementary school, but its headmistress had a reputation for getting good results from unpromising material, and my mother chose it on this basis. On my first day, she generously came with me as I was introduced to the class of mixed infants before she surrendered me to Mrs Fidler, the teacher in charge. I was the only child starting school that day, and so was marked out from the first, standing in front of the class as the others all stared while the pocket-size chairs were reorganised around the low tables to make space for me to sit down. Were they not expecting me? I suppose my mother must also have collected me at the end of that first afternoon. After that, however, I was on my own. Each morning I would walk half a mile down the hill from home to the main road, cross the broad, zig-zag expanse of tramlines, and board the tram for the two-and-a-half-mile journey to school. At the end of the day, I did it all in reverse, a rather more arduous exercise because Dobcroft Road involved a pretty steep climb by any standards. Trams were a great form of transport. Powered by electric trolley cables, they were incapable of turning around so at the end of each one-way journey, the driver and conductor would merely swap ends, clicking the backs of all the seats as they walked down the length of the car so that they moved into a facing forward position. On one occasion, when I was eight, I was rushing across so as not to be late, and although I swear to this day that I looked carefully both ways, somehow I never saw the monster looming out of nowhere to knock me flying as I raced in front of it. While the badly shaken driver was being comforted by his passengers, the father of another child, who had delivered his offspring to the tram-stop by car, gathered up my limp body and took me home. My only permanent fatalities were my two front teeth. I was lucky. Trams are big, heavy things.

In general, however, my travels were without incident, and my mother was right about the quality of the schooling. We were taught according to a rigorous system, and our results completely put paid to modern theories that chart the correlation between small class sizes and pupil achievement. Almost all the way through my time at Abbey Lane, there were fifty-six children in my class, with a single teacher, and fifty-five of us passed the eleven plus. As we all now shamefully recognise, in the 1950s this exam was the key to every child's future. A pass meant that you could go to grammar school for what was considered to be an elite education. A fail consigned you to a secondary modern, the educational scrap heap, from which your chances of getting to university or college and then a white-collar job were severely limited. Betsy, the one girl in my class who failed the exam, was I think from a family of travellers. At any rate, she was an intermittent attender at school. Her hair was matted and her clothes were stained and often in rags. She ponged so badly that we all fought not to sit next to her. With that single exception, our wholescale success could well have been down to the discipline we never thought to challenge, and the inevitable learning by rote, which was remarkably effective and which I personally found quite comforting. I've always welcomed the security of ritual. We chanted times tables in unison every day and had a test each week from Miss Davis, the formidable head teacher my mother had such faith in. She was a stocky, grey-haired lady, who wore steel-rimmed spectacles, and carried a ruler, which she didn't hesitate to use on the knuckles or open palms of disobedient children. We all dreaded being summoned to her office, where the cane was kept. We learned how to spell on the same system, with a test of twenty spellings at the start of the morning. You knew you had done well when the ultimate gauntlet was thrown in front you, the word "phthisis". Somewhat poignantly, although I didn't know it at the time, this was the disease that had killed my forty-year-old grandfather in 1915.

Spellings followed daily prayers, which we recited together in our classroom, ending with the Lord's Prayer. I had been instructed by my mother to remain silent during these prayers as we stood at our desks with heads bent and hands together. I just hoped that no one would notice I wasn't joining in. The odds were in my favour as the other children were all looking at the floor rather than at me, and most had their eyes closed anyway. In class, we never dreamed of speaking out of turn – we could be caned for talking – and we sat mute with our hands on our heads when the command was barked. We often sat like this for several minutes until the teacher was satisfied that we were all suitably browbeaten. I became terrified that I would die in singing lessons because we had been ordered to sing with our arms folded across our chests, presumably so that our hands were clearly visible and not pinching anyone under the desk. When one day Mrs Fidler told us sternly that folding our arms stopped our breathing, I took her literally, and waited for the fatal moment, convinced that each note would be my last.

The school was by no means in a salubrious area and its intake was more socially diverse than most, though this still meant that the catchment was entirely white. Afro-Caribbean immigration had not extended much beyond London or Liverpool in the immediate post-war years, and the wave of Asian exiles did not hit the provinces until the 1960s in the wake of expulsion from Idi Amin's Uganda. I was the only Jewish child in my year, and one of only two in the whole school until my brother swelled the number by fifty per cent in 1953. When we marched into the weekly assembly to the jangling strains of the ancient upright piano, I joined enthusiastically in "The British Grenadiers", although the words meant absolutely nothing to me. The comparative eminence of Hercules, Hector and Lysander was a tricky concept for a five-year-old with no background in classical literature. As my mother had strictly banned anything that mentioned Jesus, hymns were definitely out. I was a bit perplexed by whether "All Things Bright and Beautiful" counted in this category, and if I sang it, would a thunderbolt drop out of the sky and hit me on the head, but as the lyrics didn't seem too harmful, I risked it, and at least the words made sense. I was not attuned at that stage to the political implications of asking God to keep the rich man in his castle and the poor man at his gate.

It wasn't often that I was called a dirty Jew, and although I was a bit taken aback when one girl confronted me and accused me of killing her God, I bore it with remarkable self-control. The school had been informed that I was to be removed from all religious education, so I was duly sent out of the classroom most days to mooch around in the corridor while everyone else listened to the stories of the Nativity, the parables, miracles and the like. This meant that when I eventually went to university to study English I had to give myself an instant crash-course in New Testament theology or the literary canon would have remained a complete enigma.

Bizarrely, given this exclusion and the fact that my parents kept a strictly kosher home, I was signed up for school dinners, on the strict condition that I steered clear of pork or bacon. I suppose it was too far for me to go home for lunch – most of those who did lived in the streets that bordered the school – and my mother clearly wasn't up to the task of making sandwiches first thing in the morning. On the occasions when forbidden foods in their various incarnations were on the menu, one of the dinner ladies would march off to the kitchen to find a solid lump of cheese to accompany the mashed potatoes and carrots. These meals were heavily subsidised by the welfare state, and often were the only hot food that some children would have in a day. In 1951, when I was six, they were consumed by nearly half the school population. They cost five pence when I first started school, later increased to seven pence, and we lined up with our weekly dinner money every Monday morning, while the teacher ticked our names off in the special blue book. We ate sitting at our desks, which were covered with neat little cloths that once upon a time had been hemmed and embroidered by the girls in the top form. These cloths were laundered once a week so while they were spotless on Mondays, by Thursday they were covered with spilt gravy, grease and splashes of custard. As a monitor doled them out, you could plead for a clean one but there was no guarantee that you wouldn't be faced with a week's worth of congealed splodges from messy eaters.

The cloths apart, I thought school dinners were a huge treat. They introduced me to all sorts of delicious foods that we never had at home. Meat and potato pie was my absolute favourite, and I looked forward to the fish and chips, which appeared on Fridays as a sop to Catholic sensibilities, although sometimes we got a lump of chewy, fishy substance, which stuck in your throat, smothered in white glue with green specks, theoretically a parsley sauce, which was much less appetising. We were supposed to eat milky foods for their health benefits so sago pudding, known by us as frogspawn, featured prominently on our diet plus rice, semolina and tapioca, all of which came with a dollop of strawberry jam, which made a pretty pink river across the pallid surface if you pushed it gently with your spoon. The real downside of the nutritional regime was the mid-morning milk, a benefit introduced by the Labour government in 1946 to build our bones in the post-war years, and which was delivered in crates of little bottles, a third of a pint each. These were stacked against the radiators in winter which meant that the contents would curdle and become disgusting, while in summer they were often left outside, where they could take full advantage of the sun's rays, with much the same effect. Fortunately Sheffield was not known for its tropical climate.

The school was a Victorian three-storey, red-brick building, standing in a large concreted yard, surrounded by railings, and with gates that were kept locked during the school day to give the whole structure a prison-like aspect. The yard was divided into three. As mixed infants, we had our own walled space, presumably to protect us from the savagery of the older children's games. At seven, having moved up into the juniors, I was promoted to the girls' playground. The boys had a further separate area from which the deafening yells indicated that several murders were taking place on a daily basis, although in fact it was just unrefereed football or the habitual fistfights in which teachers only intervened if they looked potentially life-threatening. There was always a teacher on yard duty at every break time. They must have loved that. Our girls' section was more decorous, though still scary if you got in the way of an aggressive skipping rope or caught the sharp edge of whirling leather from the whips and tops that we spun around the yard in summer. We drew squares with coloured chalk on the ground to play hopscotch, stood in pairs with bits of string over our fingers to play cats' cradle, and crouched down to throw jacks, our term for knucklebones, in a convoluted sequence according to rules I've now forgotten. As fresh air was thought to be good for us, we were sent outside in all weathers. The rain had to be truly torrential for us to be kept indoors.

We were also allowed to use the toilets during playtime, though not at any other time, a stricture that demanded great self-control and resulted in the occasional mortifying accident. The toilets, which served the whole school, apart from the infants, who, lucky things, had their own indoor facility, were housed in a block at one side of the yard. They consisted of ten adjoining cubicles, nine for girls and one for boys at the end of the row, next to a communal urinal, which had a channel round the base. As the block was only partially roofed, the boys vied with one another to pee as high as possible against the wall so that the stream projected over the top into the girls' area. A visit to the loo consequently became a wet obstacle course, and we all frantically tried to avoid the end cubicle. The block was not equipped with toilet roll. This was thought too precious to be kept where it was most needed, doubtless because it would be immediately nicked. Instead, a roll of scratchy Izal paper was secured in a locked cupboard in the infants' classroom to be handed out on request, a humiliation that was compounded if a class happened to be in progress at the time. "How many sheets do you need?" Mrs Fidler would ask. The listening mixed infants would snigger loudly if you said any number higher than one.

Learning how to navigate these trials were by far the most important lessons that school had to offer and took precedent over any academic hurdles. I was naturally obedient, found sums relatively painless, and, as I had been reading since I was three, English was a doddle. Once I graduated to the junior class, we were issued with ruled exercise books, which had both the English and the metric system of weights and measures on the back as well as a verse reminding us of how many days were in each month. Any child who went to school in this period will be familiar with rods, poles and perches as measures of length, and knows how many pecks make a bushel, arcane data that virtually none of us would ever need to refer to but nonetheless were obliged to memorise. We studied the rules of grammar from *The King's English*, a textbook originally published in 1906, and now on the Oxford English Classics list. The title had to be rapidly changed for the Coronation in 1953 but its basic principles of language use continue to apply – always use a short word rather than a long one and stick to concrete rather than abstract nouns. If we floundered a bit when advised to choose a Saxon word over a Romance one, it made no real difference to our juvenile compositions, and our eleven plus results vindicated the approach, even if it all looks highly over-prescriptive nowadays. The Coronation itself was a huge event in our lives. It meant a whole day holiday from school, a shiny Coronation penny, and a mug with a picture of the young queen on the side. And Greenfields, the sweet shop a couple of doors down the road from school, sold red, white and blue iced lollies all week.

At Abbey Lane, each class had its own mini-library, and once the teachers were confident we could advance beyond the Janet and John reading scheme, we were encouraged to branch out on our own. It was here I first encountered the English classics, including *Oliver Twist* and *The Pilgrim's Progress*, a pre-requisite for any girl who wanted to grow up to be Jo in *Little Women*. It didn't matter a jot that most of these works were in watered-down versions with much of the nineteenth-century, prosy moralising removed. The story was the thing. I was especially fascinated by tales of children who were unfairly treated, and whose inner virtue was eventually recognised as they triumphed over their evil antagonists, who were then duly punished. They gave me the conviction that one day my hidden talents too would be rewarded. There were lots of stories like this from *David Copperfield* to *The Water Babies*. It never fully registered that Kingsley's hero, Tom, the little chimneysweep, actually died quite early on the narrative, or not enough to spoil the vicarious enjoyment. Heavenly retribution seemed perfectly satisfactory to me. We were also urged to write our own stories, and the completed versions, together with all their crossings-out and crayoned illustrations then joined the printed collection and were available for other children to borrow. Despite the fact that one of my own volumes ended with the boast that "I got the facts and the knowledge in this book from my brain", my own efforts were highly derivative, and mostly reliant on Enid Blyton, whose peak output coincided with my early reading years.

Blyton's works were a staple of most children's literary intake at that time, and carried none of the associations of political incorrectness, racism, class snobbery or xenophobia with which they are now saddled. Not only did I eagerly devour the Famous Five series *et al* but I also polished off *Sunny Stories*, a weekly magazine that Blyton produced until 1952, together with the subsequent *Enid Blyton's Magazine*, which came out after she parted company with her original publishers. I managed to miss Noddy and his mate, Big Ears, thank goodness. By 1949, the year of his first appearance, I had already outgrown such babyish tales, and was almost ready to progress to the boarding school adventures of St Clare's and Malory Towers. "I must pay attention" "I must pay attention", wrote Vera Saunders, "Oh, good, that's the last, what about you Daphne?" cringingly began one of my own versions in a stapled-together tome written when I was nine and for some reason kept by my mother all these years. I was just dying to go to boarding school. I also lapped up the serialisation of Marion Crawford's reminiscences of her time as governess to the two little princesses, Elizabeth and Margaret Rose. We were all passionate Royalists then.

Books offered an alternative existence, one that was far more rewarding than my own. They took me to places I could never have visited in real life and introduced me to people who seemed far more thrilling than anyone I actually knew, and who certainly had more fun. It was only later, looking back, that I came to see how wrong I was. On Friday evenings, when my father came home from work, we would have a family outing to the Ecclesall lending library, which had an extensive children's section. Children were assigned three tickets, a paltry allocation for a bookworm like me. I waited impatiently for Fridays when I could change my books, though frequently I would have finished them by the end of the weekend. Steadily I made my way through the collection, progressing from the school stories to mysteries, historical novels and non-fiction. Any information that was presented as a series of adventures got my vote.

As a result, my grasp of British history during my primary school years was almost entirely drawn from Henrietta Elizabeth Marshall's *Our Island Story*. Subtitled *A History of Britain for Boys and Girls from the Romans to Queen Victoria*, this was first published in 1905, and touted the version of international power relations that predominated throughout the 1950s, when Great Britain and its territories were still coloured pink on the map. I also possessed a globe that could be twirled around on its stand so that all the colours merged into a kaleidoscopic rainbow. Marshall's vivid renderings of the chronicles of kings and queens were utterly magnetic, and I was riveted by the unsolved mystery of the poor little princes in the tower, and the gruesome details of the tortures and burnings of heretics by the brilliantly named Bloody Mary, even if she didn't personally light the pyre herself. I borrowed this book repeatedly, though now it is hotly contested for the way in which it promotes the UK's colonial past in unequivocally positive terms. It later joined forces with *Gone With the Wind* in forming my view of the rights and wrongs of political events, and for years I remained convinced that the Southern States were the good guys in the American Civil War. I was completely on the side of dazzling, plucky Scarlett O'Hara, up against those uncivilised Yankee louts, and who wouldn't be? Marshall did, however, give me a pretty accurate grasp of the events leading up to Queen Victoria's ascension to the throne, together with the other historical fiction I devoured, *And So Victoria*. My impressions of the young, self-willed teenage queen were reinforced by acting out with my father scenes from Laurence Housman's *Victoria Regina*, a 1934 dramatic biography that had been a great hit on the London stage. Now there was a girl who managed to defy her mother and emerge triumphant.

While my mother was quite content to let me feed my hunger for reading when I was small, by the time I was eleven, she became convinced that I was becoming socially inadequate and would be consigned to a future of friendless oblivion. Such a destiny seemed not unappealing to me. I consoled myself with thoughts of misunderstood heroines who also loved books, such as Jane Eyre, while my despairing mother signed me up for tennis coaching and other activities that she had enjoyed as a youngster and that would guarantee entrée into decent society. I was generally hopeless at sport and knew no one at the tennis club so I sulked persistently for several weeks and got back to the Brontë sisters as soon as I could.

I was part of that lucky generation to have been born at the end of the Second World War. I grew up in peacetime in an enlightened, liberal democracy, which gave me free school milk, a health service and educated me all the way up to university graduation. As a Jew, I did not live in fear of the footstep on the stairs or the dreaded knock on the door, as had been the case with my European counterparts, such as Anne Frank, less than ten years earlier, and I have never had to assess my friends on the basis of whether or not they would hide me. Despite my mother's fears, I did manage to make lasting relationships, which I treasure, and I didn't have to give up books in order to do so. My big mistake though was in assuming that the tales in those books were more inspirational than those around me. For as I have pieced together the fragments of yellowing paper in my mother's boxes, and scrutinised the dog-eared photographs for clues, I have been astounded at the stories stashed away in my own family that have come to light.

It is my twelve-year-old grandmother, travelling alone across Eastern Europe, who is the Jo March of my personal past, and her daughter, my mother, who is Alice in *Through the Looking Glass*, a book she first read with me, supremely alive to the jokes of an upside-down world in which she manages to remain a rational observer. My orphaned father, dropped unwanted into a war-time Sheffield jungle, somehow miraculously reinvents himself from being Rudyard Kipling's Mowgli to a latter-day Atticus Finch. His sterling maiden aunts are the Betsy Trotwoods of their generation, rescuing their very own David and instilling him with the innate sense of justice that made him into the hero he became. Too many of my sad, lonely and abandoned aunts, trapped by their time and circumstance, are twentieth-century Bertha Masons, carrying a troubled inheritance of repression and denial that led them to the madhouse or worse. Their stories are just as sensational as any of those in the library books I borrowed each Friday evening. I know that there are still mysteries

I have not been able to unlock, and tales waiting to be told. I have mapped the gossip and chance snippets of information gathered over the years against the official facts and discovered that the authorised records are by no means infallible. I possess photographs sent from New York in 1905 with pictures of little boys in bar mitzvah outfits, inscribed with affectionate messages. I have no means of tracing who they are. Despite my painstaking researches, which have uncovered a lot of surprises, in many cases I have to be content with the bare outlines from which to reconstruct the emotional lives of my long-gone ancestors. Oh, why didn't I ask them more questions when they were alive? In the end, however, and despite my passion for neatness, I have to accept the fact that my jigsaw will always have pieces missing. It is this lack of closure after all that makes history continuously enthralling. So, even though its edges can never be as tidy or as finished as I would really like, I hope that there's enough here to create the picture that shows just what a lucky girl I have been amongst my ordinary family and their extraordinary lives.

Sources

The primary sources for this book are the diaries, letters, photographs and unpublished scraps of memoir left behind by my predecessors. I have also drawn heavily on the archives of the *Sheffield Jewish Journal* 1944–80. Background information and additional materials came from my visits to libraries, records offices, museum collections and in particular from consulting the sources listed below.

Almonds and Raisins: The Rise and Fall of Manchester's Jewish Quarter, Manchester Jewish Museum, Manchester, 2006

Tomas Balkelis, *The Making of Modern Lithuania,* Routledge, London, 2009

Tobias Brinkmann, 'From green borders to paper walls: Jewish migrants from Eastern Europe in Germany before and after the Great War', *History in Focus*, The Institute of Historical Research, London, 2006

'Brushed Aside by the Nazis', *Camden New Journal*, 27 May 2005

David Cesarani (ed), *The Making of Modern Anglo-Jewry*, Basil Blackwell, London, 1990

David Englander (ed), *A Documentary History of Jewish Immigration into Britain 1840–1920*, Leicester: Leicester University Press, 2001

Elizabeth Furness, *The Etchings of Erich Wolfsfeld,* Belgrave Gallery Ltd, London, 1979

Deborah Glassman, 'A quick look at records from European ports', JewishGen KehilaLinks, 2005

Olga Goldberg-Mulkiewicz, 'Dress', in Gershon David Hundert, *The Yivo Encyclopaedia of Jews in Eastern Europe*, The Yivo Institute of Jews in Eastern Europe, 2008

Glossop Road Spa Brochure, Sheffield, 1877

'The Sheffield Skating Tragedy – Killamarsh', *The Telegraph*, Monday 29th November, 1915

International Jewish Cemetery Project, iajgscemetery.org, 2010

Jewish Communities and Records, www.jewishgen.org/jcr-uk

Sharman Kadish, 'Ironing out the Ghetto Bend': The origins and ethos of the Jewish Lads Brigade, 1895–1914, *Proceedings of the World Union of Jewish Studies*, 1993

Barry Kosmin, Marzy Bauer, Nigel Grizzard, *Steel City Jews: A Study of Ethnicity and Social Mobility in the Jewish Population of the City of Sheffield, South Yorkshire*, Board of Deputies of British Jews, London, 1976

Dr Montagu Lomax, *The Experiences of an Asylum Doctor*, Allen & Unwin, London, 1922

Sidney Pollard & A.J. Hunt, 'The Growth of Population', in David Linton (ed), *Sheffield and its Region*, Sheffield, 1956

'The Curious Tale of Horatio Bright's Mausoleum on the Moors', *sheffieldforum. co.uk*, 2008

Manchester Jewry Database: *City Directories* for 1855, 1888, 1927 and 1934 by Ann Rabinowitz, 2001

'Moving Here: Migration histories', The National Archives, UK Government www. movinghere.org.uk/galleries/histories/Jewish/journeys/humber5htm

Safety in Numbers: Life Inside Prestwich Asylum in 1900, Greater Manchester County Record Office, Bury Archives Service and Bury Church of England High School, with the support of Greater Manchester West Mental Health Trust, 2008

Minutes of the Committee for Prestwich Lunatic Asylum 1894–1921, Preston Records Office, Archives and Special Collections

Patient Admissions Records, Manchester City Council Archives

Private William Roberts' Diary, Durham Light Infantry, 1916

Richard Salmon, 'The Development of the British Railway Carriage', bluebell-railway.co.uk, 2005

BBC News, 'Were trains any better 100 years ago?', news.bbc.co.uk/2/hi/uk_news/992144stm

Jurgen Sielemann, 'Eastern European Jewish Emigration via the Port of Hamburg 1880–1914', JewishGen KehilaLinks

The Sheffield Telegraph, 16 December 1938

I. Simons, Letter, *The Jewish Chronicle*, 1901

Malcolm Shifrin, *Victorian Turkish Baths*, Historic England, 2015

Isaac Slater, *Royal National Commercial Directory of Manchester and Salford, with their vicinities*, 1884, and *Kelly's (Slater's) Directory of Manchester, Salford and Suburbs, 1927*, Kelly's Directories Ltd, London 1927

L. Stoller, 'A Communal Dispute at Barrow', *The Jewish Chronicle*, 22 May, 1914, p.24

Jan Vallance (ed), *They Came from the Haim: A History of Manchester Jewry from 1867*, Manchester Social Services, Manchester, 1995

'The Way We Were: Belle Vue – Showground of the World', *Manchester Evening News*, 11 January 2013

Bill Williams, *The Making of Manchester Jewry*, Manchester University Press, Manchester, 1985

Bill Williams, *Manchester Jewry: A Pictorial History 1788–1988*, Archive Publications, 1988

Terry Wilson, *Prestwich Hospital ("Asylum"), a Brief History*

Robert Winder, *Bloody Foreigners: The Story of Immigration to Britain*, Hachette Books, Little Brown, London, 2004

Yiddishsong.wordpress.com

Acknowledgements

Special thanks go to those from the different sides of my family who helped me with information about the past and gave me original materials, in particular Julie Harris for the stories of her father Harry Lowit, the late Maureen Horwich for handing over the carrier bag full of Ada Goldstone's papers, and to my daughters – Juliet for help with the family trees, and Victoria, who never thought that her student project on Jewish refugees in Sheffield would prove so useful. I am grateful to Sheffield Jewish Friendship Club for allowing me to share some of my early researches with them and who in turn shared with me their memories of early Sheffield. I am indebted to the Imperial War Museum, the Jewish Museum London, Manchester Jewish Museum, Greater Manchester County Record Office, the Preston Records Office and Sheffield Local Studies Library for the access to their special collections. Rick Rylance read the manuscript and encouraged me to publish, and Hilary Fraser came up with the perfect title. And of course, as ever, thanks go to David who has travelled with me on this journey into the past.

Judy Simons, June 2020

 **Matador**

For exclusive discounts on Matador titles,
sign up to our occasional newsletter at
troubador.co.uk/bookshop